ALS research : From stopping the disease to restoring the motor function.

Table of Contents

What is this book about ?

This book is about tracing the main steps in ALS research during the last 30 years, presenting information on new drugs in the pipeline. It offers some glimpses on treatments that could block the disease in a first step and helping to heal from it in a second step. It is also the report of astonishment of an observer outside the field.

There are three parts in this book. The first deals with research in its historical aspect, as well as drugs and clinical trials. The second part deals with a therapy that does not yet exist but is state-of-the-art in 2019, so it could heal pALS[1]. The third part of the book shows how current research could offer therapeutic solutions in one or two decades.

The author of this book is a retired R & D engineer with no academic credentials in biology or medicine. However he had recently studied bioinformatics at Rennes university, got a Mount Sinai online certificate in system biology and a Duke university online certificate in medical neuroscience. If the author welcomes comments or questions about this book, any medical questions should be asked to a physician.

The author is not an English native speaker, so he apologizes for any mistake he may have done in Shakespeare's tongue.

You can contact the author at : jeanpierre.lerouzic@wanadoo.fr

His web site is available at : https://padiracinnovation.org

This book is revised every few months. This version was written in February 2019.

---

1   pALS is an acronym for ALS patient

First part : History of ALS research

1. History of ALS research

1.1. Research and clinical trials

1.1.1. Research carries the hopes of the sick.

Having ALS means different things for different people. There are patients with slow progressions and other that are too fast, and no one really knows why. The bulbar form is different from other forms. Why does this disease start in only a few areas, then progress slowly ? Why some motor neurons, such as eye and bowel motions, are usually spared from ALS ?

And as is the case for all rare diseases, there are few doctors who have a good knowledge of ALS, which is a disease of rare complexity. In addition, drugs are coming to the market. They are targeted on one form of the disease but ineffective for others. It requires of doctors, an information effort that is not trivial.

For all people with ALS, it is of utmost importance to know if it is possible to get a treatment that could improve their condition, so it will give them time to see their grandchildren graduate, or maybe even cure them of this horrible disease.

We are living an interesting moment in the research on ALS, where there seems to be an effervescence of results. It gives hope that a more effective treatment without too many side effects will be available in the coming years.

1.1.2. A lack of interest in society.

ALS patients are often disappointed with the lack of progress in ALS research. Indeed from 1995 to 2017, there was only one drug which was authorized by the various regulatory authorities and that this drug is only slowing the progression. When patients and their families read in the press almost every week that a major breakthrough[2] happened in the field of cancer, they wonder why there is so little progress in ALS research.

In 1981, 81 scientific articles were published on ALS. Today this number has multiplied by 20. The number of articles also reflects the number of people involved in ALS research. So why is there not more progress ? The usual answer is that ALS is a rare disease, so it is difficult to interest the public in it.

The pharmaceutical industry and investors know that a rare disease means an unprofitable market, so there is little incentive to develop new drugs. It is more rational for a society to spend money on saving young people than seniors, especially if the survival of these people will lead to other costs related to old age. The year 2019 confirmed this interpretation because it saw the arrival on the market of two drugs[3] for spinal muscular atrophy (SMA), a kind of ALS that strikes children.

---

2 Of course, there is no revolutionary breakthrough every week in cancer research, but it is reported as such by the PR services of universities and by the media.
3 Zolgensma and Spinraza

1.2. Brief description of ALS phenotypes.

1.2.1. Is ALS a single disease or a spectrum of symptoms ?

Amyotrophic lateral sclerosis is a strange disease whose symptoms seem to be different for each patient. There is no strict medical definition of ALS, which is diagnosed by exclusion. This means that a diagnosis of ALS is only made when any other disease that causes the same symptoms has been excluded.

Different countries[4] have different criteria for what is ALS and there is a great diversity of practice among neurologists. It is not uncommon for two neurologists to have different opinions on the same case, or that the initial diagnosis is revised after some time. Among the many diseases causing symptoms similar to those of ALS, some also have similarities at the genetic level[5] and have no recognized biomarkers. The risk of confusion is therefore important.

Scientists are circumventing the problem by working on animal models of the disease, but there is no formal way to assess how well those models reflect ALS in humans.

The duration of the diagnostic process is measured in years and this causes a lot of distress in the patients. The proportion of misdiagnosis is of the order of 10 %. There are no biological markers of ALS which is making it difficult to diagnose and also

---

4 In the United States, the term "ALS" refers to all forms of the disease, including classical ALS, progressive bulbar palsy, progressive muscular atrophy and primary lateral sclerosis, but each of these diseases are identified in classifications. medical. In Europe and particularly in France, the term "ALS" also refers to all forms of the disease. In the United Kingdom and Australia, the term « motor neuron disease » refers to all forms of the disease and "ALS" refers only to classical ALS, that is, the form associated with upper and lower motoneurons.

5 https://www.ncbi.nlm.nih.gov/pmc/articles/PMC6089690/

to measure the progression of the disease. The ALS Functional Rating Scale (ALSFRS-R) is an assessment tool for tracking the disease progression in patients with Amyotrophic Lateral Sclerosis (ALS). This scale is used in most clinical trials, but is criticized.

On the Internet, crooks flourish who sell ersatz medications, remedies of their own design, and are boasting cure cases they attribute to their remedies. As with other diseases, for example cancer, some doctors are not the last to give recipes to defeat ALS with "natural" medications[6].

All this is surprisingly nebulous, and finally quite disturbing in our society which thinks it is rational and prides itself on mastering from the infinitely small to the infinitely large.

1.2.2. Familial ALS

Familial ALS is of genetic origin, but even sporadic forms of the disease may have gene mutations. Familial ALS cases account for 10 % to 20 % of all cases. A doctor will diagnose familial ALS if there are other cases of ALS in the family. Yet the risk for a parent with ALS to have a child who develops ALS is very limited, in the order of 1.5 %.

- SOD1. Mutations (there are dozens) of this gene account for about 2 % of all cases of ALS in Western populations, but less than 1 % in Eastern populations. Curiously it is the most cited gene when talking about familial ALS, while the most common gene is actually C9orf72. We are very close to the commercialization of a treatment for this type of ALS.

- C9orf72. Mutations in this gene are found in about 80 % of familial ALS cases. When there is a mutation in a gene, the resulting proteins are altered and diseases occur. In the case of C9orf72, the produced proteins

6   https://www.tandfonline.com/doi/full/10.3109/21678421.2015.1039240

have dipeptide repeats (DPR). Poly(GR) is an example of dipeptide repeats that is particularly damaging to vesicles inside cells, the mitochondria. They are essential for cellular metabolism. Scientists have recently shown that reducing the amount of Poly (GR) can help cells to regenerate. As for SOD1, we are very close to the arrival on the market of a treatment for this type of ALS.

- FUS (« Fused In Sarcoma »), is a gene encoding an RNA-binding protein found in human cancers. Some scientists have suggested that it would be beneficial to stimulate PARP activity in FUS ALS.

- There are many other genes involved in ALS (from 30 to 120 depending on the criteria), but they are less common and are not exclusive of SOD1 or C9orf72. It is unlikely that specific treatments will be designed for those mutated genes and patients will probably benefit from growth factor based therapies, like Nurown.

1.2.3. Sporadic ALS

This section presents signs and symptoms that are usually associated with sporadic ALS. It is a blurrier category than familial ALS.

Sporadic ALS affects about 90 % of people with this disease. It is due to a TDP-43 proteinopathy in most cases. But it can also be genetic origin if there was no parent with this disease[7].

Proteopathy or proteinopathy, refers to a class of diseases in which certain proteins disrupt the function of cells, tissues and organs of the body. Often, those proteins, instead of being in the nucleus, are not folded correctly and are localized in granules in the cytoplasm of neurons. Proteinopathies include diseases such as Alzheimer's disease, certain dementias (such

---

7Incomplete disease penetrance.

as frontotemporal lobar degeneration, also known as frontotemporal dementia), Parkinson's disease, amyloidosis, multisystemic atrophy and a wide range of other disorders.

On a very general level, the various molecules incriminated in ALS, are often involved in protection or repair processes. Their presence, even in a degraded form, in ALS is not necessarily a sign of deleterious behavior.

1.2.4. ALS classical form.

The classic ALS form accounts for about 70 % of all cases of familial and sporadic ALS. It can subdivided into ALS with spinal onset and bulbar onset.

ALS with a spinal beginning, starts with weakness in the arms and legs and accounts for about two-thirds of all classic ALS cases.

Bulbar onset ALS begins with weak speech, chewing and swallowing muscles and accounts for about one-third of classic ALS cases. Its prognosis is more serious than that of ALS with a spinal beginning.

A population study showed that bulbar onset ALS had a 10-year survival rate of 3 %, whereas spinal onset ALS had a 10-year survival rate of 13 %.

There are also regional variants to ALS.

1.2.5. Pseudobulbar palsy :

Pseudobulbar palsy is the result of bilateral lesions of the corticobulbar pathways. They extend from the cerebral cortex to the nucleus of the cranial nerves of the brainstem. Those damages can occur during various neurological conditions, further complicating the diagnosis.

Patients experience difficulty chewing and swallowing. They have increased reflexes and spasticities[8] in the tongue and bulbar region, and they have a speech disorder (which is often the initial symptom).

Those patients find it difficult to control their emotions, for example they may cry in front of something that is only moderately sad, or laugh uncontrollably when angry or frustrated.

1.2.6. Primary lateral sclerosis

Primary lateral sclerosis (PLS) is a rare neuromuscular disease (~5 % of cases) characterized by progressive muscle weakness in voluntary muscles. PLS only affects upper motor neurons. The degeneration of the lower motoneurons and the muscular atrophy that occurs in classical amyotrophic lateral sclerosis, are absent in the PLS.

The onset of PLS usually occurs spontaneously after age 50 and progresses over several years or even decades. The disorder usually begins with the legs, but can occur in the tongue or in the hands. Symptoms may include balance difficulties, weakness and stiffness in the legs, and clumsiness. Other common symptoms include spasticity (involuntary muscle contraction) in the members, as well as speech and swallowing problems.

Patients can often live with PLS for many years, some people may still be able to walk without assistance, but others may need wheelchairs, canes, or other assistive devices.

1.2.7. Progressive bulbar palsy

Progressive bulbar palsy (PBP) is a disease that attacks the nerves supplying the bulbar muscles.

---

8   An involuntary resistance to movement, painful in some cases.

Symptoms may include progressive difficulty to speak and swallow. Patients may also experience a decrease in gag reflexes, and in weak movements of the face and tongue. In advanced cases of PBP, the patient may be unable to handle food within their mouth.

About 25 % of patients with PBP eventually develop the symptoms of ALS. Some neurologists consider this disorder as a subset of amyotrophic lateral sclerosis, but others do not agree with this classification. In 2019 an important step towards the recognition of this disorder as a subset of ALS, seems to have been done[9].

1.2.8. Progressive muscular atrophy

Progressive muscular atrophy (PMA) is a rare subtype of motor neuron disease that affects only lower motor neurons. PMA is thought to account for about 5 % of all ALS cases. This contrasts with the classic form of amyotrophic lateral sclerosis, or primary lateral sclerosis. Amyotrophic lateral sclerosis affects both upper and lower motor neurons, while primary lateral sclerosis only affects higher motor neurons. The distinction is important because PMA is associated with a better prognosis than classical ALS.

As a result of less significant degeneration of the motor neuron, symptoms of PMA include :

- atrophy
- fasciculations
- muscular weakness

Some patients have symptoms that are limited to the arms or legs (or in some cases to one or the other). These cases are associated with a better prognosis.

---

9   https://www.ncbi.nlm.nih.gov/pmc/articles/PMC6706345/

1.2. Brief description of ALS phenotypes.

Unlike amyotrophic lateral sclerosis or primary lateral sclerosis, PMA is distinguished by the absence of :

- Quick reflexes
- Spasticity
- Babinski sign
- Emotional lability (they experience rapid change of emotional state)

Some patients with PMA live for decades after diagnosis, which would be unusual in the case of a typical ALS.

2. Biology notions related to ALS

2.1. General organization of the cell

As most ALS publications discuss about the cell and its internal mechanisms, it may be helpful for some of us to refresh our knowledge. The others will be able to move on to the next chapter directly.

Since 1990, most publications on ALS have focused on genetic mutations, but starting in 2006, researchers have increasingly understood the near universality of protein disorders in neurodegenerative diseases.

In proteinopathies, there is a disruption of protein expression in the cell by RNA and, instead of producing a useful protein, the protein is blocked in an intermediate state in the cytoplasm. The normal location of many of these proteins should be in the nucleus. These proteins agglutinate and form the granules found in most degenerative diseases. For example, TDP-43 (the most common form of ALS proteinopathy) is also found in one third of Alzheimer's cases. Since these aggregates can result from dysfunction of the major organs of the cell, such as the endoplasmic reticulum or the Golgi apparatus, it is important to know more about them.

2.1. General organization of the cell

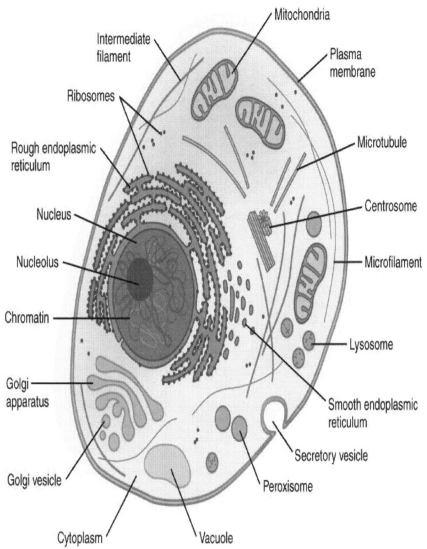

Source : *https://cnx.org/contents/FPtK1zmh@8.25: fV7KwqTE@5/The-Cytoplasm-and-Cellular-Organelles*

2.1. General organization of the cell

Although the image above does not represent any particular human cell, it is a prototypical example of a cell containing the main organelles and internal structures. But from the morphological point of view, a neuron is very different from this cell, as it has very long projections and even decentralized organelles.

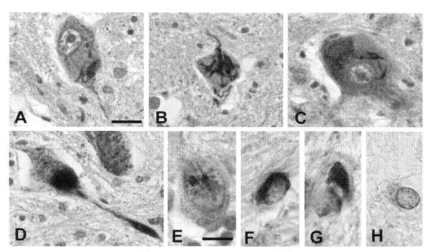

T. Arai et al. / Biochemical and Biophysical Research Communications 351 (2006) 602–611

Motor neurons with TDP-43 inclusions (in brown)

Contrary to what is shown by the superb educational videos on molecular biology where biological phenomena take place essentially in a nearly empty space, the cell is both tiny and congested and molecules are violently agitated and interact at every moment with their environment, through their multiple fields (electrostatic, Debye force, Van der Walls, etc.).

In these incredibly small volumes, there are molecules, that if they were not folded, would be very long. All the proteins (which are long molecules) are thus folded on themselves. This folding confers them specific properties. The cell has a very complex vesicle whose role is to fold those proteins : the endoplasmic reticulum.

All the cells of the same organism are not similar, there are about 200 types of cells in our body. And the cells are different between different organisms, mammals have very complex cells. Even in mammals, the biology of mice is very different from that of primates. In particular mice and primates central nervous system differ significantly. This difference partly explains why it is so difficult to translate laboratory results into clinical trials. Curiously, this has only been recognized recently. For example, swine (but still not primate) models of ALS exist only since 2014[10].

The organization of organelles in a cell is not static, new organelles are created depending on environmental changes. They are transported where needed by the mean of several internal mechanisms using special proteins. Organelles can die and are then recycled by the cell.

---

10 https://www.ncbi.nlm.nih.gov/pubmed/24157939

2.1.1. DNA and mutations

The main task of any cell is to produce tens of thousands of protein types necessary for its survival and the formation of the tissue that hosts it. DNA, a long molecule located in the nucleus of the cell, contains all the information necessary for the building of the cell's proteins.

It makes not much sense to incriminate a mutated gene as the sole cause of the disease, because in this case, the disease would appear much earlier (as in the SMA). Except to think that, as in cancer[11], the mutation appears only late in life.

In addition, there are about ten genes that are commonly found to be mutated in ALS patients. Each of them can undergo dozens of mutations, so several hundred different mutations would lead to the same disease ? It looks rather improbable. The mutations are part of the overall puzzle, but other elements are to be considered.

Biology books and articles discuss essentially of cellular reproduction, less so of DNA transcription and translation. They discuss only a bit of cellular metabolism and almost never to what happens to those newly created proteins. In fact the cell spend most of its time and energy to produce proteins from

---

11 There are some strange facts about the relationship between cancer and ALS.

* Rilutek (an ALS drug) induces two different anticancer effects on hepatocellular carcinoma (HCC).

* Some anti-cancer drugs (ITKs) can slow the progression of ALS.

* There is an inverse relationship between the onset of cancer and the onset of ALS.

* The FUS gene orchestrates the response to DNA defects

* Myasthenic Lambert – Eaton Syndrome (LEMS) is a rare autoimmune disorder characterized by muscle weakness of the limbs. About 60 % of people with LEMS have underlying malignancy, most often small cell lung cancer ; it is therefore considered a paraneoplastic syndrome (a condition resulting from cancer elsewhere in the body).

* Many genes in ALS are linked to transcription or translation.

DNA, in order for the cell to live, develop, move, interact with their environment and especially with other cells.

Neurons in particular are unable to survive in isolation, they need support from other cells types that are collectively called *"glial cells"*. For example, myelin, which isolates axons from neurons, is formed in the central nervous system (CNS) by glial cells called oligodendrocytes. In the peripheral nervous system (PNS) myelin is produced by Schwann cells.

Even if the DNA of an organism is the same in any of its cells, the expression of the proteins is different in different tissues. This is what actually differentiate tissues between them. Our nearly 200 types of cells differ widely from each others in their role and phenotype. Some of these cells are microscopic, others like neurons can measure one meter long. Some cells only live for a few hours and others (like neurons) survive as long as their host.

There are five steps involved in protein expression, but the last three are almost never discussed.

- Transcription
- Translation
- Post-translational modifications (specially in the mammalian cell)
- Folding (which confers its biological properties to the molecule)
- Delivery (the new protein must be sent where it is needed)

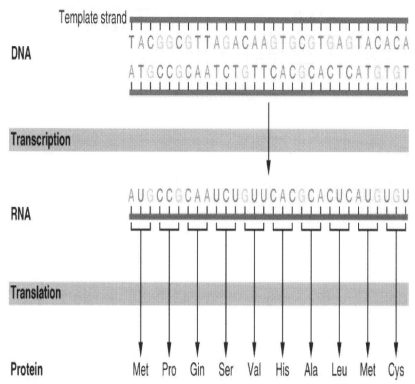

Source : https://cnx.org/contents/FPtK1zmh@8.25:
lyDdZqp4@6/Protein-Synthesis

2.1.1.1 From DNA to RNA : Transcription

The DNA is located inside the nucleus and the protein is synthesized in the cytoplasm. There must therefore be an exchange of information between the two cellular compartments. This is achieved thanks to a molecule called messenger RNA (mRNA), it carries a copy of a small part of the genetic code[12] from the nucleus to the cytoplasm. This

12 This is often loosely called « a gene ». Although we will use this term, "locus" is a better term. And sometimes, it is even difficult to associate a protein with a single corresponding gene. For example, the protein « Motor

information will be used by ribosomes to produce proteins. Ribosomes are either free or attached to the endoplasmic reticulum.

There are several types of RNA, each having different functions in the cell.

Gene expression begins with a process called transcription.

2.1.1.2. Transcription : from DNA to mRNA

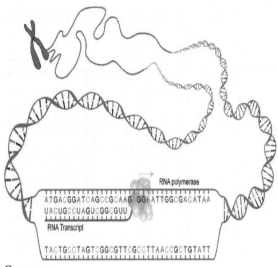

Source :
https://cnx.org/contents/FPtK1zmh@8.25:
lyDdZqp4@6/Protein-Synthesis

Before the mRNA molecule leaves the nucleus, it is modified in several ways. For this reason, it is often called a pre-mRNA at this stage.

DNA contains long regions, called « non-coding regions », that often indirectly influence amino acid coding. We will see an

Neuron Survival » (SMN) is a protein that in humans is encoded by the SMN1 and SMN2 genes.

example of the role of some of those regions, with the C9orf72 gene that is involved in familial ALS. The process called splicing removes these non-coding regions from pre-mRNA transcription.

The deleted segment of the transcript is called intron[13].

An exon is an RNA segment that is used after splicing. The remaining exons are glued together. When different coding regions of the mRNA are spliced, it produces different proteins. This process results in a great variety of proteins and possible protein functions. When the transcription of the mRNA is ready, mRNA moves out of the nucleus and into the cytoplasm.

2.1.1.3. From RNA to Protein : Translation

Inside the cytoplasm, the strand of mRNA is translated into a chain of amino acids. The substrate on which the translation takes place is the ribosome. In most cases mRNA will be translated simultaneously by several adjacent ribosomes. This increases the efficiency of protein synthesis.

There are two types of ribosomes :

- Free ribosomes can move anywhere in the cytosol, but are excluded from the cell nucleus and other organelles. Proteins that are formed from free ribosomes are released into the cytosol and used in the cell.

- Membrane ribosomes are confined to the endoplasmic reticulum (ER). The newly produced polypeptide chains are inserted directly into the ER by the ribosome and are then transferred to the Golgi apparatus.

Free ribosomes are transported to peripheral axonal domains by microtubule-based, fast axonal transport. A common

---

13 During RNA splicing, the introns are removed and the exons are joined together to create the mRNA. Introns are still referred to as « *noncoding regions* », and exons are still called « *coding regions* », even though introns also indirectly participate in the coding of a protein.

consequence of neuropathies is disruption of the ability of neurons to transport cargo along the entire length of the axon. An alternative source for axonal ribosomes might be the periaxonal Schwann cells. These cells bud off so-called ribosome-containing vesicles, from the peri-axonal Schwann cell cytoplasm and into the axonal compartment.

2.1.1.4. Post-translational modifications

Heterogeneous nuclear ribonucleoproteins (hnRNPs) are complexes of RNA and protein. They are present in the cell nucleus during gene transcription and subsequent post-transcriptional modification of the newly synthesized RNA (pre-mRNA). The presence of the proteins bound to a pre-mRNA molecule, serves as a signal that the pre-mRNA is not yet fully processed and therefore not ready for export to the cytoplasm. After splicing has occurred, the proteins remain bound to spliced introns and target them for degradation.

hnRNPs affect several aspects of the cell cycle by recruiting, splicing, and co-regulating certain cell cycle control proteins. Much of hnRNPs' importance to cell cycle control is evidenced by its role as an oncogene, as the loss of its functions results in various common cancers.

The multiple roles played by RNA binding proteins in neurodegeneration have become apparent after the discovery of TDP-43 and FUS/TLS involvement in amyotrophic lateral sclerosis and frontotemporal lobar dementia. TDP-43 and FUS/TLS control several aspects of an mRNA's life, but they can also participate in DNA repair processes and in non-coding RNA metabolism. Although their regulatory activities are similar, they regulate mainly distinct RNA targets.

Like all hnRNP proteins, TDP-43 binds to nascent pre-mRNA molecules as soon as they emerge and regulates their processing steps either through sequential interactions with binding partners or in collaboration/antagonism with neighboring RNA binding factors. However, TDP-43 has been identified to play a role not only in splicing but also in all steps of mRNA life cycle and to regulate also non-coding RNAs (miRNAs, lncRNAs, etc.).

Similar to TDP-43, FUS/TLS is a hnRNP protein, which belongs to the FET protein family.

2.2. Organelles of the endomembrane system

A set of three organelles form a major system within the cell. These organelles work together to perform various cellular work, including the production, conformation and export of proteins. These organelles include the endoplasmic reticulum, the Golgi apparatus and the vesicles.

They play a central role in proteinopathies such as TDP43.

2.2.1. Endoplasmic reticulum

The endoplasmic reticulum (ER) is a large folded membranous surface that supports many functions. This membrane creates a system of channels through most of the cell. These channels provide passages through most of the cell for transport, synthesis and storage of materials.

The endoplasmic reticulum exists in two forms : rough ER and smooth ER. These two types of endoplasmic reticulum perform very different functions. Depending on the type of cell, they are found in very different amounts. The rough endoplasmic reticulum (RER) is so called because its membrane is dotted with ribosomes. The ribosomes on the membrane confers the RER its bumpy appearance.

A ribosome is composed of two ribosomal RNA subunits that wrap around the mRNA to start the translation process, followed by protein synthesis. The smooth endoplasmic reticulum (SER) is devoid of these ribosomes.

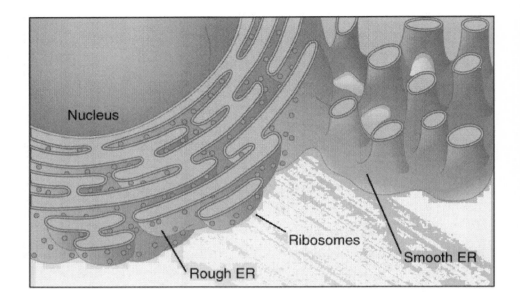

Nucleus

Ribosomes

Smooth ER

Rough ER

Source : https://cnx.org/contents/FPtK1zmh@8.25: fV7KwqTE@5/The-Cytoplasm-and-Cellular-Organelles

2.2.2. The Golgi apparatus

The Golgi apparatus is responsible for sorting, modifying proteins coming from the rough endoplasmic reticulum and exporting them to their final destinations. The Golgi apparatus resembles a stack of hollow, membranous disks. It has two distinct sides, one side of the Golgi apparatus receives proteins contained in vesicles.

These proteins are sorted through the Golgi apparatus, then released on the opposite side after being reconditioned into new vesicles. If the protein is to be exported out of the cell, the vesicle migrates to the surface of the cell and fuses with the cell membrane. The cargo is then secreted. Cargo can also be returned to other locations in the cytoplasm (axonal transport case) or to the nucleus (which happens to TDP-43 when it is normally formed).

During neurodegenerative diseases, the Golgi apparatus may be fragmented.

Golgi fragmentation alters protein transport. Moreover, the Golgi apparatus in neurons is an important microtubule-organizing center and its alteration may significantly alter the cytoskeleton and associated activities. Thus, fragmentation may induce failures in transport to axons and synapses as well as dendrites.

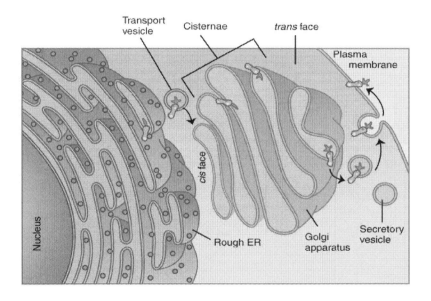

Source : https://cnx.org/contents/FPtK1zmh@8.25:
fV7KwqTE@5/The-Cytoplasm-and-Cellular-Organelles

2.2.3. Mitochondria

2.2.3.1. Providing energy to the cell

A mitochondrion is a membranous organelle. Its inner membrane is strongly folded in sinuous structures so as to have a maximum of surface in a minimum of volume. It is along this inner membrane that cellular respiration takes place. Chemical reactions convert the energy stored in nutrient molecules (such as glucose) into adenosine triphosphate (ATP). ATP provides the cell with usable energy for the various chemical operations it will have to carry out. The cells constantly use ATP, so mitochondria are constantly at work.

One of the body's organic systems that use a lot of ATP is the muscular system because it is necessary to maintain muscle contraction. As a result, muscle cells are largely provided with mitochondria. Nerve cells also need large amounts of ATP to operate their sodium-potassium pumps. Therefore, a neuron will have more than a thousand mitochondria that are mobile inside the cell to adapt to changing energy needs. On the other hand, a bone cell, which is not as metabolically active, could contain only a few hundred mitochondria.

The number of mitochondria is dynamic, if there is a need somewhere in the neuron, they are created and transported by a specific axonal transport mechanism in a few minutes.

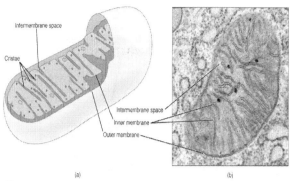

Source :
https://cnx.org/contents/FPtK1zmh@8.25:
fV7KwqTE@5/The-Cytoplasm-and-
Cellular-Organelles

2.2.3.2. Genetic information and inheritance

Mitochondria carry also genetic information, and influence inheritability as they are inherited from the mother. It is yet another mystery that no scientist seems to have investigated maternal inheritance in familial ALS. It seems there is only one study[14] on this subject out of more than 25,000 articles.

2.2.3.3. Extracellular space

Mitochondria can also be found in the extracellular space, in vesicular structures and fragments being able to elicit regenerative effects, or act as a danger signal when interacting with other cells.

Forms of extracellular mitochondria can be found free, enclosed by a membrane as inside platelets or vesicles, or as cell free circulating mitochondrial DNA (ccf-mtDNA).

These free mitochondria have been implicated recently in ALS.

---

14 https://www.ncbi.nlm.nih.gov/pubmed/15883330

2.3. Neurons are not ordinary cells

ALS researchers are studying the progression of the disease in different contexts, either in-vitro or in animal models such as flies, fish or mice. The very special characteristics of a human neuronal cell are often ignored.

Neurons are not the average cell described in biology textbooks, for example they do not divide every few hours, they have to survive as long as the body lives. They are very long, so the protein transport time takes hours instead of milliseconds on its travel from the soma to the neuromuscular junction.

Homeostasis is very difficult to maintain for a neuron. Neurons are thus aided by other cells such as astrocytes, oligodendrocytes, ependymal cells that nourish them, assist them in different ways, and protect them from pathogens.

A particularity of neurons is that they have many extensions. A neuron has a large cell body branching into short extensions called dendrites, and a long extension called axon.

Dendrites receive information from other neurons in specialized contact areas called synapses. Dendrites are usually highly branched extensions, providing interfaces for other neurons to communicate with the cell body. A special dendrite, the axon of a motor neuron is connected to many supporting cells. Those supporting cells are themselves connected to other motoneurons. This is one mechanism that might explain how ALS propagates from neuron to neuron.

The axon propagates the nerve impulse to one or more other cells. At the end of the axon is the terminal axon, where there are usually several branches that extend to the target cell, and each end has an enlargement called a synaptic end bulb. In the case of a motor neuron, the axon innervates the cells of a muscle. The set consisting of a motor neuron and the muscle fibers it supplies is called a motor unit.

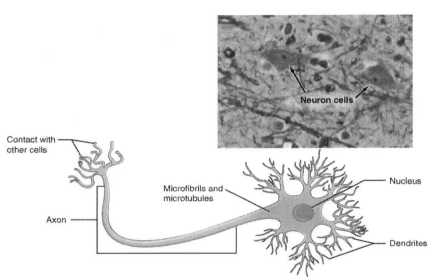

Source : https://cnx.org/contents/FPtK1zmh@8.25: yEs2p8R_@6/Basic-Structure-and-Function-of-the-Nervous-System

When a neuron is sufficiently stimulated, it generates an action potential that propagates along the axon towards the synapse. It is through the synapse that the pulse is transmitted by chemical compounds known as neurotransmitters.

2.3.1. Chemical imbalances

The ion concentrations in the extracellular fluid are the basis of how the membrane potential is established. If the ionic balance is disrupted, dramatic results are possible. Glial cells, particularly astrocytes, are responsible for the maintenance (homeostasis) of the chemical environment in the central nervous system.

In order to maintain the potential of the cell membrane, the cells maintain a low concentration of sodium ions and high levels of potassium ions in the cell. This is called the sodium/potassium pump. One of the earliest signs of a cellular disease is a "leakage" of sodium ions into the body's cells and an excess of potassium-positive ions into the intercellular medium.

After the repolarization phase of the action potential, the potassium positive ion leakage channels and the sodium/potassium pump guarantee the return of the ions to their original location.

After a stroke or other ischemic event, potassium ion levels may remain high in the intercellular medium. Astrocytes then remove excess ions to help the sodium/potassium pump.

But when the level is very unbalanced, the effects can be irreversible. Astrocytes can become reactive in such cases, affecting their ability to maintain a healthy environment. This reactive behavior has been implicated in ALS, notably by Boillée[15]. Reactive astrocytes expand and their extensions swell, they now look like senescent cells. They lose their ability to absorb potassium ions and the pump function is affected or even reversed.

_____

15 https://www.ncbi.nlm.nih.gov/pubmed/17015226

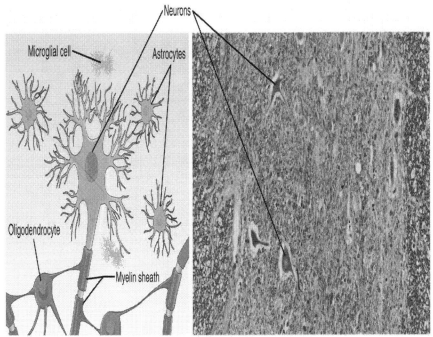

Source : https://cnx.org/contents/FPtK1zmh@8.25: yEs2p8R_@6/
Basic-Structure-and-Function-of-the-Nervous-System

2.3.2. Neural environment

Glial cells maintain the neurons' environment. Glial cells include astrocytes, oligodendrocytes, microglia and ependymal cells. Astrocytes are important for maintaining the chemical environment around the neuron and are essential for regulating the blood-brain barrier. Oligodendrocytes are the myelinating glia of the central nervous system. Microglia act as phagocytes and play a role in immune surveillance. Ependymal cells are responsible for filtering blood to produce the cerebrospinal fluid (CSF). The CSF is a circulatory fluid that fulfills some of the functions of the blood, but in the brain and spinal cord. In the peripheral nervous system, satellite cells are

38

the cells that support neurons and Schwann cells isolate peripheral axons.

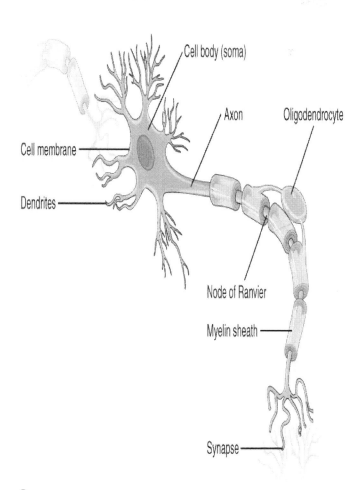

Source :
https://cnx.org/contents/FPtK1zmh@8.25:
mYoZvS9p@3/Nervous-Tissue

2.3.3. What is a motor neuron ?

A motor neuron, or motoneuron, is a neuron whose axon projects sometimes over a meter and that participates in the voluntary control of movements. There are two main varieties, upper motor neurons have their bodies in the motor cortex or brainstem, while lower motor neurons have their bodies in the spinal chord. A lower motor neuron can innerve up to 1000 muscle fibers.

Interneurons in the spinal chord help to integrate the sensory information and they control lower motor neurons in tasks such as balance control or repetitive actions like walking.

During the organism development, neurons spontaneously assemble to construct organized structures and functional circuits in various parts of the nervous system. An axonal fascicle is formed as growing axons follow and gather along the « pioneer axon » that precedes them through inter-axonal interactions.

Inside the nerve, axons targeting the same anatomical location are grouped into groups called fascicles, each surrounded by another protective sheath called perineurium. Several bundles can in turn be bundled with a blood supply and adipose tissue into another sheath, the epineurium.

This grouping structure is analogous to the muscular organization system.

The nerves are linked and often travel with the blood vessels, because the neurons of a nerve have quite high energy needs.

Motor neurons are unique in that they are highly polarized cells with long projections. Active transport of proteins and organelles along the axon, in both directions between the cell body and the neuronal synapse, is essential for their survival.

This function is particularly difficult to perform in neurons because of their polarized nature and the need for different proteins in synaptic buttons, dendrites, axons and soma. Therefore they need the support of astrocytes and other glial cells, even more urgently than other types of neurons. This dependency of neurons on the supporting cells may explain why they are the first to fail in neurodegeneration.

As all cells of the central nervous system can mutate from one type of cell to another, under specific conditions, it may be possible in the future to encourage other cells to replace neurons. We will discuss in more detail about this subject at the end of this book.

In order to transport proteins over these incredibly long distances, the neuronal nucleus, in addition to the endoplasmic reticulum, the Golgi apparatus and dendrites, also sometimes contains neuron-specific organelles : the epinic apparatus and the Golgi outposts. Long-distance transport is greatly improved in neurons by these decentralized mini-organelles.

Local production and protein supply in dendrites is a particularly effective way to enable synapses that are far away from the soma of the neuron, where the traditional organs of protein creation and maturation are located. This production in neurites is done through mRNA and encoding membranes[16].

The number of Golgi outposts increases during periods of intense dendritic growth. Although the Golgi outposts play important roles during dendritic development, the vast majority of mature cortical and hippocampal dendrites do not contain Golgi outposts. Indeed, these neurons in the brain are smaller in size than motor neurons.

---

16 Neurite is any extension of the cell body of a neuron. It can be an axon or a dendrite.

2.3. Neurons are not ordinary cells

2.4. From the cortex to the neuromuscular junction.

While the sensory cortical areas are located in the occipital, temporal and parietal lobes, the motor functions are largely controlled by the frontal lobe. The most anterior regions of the frontal lobe, the prefrontal regions, are important for executive functions. Executive functions are the cognitive functions that lead to conscious behaviors. However if there are indeed specialized areas in the brain, most brain areas are deeply interconnected and cannot function properly without inputs from other regions.

2.4.1. Primary motor cortex

In the precentral gyrus of the frontal lobe, the primary motor cortex receives information that facilitates movement planning, and uses lower motor neurons in the spinal cord to stimulate contraction of skeletal muscles. Neurons in the primary motor cortex, called Betz cells, are a type of upper motor neuron that connect to lower motor neurons of spinal cord or brainstem.

Muscles that perform fine and agile movements, such as the muscles of the fingers and lower face, receive most of the cortical space. "Power muscles » that perform coarser movements, such as the muscles of the buttocks and back, occupy much less space on the motor cortex.

The motor commands issued by the cortex descends into the brainstem and into the spinal cord to control the musculature by the lower motor neurons. Any motor order of the right motor cortex controls the muscles on the left side of the body, and vice versa. The two descending pathways taken by the axons of Betz cells are the **corticospinal tract** and the **corticobulbar tract**.

2.4.2. The corticobulbar tract

The muscles of the face, head and neck are controlled by the corticobulbar system. However it does not control the eyes movements which explains why a paralyzed ALS patient can still control their eyes.

The corticobulbar tract is a white matter motor pathway connecting the motor cortex in the cerebral cortex to the medullary pyramids. This pathway is part of the brainstem's medulla oblongata (also called "bulbar") region.

The corticobulbar tract is composed of the upper motor neurons of the cranial nerves. The corticobulbar system terminates on lower motor neurons within brainstem's motor nuclei. This is in contrast to the corticospinal tract which terminates on lower motor neurons within the spinal chord.

The corticobulbar tract directly innervates the nuclei for cranial nerves V, VII, IX, and XII. The corticobulbar tract also contributes to the motor regions of cranial nerve X in the nucleus ambiguus.

2.4.3. The corticospinal tract

The lateral corticospinal tract is responsible for the movement of the muscles of the arms and legs.

The corticospinal tract descends from the cortex through the deep white matter of the brain. Entering the marrow, this path constitutes the great expanse of white substance called pyramid.

The lateral corticospinal tract is composed of fibers that cross body's midline during the pyramidal decussation[17]. This makes the right hemisphere controlling the left part of body and vice-versa.

---

17 Le croisement des fibres nerveuses qui fait que la partie droite de notre cerveau contrôle la partie gauche de notre corps, et vice versa.

2.4. From the cortex to the neuromuscular junction.

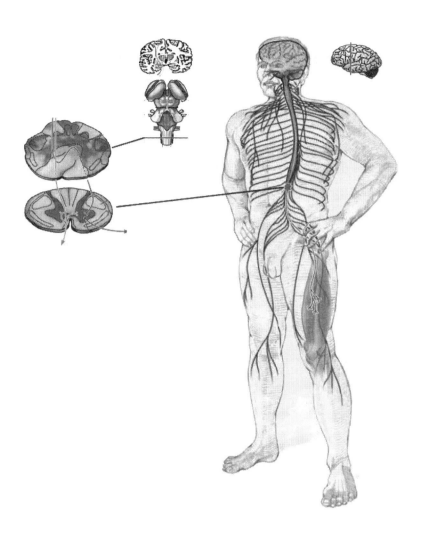

2.4.4. The spinal cord

The spine surrounds the spinal cord that moves in the spinal canal, itself formed by a central hole in each vertebra.

The dorsal or posterior horns of the gray matter are mainly devoted to sensory functions, while the ventral or anterior horns and lateral horns are associated with motor functions.

A spinal nerve is a mixed nerve that transmits motor, sensory and autonomic signals. In the human body, there are 31 pairs of spinal nerves, one on each side of the spine. These are grouped in the corresponding cervical, thoracic, lumbar, sacral and coccygeal regions of the spine.

There are eight pairs of cervical nerves, twelve pairs of thoracic nerves, five pairs of lumbar nerves, five pairs of sacral nerves, and a pair of coccygeal nerves. The spinal nerves are part of the peripheral nervous system.

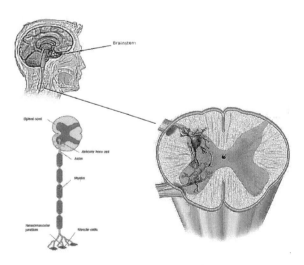

2.4.5. Exit of the ventral horn

The soma (cellular body) of the lower motoneurons, is found in the ventral horn of the spinal cord. These large multipolar neurons have a crown of dendrites surrounding the cell body and an axon coming out of the ventral horn.

This axon crosses the ventral nerve root to join the emerging spinal nerve. This axon then exits the central nervous system to enter the peripheral nervous system. The cells that will assist it are no longer astrocytes and oligodendrocytes, but satellite cells and Schwann cells. The satellite cells could play a role equivalent to that of the blood-brain barrier. Curiously satellite cells have little been studied while astrocytes have been the subject of many studies[18]. This is quite amazing in the context of ALS insofar as the axon of the lower motoneuron and its environment are obviously first class actors in the disease.

The axon is relatively long, because it must reach the muscles located at the periphery of the body, but the diameters of the cell bodies may be in the range of ten to several hundred microns. If the neuron soma were a pump as big as a fist, and the axon, a pipe where proteins were pumped, the axon would be several tens of meters (or yards) long.

Axons can branch to innervate several muscle fibers. The motor neuron and all muscle fibers that it controls then constitute a motor unit. Motor units vary in size. Some may contain up to 1000 muscle fibers, such as those of the quadriceps, or have only 10 fibers, such as those of an extraocular muscle. The number of muscle fibers forming part of a motor unit corresponds to the precision of the control of this muscle. In addition, muscles that have finer motor control have more connected motor units. This larger number of

---

18   In 2019, satellite glial cells compose 0.06 % of all ALS studies, while astrocytes compose 3.85 % of all studies.

connections requires an important topographic field in the primary motor cortex.

2.4.5.1. The axon goes out of the CNS

The central nervous system includes the brain and spinal cord, while the peripheral nervous system includes neural tissue located outside the CNS, that is, the axons of lower motor and sensory neurons. The two nervous systems are distinct, notably by barriers such as the blood-brain barrier and yet interconnected.

Motor neurons send their axons through the CNS transition areas, then they travel long distances into the peripheral nervous system and eventually create synapses on the muscles.

The CNS/PNS boundary is delimited in mammal by a thick layer of astrocytic feet that is continuous with the glia limitans that covers the surface of the spinal cord, with the exception of the perforations that allow the axons to cross.

2.4. From the cortex to the neuromuscular junction.

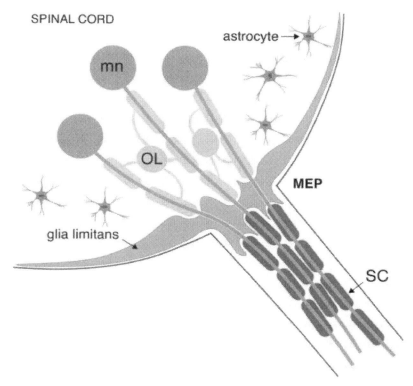

Source : Livin' On The Edge : Glia Shape Nervous System Transition Zones, Laura Fontenas and Sarah Kucenas

Glia limitans, or glial limiting membrane, is a thin barrier formed by cytoplasmic astrocyte extensions associated with the basal parenchymal lamina surrounding the brain and spinal cord. It is the outermost layer of neural tissue and one of its responsibilities is to prevent the excessive migration of neurons and neuroglia into the meninges.

It also means that outside the CNS, there are no more astrocytes or oligodendrocytes around the axon, instead there are Schwann cells. And as we will see in the third part of this book, Schwann cells promote the regeneration of nerves.

2.4. From the cortex to the neuromuscular junction.

Schwann cells organize a preferential motor reinnervation direction. If the Schwann cells are prevented from associating with the axons, axons die. Regenerating axons reach no target if the Schwann cells are not there to support and guide them. On the other hand, the rate of progression of this regeneration is slow (one cm per month), is limited to short distances[19] and does not work well in the elderly[20].

There are some astonishing publications, some well cited, that state that ALS is a distal axonopathy[21]. If ALS was a distal axonopathy, not only current therapy approaches that are targeting the CNS would be inefficient (which they are), but recovering from ALS would be possible. But most scientists would say ALS cannot be a distal axonopathy.

2.4.5.2. Blood-brain barrier

The blood-brain barrier is selective, only certain molecules can penetrate the CNS. Glucose and amino acids, sources of primary energy can enter as well as water and some other small particles, such as gases and ions, but almost everything else is excluded.

Although this barrier protects the central nervous system from exposure to toxic or pathogenic substances, it also prevents the entry of immune system cells. This means that the CNS must replace the physiological mechanisms of the body by its own mechanisms, for example the cerebrospinal fluid plays a role similar to blood. The blood-brain barrier also complicates the development and administration of pharmaceuticals in the nervous system.

This barrier is provided by the ependymal cells which are glial cells that filter the blood to produce the cerebrospinal fluid, the fluid that circulates in the central nervous system. Glial cells

19   https://www.ncbi.nlm.nih.gov/pubmed/27094884
20   https://www.ncbi.nlm.nih.gov/pubmed/27451012
21   https://www.ncbi.nlm.nih.gov/pubmed/14736504/

2.4. From the cortex to the neuromuscular junction.

resemble to epithelial cells, forming a single layer of cells with little intracellular space and close connections between adjacent cells. They also have cilia on their apical surface to help them move the cerebrospinal fluid.

Lower motor neurons are different from other neurons in that all other types of neurons are entirely within the blood-brain barrier. For lower motor neurons, only the central body is within it, the axon and the neuromuscular junctions are outside this barrier.

2.4.6. Consequences of damage to higher neurons

Signs that suggest damage to higher neurons are muscle weakness, called « pyramidal weakness" and exacerbated reflexes. And initial period named "spinal shock", happens after the upper motor neuron injury and is characterized by hypotonia. This may reflect the decreased activity of spinal circuits suddenly deprived of input from the motor cortex and brainstem. After several days, however, the spinal cord circuits regain much of their function for reasons that are not fully understood, but may include the strengthening of remaining connections and the sprouting of new connections.

- One of these signs may be a clonus. It is an involuntary and often violent cycle of contraction/relaxation of a muscle.

- Spasticity appears after the spinal shock period. A rapid stretching of a muscle, automatically causes its reflex contraction which lasts a certain time. This is called a clasp-knife response where a higher initial resistance to movement is followed by less resistance.

- There is also an increase in deep tendon reflex (DTR).

- The Babinski sign is present, where the big toe is raised rather than curved down if appropriate stimulation is done on the sole of the foot.

- Pronator drift : Also named Barré's sign, it indicates a pyramidal syndrome marking the deficit of the voluntary motor drive in the lower limb. The patient lying on his stomach, legs bent at 90°, the deficit is observed by the gradual fall of the legs because of the involvement of the flexor muscles.

- Paralysis is rare, often only mild atrophy develops.

2.4.7. Consequences of damage to lower neurons

A lesion on a lower motor neuron will result at least partially in paralysis, with a partial or total loss of muscle tone. The brain and upper neuron command the muscle, but the muscle stays inert.

In addition to paralysis and/or paresis, the lower motor neuron syndrome includes a loss of reflexes.

Damage to lower motor neurons also entails a loss of muscle tone, since tone is dependent in the link between the muscle spindles and the lower motor neurons

Other signs that characterize lower motor neuropathies are fibrillation, fasciculations where the muscle reacts to ghost signals. These spontaneous contractions can be readily recognized in an electromyogram, providing an especially helpful clinical tool in diagnosing lower motor neuron disorders.

A somewhat later effect of lower motor neuron damage is atrophy of the affected muscles due to long-term denervation and disuse.

2.4. From the cortex to the neuromuscular junction.

Manifestation	Upper motor neuron injury	Lower motor neuron injury
Reflexes	Hyperactives	Decreased or absent
Muscular atrophy	Absent at first, but will appear after a prolonged absence of use of the limbs.	Present
Fasciculations	Absents	Presents
Clonus	Present	Absent
Muscle tone	Accrue	Receding or missing

2.4.7.1. Neuromuscular junctions

The interface between the motor neuron and the muscle fiber is a specialized synapse called the neuromuscular junction.

In contact with the muscle fibers, the nerve branches out and ends with an anatomical structure contiguous to the muscle fibers : the motor plate. These motor plates are located at the junction of the nerve and the muscle fiber. The role of the motor plate is the chemical transmission of the electrochemical signal (or action potential) of the nerve.

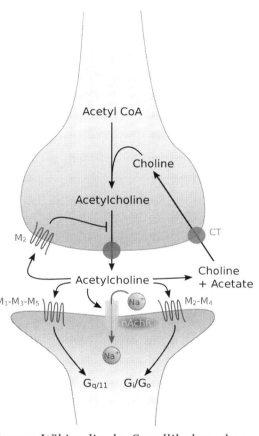

Source Wikipedia, by Smedlib, based on original work by Pancrat

For each nerve fiber, there is a corresponding muscle fiber, the whole forms a motor unit. Groups of motor units often work together to coordinate the contractions of a single muscle ; all the motor units of a muscle are considered as a motor pool.

2.4. From the cortex to the neuromuscular junction.

The number of muscle fibers in each unit can vary within a given muscle and from one muscle to another : The muscles that act on the largest body masses have motor units containing more muscle fibers, whereas the smaller muscles contain less muscle fibers in each motor unit. For example, the thigh muscles may have a thousand fibers in each unit, while the extra-ocular muscles may have ten. Muscles that have more motor units are able to control the use of force more finely.

2.4.8. Visceral motor neurons

2.4.8.1. General visceral motor neurons

These motoneurons indirectly innervate the heart muscle and the smooth muscles of the arteries.

2.4.8.2. Special visceral motor neurons

These are also known as branchial motor neurons, involved in facial expression, chewing, phonation and swallowing. The associated cranial nerves are the oculomotor, abducens, trochlear and hypoglossal nerves.

2.5. Glial cells

Glial cells, or simply glia, are of different types of cells than neurons. They are also found in nerve tissue. Glial cells were usually considered only as supporting cells of secondary importance, but neurodegenerative research tends to consider them as important as neurons. The name glia comes from the Greek meaning "glue" and was invented by the German pathologist Rudolph Virchow, who wrote in 1856 : *"This connective substance, which is found in the brain, spinal cord and special sensory nerves, is a kind of glue (neuroglia) in which the nerve elements are planted."*

There are six types of glial cells. Four of them are in the CNS and two in the PNS.

Types of glial cells by location and basic function		
Glial cells of the CNS	**Glial cells of the PNS**	**Basic function**
Astrocyte	Satellite cell	Support
Oligodendrocyte	Schwann cell	Isolation, myelination
Microglia		Immune monitoring and phagocytosis
Ependymal cell		Creation of cerebrospinal fluid (CSF)

The CNS has astrocytes, oligodendrocytes, microglia, and ependymal cells that support CNS neurons in several ways.

2.5.1. Astrocytes

One of the cells providing support for CNS neurons is the astrocyte, so named because it appears star-shaped when viewed under a microscope.

Astrocytic cells are abundant in the central nervous system. They have many functions, including the regulation of ion concentration in the inter-cellular space, the absorption and/or degradation of certain neurotransmitters and the formation of the blood-brain barrier.

Astrocytes have many extensions. These extensions interact with neurons, blood vessels or connective tissue covering the central nervous system.

The blood-brain barrier (BBB) is a physiological barrier that prevents many substances that circulate throughout the body from infiltrating the central nervous system, thus preventing blood from entering in the central nervous system. Nutrient molecules, such as glucose or amino acids, can pass through the BBB, but other molecules can not. This poses problems in delivering drugs to the central nervous system. Pharmaceutical companies are challenged to design drugs that can cross the BBB and have an effect on the nervous system.

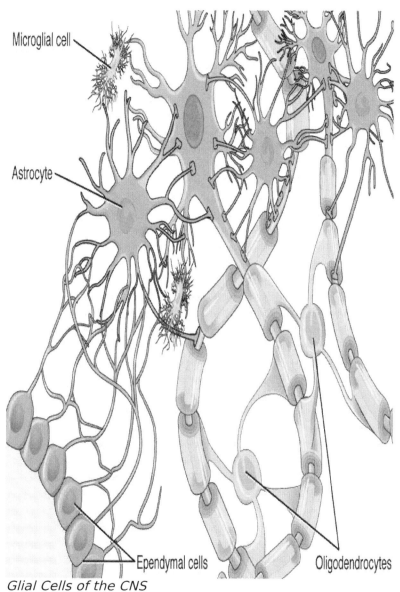

Glial Cells of the CNS
Source : https://cnx.org/contents/FPtK1zmh@8.25:
mYoZvS9p@3/Nervous-Tissue

2.5.2. Oligodendrocytes

The name of the oligodendrocytes means « cell of some branches ». They only have a few extensions that extend from the cell body. Oligodendrocyte cells produce myelin in the central nervous system (brain and spinal cord), while the Schwann cell produces myelin in the peripheral nervous system. An oligodendrocyte will provide myelin for several axon segments.

2.5.3. Microglia

Microglia cells protect the nervous system against infection and are related to the macrophages of the immune system. When they encounter diseased or damaged cells in the rest of the body, they ingest and digest these cells or the pathogens responsible for the disease.

2.6. Communication and neurons

2.6.1. Synapses

There are two types of connections between neurons, chemical synapses and electrical synapses.

- Chemical synapses involve the transmission of chemical information, ie a neurotransmitter, from cell to cell.

- In an electrical synapse, there is a direct connection between the two cells so that the ions can pass directly from one cell to another. If a cell is depolarized in an electrical synapse, the attached cell depolarizes itself as the ions pass between the cells.

All synapses have common characteristics, which can be summarized in this list :

- The presynaptic element is the axonal end of the motor neuron.

- The neurotransmitter is acetylcholine, contained in a vesicle.

- The synaptic cleft is the space between the cells where the neurotransmitter is transferred from one cell to another.

- There is a receptor (nicotinic acetylcholine protein)

- The postsynaptic element is the sarcolemma of the muscle cell and the neurotransmitter is removed by acetylcholinesterase.

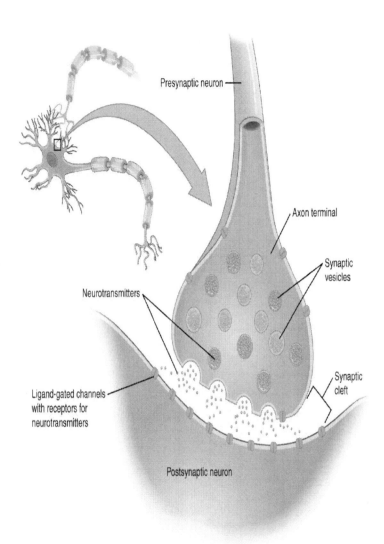

Source : https://cnx.org/contents/FPtK1zmh@8.25:
p74vr6PZ@3/Communication-Between-Neurons

2.6. Communication and neurons

2.6.2. Neurotransmitters

Neurotransmitters are released by the synaptic vesicles of the synapses into the synaptic cleft and are received by neurotransmitter receptors on the target cells. The important thing to remember about neurotransmitters, is that the effect depends on the receptor.

The sodium pump (sodium-potassium ATPases) plays an essential role in the maintenance of an electrochemical membrane potential. The pump is used to exchange sodium ions (Na+) from the intracellular medium with K+ potassium ions from the extracellular medium in a precise ratio. The potassium current "leakage" defines the membrane potential. In neurons, this electrochemical potential allows the triggering of action potential and postsynaptic potential.

Hyperpolarization is a modification of the membrane potential of a cell that makes it more negative. This is the opposite of a depolarization. Hyperpolarization increases the stimulus needed to shift the membrane potential to the action potential threshold.

In neurons, the cell enters a state of hyperpolarization immediately after the generation of an action potential. When hyperpolarized, the neuron is in a refractory period of about 2 milliseconds, during which time it is unable to generate subsequent action potentials.

The sodium-potassium ATPases redistribute the potassium and sodium ions between the extra and intra-cellular media until the membrane potential returns to its quiescent potential of about -70 millivolts, at which time the neuron is again ready to transmit another action potential.

Excitatory neurotransmitters cause depolarization of the postsynaptic cell, while hyperpolarization produced by an inhibitory neurotransmitter will attenuate the effects of an excitatory neurotransmitter.

When an action potential reaches the axon terminals, the voltage-gated Ca2 channels open into the membrane of the synaptic end bulb. The neurotransmitter is released by exocytosis in the small space between cells, which is called synaptic cleft.

Once in the synaptic cleft, the neurotransmitter spreads over the short distance separating it from the postsynaptic membrane and can then interact with the neurotransmitter receptors. The receptors are specific to the neurotransmitter.

The neurotransmitter is removed from the synapse by either enzymatic degradation, neuronal reabsorption or glial reabsorption.

- **Cholinergic system as neurotransmitter**

   The cholinergic system is based on acetylcholine. The neuromuscular junction is an example of a cholinergic synapse, but cholinergic synapses are found in other parts of the nervous system. Many drugs, as well as venoms and toxins exert their effects by altering cholinergic transmission.

   The cholinergic system has two types of receptors, the nicotinic receptor and the acetylcholine receptor called the muscarinic receptor.

- **Amino acids as neurotransmitter**

   Amino acid neurotransmitters include glutamate (Glu), GABA (a glutamate derivative) and glycine (Gly). They play a very important role in ALS.

   Each amino acid neurotransmitter has its own receptor and they do not interact with each other. A pump in the cell membrane of the presynaptic element, or sometimes a nearby glial cell, will remove the amino acid from the synaptic cleft so that it can be recycled, reconditioned into vesicles and released again.

Glutamate is considered to be an excitatory amino acid, but only because Glu receptors in adults cause depolarization of the postsynaptic cell. Glycine and GABA are considered inhibitory amino acids because their receptors cause hyperpolarization.

○ Glutamic acid is an α-amino acid used by almost all living things in protein biosynthesis. It is also the most abundant excitatory neurotransmitter of the vertebrate nervous system.

○ Glutamate is a key compound in cellular metabolism, it also plays an important role in eliminating excess nitrogen or waste from the body. Ammonia produced is mainly excreted as urea synthesized in the liver. One article suggested that ALS could be induced by ammonia production[22] but it is a fringe proposal.

○ Glutamate serves as a precursor to the synthesis of the inhibitor GABA in GABA-ergic neurons. This reaction is catalyzed by glutamate decarboxylase (GAD), which is abundant in the cerebellum and pancreas.

• **Biogenic amine as neurotransmitter**

Biogenic amines are a group of neurotransmitters made enzymatically from amino acids. Serotonin is made from tryptophan. It is the basis of the serotonergic system, which has its own specific receptors. Serotonin is transported into the presynaptic cell for reconditioning.

Other biogenic amines are made from tyrosine and include dopamine, norepinephrine and epinephrine.

• **Neuropeptides as neurotransmitter**

---

22 https://www.ncbi.nlm.nih.gov/pmc/articles/PMC5063041/

2.6. Communication and neurons

A neuropeptide is a neurotransmitter molecule consisting of amino acid chains linked by peptide bonds. Neuropeptides are often released at synapses in combination with another neurotransmitter and they often act as hormones in other organs of the body.

2.6.3. The cell membrane

The cell membrane controls the movement of substances entering and leaving cells and organelles. Cell membranes are involved in various cellular processes such as cell adhesion, ionic conductivity, and cell signaling and serve as a binding surface for several extracellular structures, including the cell wall and the intracellular network of protein fibers called the cytoskeleton.

The lipid bilayer forms the base of the cell membrane, but is dotted with various proteins. Two different types of proteins commonly associated with the cell membrane are integral proteins and peripheral proteins.

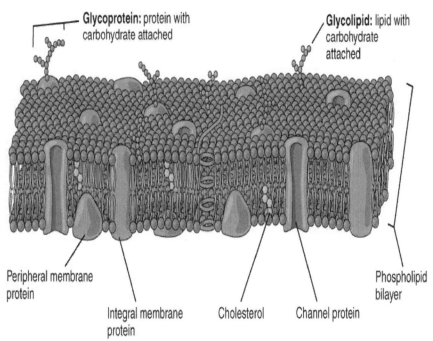

Source : https://cnx.org/contents/FPtK1zmh@8.25:
q2X995E3@11/The-Cell-Membrane

2.6.3.1. Membrane receptors

Cell surface receptors (membrane receptors, transmembrane receptors) are receptors integrated into the plasma membrane of cells. They are one of the actors of cellular signaling, controlling the exchanges between the inside of the cell and the extracellular molecules. They have generated considerable interest from ALS researchers, both because they may be part of the etiology of the disease and because they are an obvious target for drugs.

Extracellular molecules can be hormones, neurotransmitters, cytokines, growth factors, cell adhesion molecules or nutrients.

Membrane receptors are mainly divided by structure and function into 3 classes.

- **Ion channel-related receptors** participate in the fast signaling events typically found in neurons. They have been the subject of many studies in the field of ALS. They are also called ligand gate ion channels. The opening and closing of ion channels is controlled by neurotransmitters.

  ○ The AMPA receptor is an ionotrophic glutamate transmembrane receptor that provides rapid synaptic transmission in the central nervous system. It is one of three receptors with the NMDA receptor and the kainate receptor. The AMPA receptor is the most common receptor in the nervous system. It plays a key role in the generation and spread of epileptic seizures. Kainic acid, a convulsive widely used in epilepsy research, causes convulsions, in part, through the activation of AMPA receptors.

  ○ GABA receptors are chloride channels activated by a ligand. When activated by GABA, they allow the flow of of either negatively charged chloride ions into the cell or positively charged potassium ions out of the cell. This action results in a negative change in the transmembrane potential, usually causing hyperpolarization. When the net flow of chloride is close to zero, GABA has no action.

- **Enzyme-related receptors** are either enzymes themselves or activators of the associated enzymes. They are generally transmembrane receptors with a single direction of passage, the enzymatic component of the receptor being maintained intracellularly. The majority of enzyme-linked receptors are protein kinases or are associated with these proteins. Some drugs target this type of receptor.

- **G-protein coupled receptors** are integral membrane proteins that activate G protein in agonist binding, and G protein acts on intracellular signaling pathways.

3. Research on ALS

3.1. Main themes of ALS research

For a long time (2008), it has become increasingly clear that ALS is more than just a disease of upper and lower motor neurons. Cytoplasmic inclusions[23] of the protein TDP-43[24], a protein found in both familial and sporadic[25] forms of ALS, have been found in the brains of patients, indicating that the disease damages other neurons than motor neurons as well as non-neuronal cells.

The cause of ALS, which has both a sporadic form and an inheritable form, is mysterious. There is no known cause of ALS and at least a dozen credible theories clash in this area. It is good that there are some teams that have been working on ALS or neurodegenerative diseases for decades. But this creates a kind of mental rigidity, a team sticks to its culture, including its favorite theories about ALS.

In the next sections we will study two main but incompatible, themes of ALS research. Maybe the "dying forward" theme is related only to the bulbar-onset form, and the "dying back" is related only to the spinal-onset form, but scientists have never explored this possibility.

---

23   The cells have two main areas, the nucleus where the DNA is located and the cytoplasm where the proteins produced by the DNA are folded and "decorated" with signaling proteins. You may associate proteins with muscle tissue, but in fact, proteins are critical components of all tissues and organs.

24   TDP-43 is a protein that has many functions, but in ALSSLA, Alzheimer's disease and other neurodegenerative diseases, its mutated form aggregates into granules in the cytoplasm. Although the exact mechanism is not known, it is believed that these aggregates are toxic to the cell.

25   "Familial" means that the disease is hereditary (the patient has mutated genes inherited from her ancestors), while "sporadic" means that the causal event is not known.

3.1.1. Where does ALS begin ?

Many neurodegenerative diseases, including Alzheimer's disease and Parkinson's disease, begin years or decades before people experience the first symptoms.

But where does ALS really start ? Despite initial observations by Charcot on the concurrent pathological changes in ALS of upper (upper motor) and lower (lower motor neuron) motor neurons, and observation fifty years ago in the post mortem examination of motor neurons corticospinal (CSMN) in patients with Golgi staining, significant abnormalities, including late arborization of nodular dendritic and apical dendrites and loss of spine (Hammer and colleagues, 1979[26]), the question of the beginning of ALS has not been definitively established.

Many scientists subscribe to the "***dying back***" hypothesis[27], that degeneration begins at the neuromuscular junction when motor neurons retreat from the synapse. Others prefer the "***dying forward***" hypothesis[28]». They believe that ALS starts in the brain before spreading to lower motor neurons.

It is important to address this question, as it is difficult to see how a treatment could be designed for ALS if we do not know if it starts in the brain or at the neuromuscular junction. As the molecular mechanisms are very different, the drugs that act on these mechanisms will necessarily be very different.

Can we infer some information from the relatively success of drugs in ALS ? Nurown is injected in the spinal chord, so there is no clear answer as both the upper motoneurons axons and soma of lower motoneurons lie in the spinal chord. Riluzole, Cu(II)ATSM, Masitinib, Tudca or Arimoclomol on the other hand probably reach more easily the axons of the lower motoneurons than their soma or the upper motoneurones.

---

26 https://www.ncbi.nlm.nih.gov/pubmed/437007
27 « **Dying back** » en Anglais.
28 https://www.ncbi.nlm.nih.gov/pubmed/18469020

Another aspect is that any intrathecal treatment is not possible on the long run, as each time the injection is made, the dura mer is injured. So if the hypothesis "dying forward" is true, and if there is a need for repetitive treatment, which is quite probable, oral treatments must be used. It is well known that oral treatments have a reduced efficiency, due to poor bioavailability.

3.1.2. Dying forward hypothesis.

The « Dying forward » hypothesis indicates that dysfunction in the brain precedes the clinical phase of the disease involving muscles and neuronal cells. This would make ALS very similar to other neurodegenerative diseases such as Parkinson's disease. However, the lack of animal models incorporating direct cortico-motoneuronal (CM) control of muscles, which is specific to higher primates, makes this hypothesis difficult to study.

Cortico-motoneurons are neurons in the primary cortex that project directly onto the motoneurons of the ventral horn of the spinal cord. The axons of cortico-motorneurons terminate on spinal motor neurons of multiple muscles as well as on spinal interneurons. They are unique to primates and it has been suggested that their function is adaptive control of distal ends (for example hands), including relatively independent control of individual fingers. Cortico-motorneurones have so far been found only in the primary motor cortex and not in the secondary motor regions.

The « Dying forward » hypothesis suggests that ALS is mainly due to failure of cortico-motoneurons. As cortico-motoneurons connect to anterior horn cells, this lead to degeneration of anterior horn cells. The « dying forward » hypothesis is supported by the results of transcranial magnetic stimulation studies showing that cortical hyperexcitability is an early feature in patients with sporadic ALS and precedes the clinical onset of familial ALS, but indeed the "dying back" proponents can provide similar studies showing that lower motoneurons fail early in the disease.

The clinical support for this hypothesis comes from observations that motor neurons without a monosynaptic link with cortico-motoneurons, such as those that manage ocular or intestinal movements, are generally spared in ALS ; and that the pure forms of lower motor neurons of ALS are rare, while the subclinical involvement of higher motor neurons is invariably detected.

The scientists that found mutations in the SOD1 gene have pointed out early on that the motoneuron subsets innervated by cortico-motoneurones in humans are generally the most vulnerable to degeneration in ALS patients, while those with low corticosteroid motor neurons are spared. (Eisen and colleagues, 1992[29]).

There were two main points in this remarkable article, one was that ALS is primarily a cortico-motor neuron disease. The second point was that the hyper-excitability of glutamate-induced cortico-motoneurons is the cause of ALS. Scientists have lost sight of the first point and, curiously, in the current theory of motoneuron excitotoxicity, upper motor neurons are not critical for the pathology of ALS, and their degeneration is secondary to lower motor neuron loss. Which is the opposite of what Eisen said!

Ozdinler and colleagues at Harvard demonstrated degeneration of apical dendrite in cortico-motoneurons, decreased spinal density, and decreased cortico-motoneuron numbers in a mouse model (Jara and colleagues[30], 2012 ; Ozdinler and colleagues, 2011[31]).

The trajectory of the ALS progression pattern is consistent with the dissemination of TDP-43 pathology from cortical neuronal

---

29 https://www.ncbi.nlm.nih.gov/pubmed/8096792
30 https://www.ncbi.nlm.nih.gov/pubmed/22521461
31 https://www.ncbi.nlm.nih.gov/pubmed/21411657

projections, via axonal transport, via synaptic contacts to the spinal cord and other brain regions (Braak and colleagues, 2013[32]).

The lower motor neurons are hyperexcitable according to many studies but this has been disputed recently[33] and in 2015, Matthew Fogarty[34] while still a doctoral student, wanted to know if the upper motoneurons were also hyperexcitable. He examined neuronal signaling in mice overexpressing human SOD1 with a glycine-93-alanine mutation. The disease is evolving rapidly in this model. Motor neurons in the spinal cord begin to degenerate at 1-2 months of age and mice develop visible symptoms, such as tremor of the hind leg, approximately 90 days after birth.

Fogarty has observed more than twice as many excitatory neural signals arriving in superior cortical motor neurons in brain slices as in slices from animals that have not been genetically modified. "*The cells are not yet dying, but they are definitely disrupted*," according to Fogarty. These dendritic abnormalities reflect some of the first signs of degeneration in the higher motoneurons.

These results are the first evidence of a cortical circuit disruption in ALS well before the onset of symptoms.

Some ALS familial forms seems to fit well with this hypothesis. This is the case of the bulbar-onset, and it was shown that C9orf72 carriers have a higher incidence of bulbar onset disease[35], as well as FTD and sometimes Parkinson.

---

32 https://www.ncbi.nlm.nih.gov/pubmed/24217521
33 Van Zundert and colleagues, 2008 : http://www.ncbi.nlm.nih.gov/pubmed/18945894
34 http://www.ncbi.nlm.nih.gov/pubmed/25589758
35 https://www.ncbi.nlm.nih.gov/pmc/articles/PMC3925297/

3.1.3. Dying back hypothesis.

The hypothesis of « dying back » is the classic thesis of research on ALS, it says that the loss of lower motoneurons is the cause of the motor problems. Because ALS is a focal disease that often begins with the loss of a minor muscle and then spreads, it is natural to think that the causal event happened near that muscle.

Implicitly, this hypothesis postulates a prodrome event that may be completely foreign to the motoneurons, for example a virus or a bacterial infection, a wound, etc. It is true that there are many diseases that mimic the effects of ALS, they could be initiating events of ALS. They include the human immunodeficiency virus (HIV), the human T-lymphotropic virus (HTLV), Lyme disease and syphilis.

Neurological disorders such as multiple sclerosis, post-polio syndrome, multifocal motor neuropathy, spinal muscular atrophy, and spinal and bulbar muscular atrophy may also mimic some aspects of the disease and should be accounted. Lambert-Eaton syndrome can mimic ALS as well and it could also be genetic disorders such as Wilson's disease, in which copper accumulates in the body.

The problem then is: if we put apart the prodrome event, what subsequently causes the death of motor neurons ? We need another hypothesis. One of the first hypotheses was that superoxide radicals resulting from metabolism damage motor neurons in sporadic ALS. But in 2006, a first misfolded and poorly localized protein, TDP-43, will soon be found.

Misfolded and misplaced protein can cause a loss of function in the cell, therefore a possible cause of cell death but it can also result in functional gain. This functional gain can be quite toxic to the cell. It has also been found that even SOD1 mutations create aggregates of proteins.

In support of the dying back hypothesis, we find results obtained on humans in 2014 by Brettschneider and scientists like Albert C. Ludolph, Virginia M.-Y. Lee (and her husband John Q. Trojanowski), Heiko Braak.

For Brettschneider and their colleagues:

- columns of dorsolateral motor nuclei of the cervical and lumbosacral anterior horn may be the first foci of TDP-43 pathology in the spinal cord. The researchers particularly cite the interneurons found in the medial part of the lamina VII. This intermediate zone of the spinal cord is mainly located from the cervical vertebra C8 and up to the lumbar levels L3-L4.

- oligodendroglial involvement of the gray matter could possibly occur before neuron involvement by the pathology TDP-43.

However, the authors do not know how the pathology extends spreads between neurons, nor what causes it.

This article[36] has been cited 48 times, which is a very good result in the small world of ALS research.

But today, in 2019, we still do not know exactly what causes the death of neurons, or even if there is only one cause of the death of these motor neurons.

It could also be that the muscle cell or neuromuscular junction dies first and triggers the death of the lower motor neuron that is associated with this muscle fiber. The third most cited article on ALS[37] just tells that, with credible proofs on based humans not ad hoc animal models. Those proofs were verified by different teams, but most scientists still do not adhere to this idea.

---

36 https://www.ncbi.nlm.nih.gov/pmc/articles/PMC4384652/
37 https://www.ncbi.nlm.nih.gov/pubmed/14736504

3.1. Main themes of ALS research

3.2. Guiding hypotheses in ALS research.

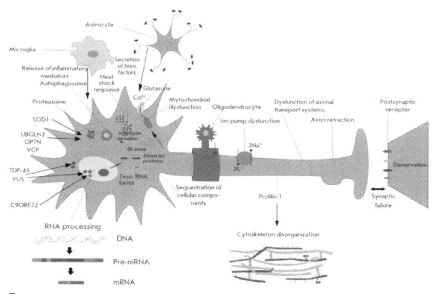

Source :
https://www.ncbi.nlm.nih.gov/pmc/articles/PMC4410393/

3.2.1. Excitotoxicity related to glutamate / calcium permeability.

3.2.1.1. The classical excitotoxicity hypothesis in ALS

It was suspected since several decades that excitotoxicity was implicated in ALS, by analogy with other pathologies such as cerebral infarction or with neurotoxins from food poisoning[38]. Excitotoxicity has been also invoked to explain the etiology of several other neurodegenerative diseases.

Starting in 1990, several articles[39] initiated the hypothesis of excitotoxicity. But other articles rejected it soon afterwards[40]. Soon more and more scientists published articles on excitotoxicity, and in 1996, Riluzole, a pharmacological agent that reduced glutamate release through nerve endings, was administered to patients with ALS. Riluzole is an anticonvulsant and a neuroprotective agent that specifically blocks sodium channels in their inactivated state. In this context, Riluzole has proved very effective. After 1 year of treatment, 58 % of patients treated with placebo were still alive, compared to 74 % of patients treated with Riluzole. Today, it is estimated that Riluzole prolongs survival up to 3 months, which may correspond to the initial findings.

Here are the main stages of neuron death according to this theory, which dates from 1987 and some aspects of which were discovered as early as 1969[41]:

---

38 https://www.ncbi.nlm.nih.gov/pubmed/16806844
39 https://www.ncbi.nlm.nih.gov/pubmed/8375434
https://www.ncbi.nlm.nih.gov/pubmed/7906190
40 https://www.ncbi.nlm.nih.gov/pubmed/8095977
41 Olney, J.W. (1969) Brain lesion, obesity and other disturbances in mice treated with monosodium glutamate. Science 164, 719–721

Choi, D.W. and colleagues (1987) Glutamate neurotoxicity in cortical cellnculture. J. Neurosci. 7, 357–368

- (1) Defects in cellular respiration cause failure of the normal ATP manufacturing process.

- (2) ATP-dependent ion transport pumps fail, causing depolarization of the cell, allowing ions, especially calcium ($Ca2+$), to enter the cell.

- (3) Ion pumps can no longer carry calcium out of the cell and intracellular calcium levels become too high.

- (4) The presence of calcium triggers the release of the neurotransmitter glutamate, an excitatory amino acid.

- (5) Glutamate stimulates AMPA receptors and $Ca2+$ permeable NMDA receptors, which open up to allow more calcium to enter the cells.

- (6) An excessive intake of calcium over-excites the cells and causes the production of harmful chemicals such as free radicals, reactive oxygen species and calcium-dependent enzymes such as ascalpain, endonucleases, ATPases and phospholipases. Calcium can also cause the release of more glutamate.

This is a well-known process that causes death of neurons in cerebral infarction, but there is no evidence that this is happening in sporadic ALS. For example, cerebral infarction is a phenomenon that occurs very quickly, not for months or years. This does not explain the proteinopathies, the local appearance of early ALS (a defect in cellular respiration should kill all motor neurons immersed in the cerebrospinal fluid), nor the progression of the disease, nor how mutations play an important role. And this is a hypothesis that focuses exclusively on the roles of glutamate and calcium.

Nevertheless, this is the theoretical basis of Riluzole, which reduces glutamate signaling and induces indirect antagonism without acting on the glutamate receptors themselves. Riluzole is only slowing the progression of ALS.

3.2.1.2. An interesting twist to the excitotoxicity hypothesis

The Japanese researcher Shin Kwak[42] and his colleagues, but also other researchers[43], think they have discovered interesting developments to this theory : For them the stimulation of AMPA receptors causes the generation of calpain. A calpain is a proteolytic enzyme expressed ubiquitously in mammals and many other organisms. Calpains have been shown to be active participants in processes such as cell mobility and cell cycle progression. Calpains have been implicated in apoptotic cell death, and appear to be an essential component of necrosis. Activated calpain also disrupts nucleo-cytoplasmic transport and gene expression by cleaving molecules involved in nucleocytoplasmic transport, including nucleoporins. And to make a long story short, the disruption of cellular transport, creates TDP-43 aggregates. While very elegant this theory does not appear to have gain much traction between ALS researchers.

3.2.1.3. Completing the excitotoxicity hypothesis

It seems necessary to complement the excitotoxicity hypothesis with other hypotheses, in order to describe what happens in ALS. For example in the first step it is not specified which defect of cellular respiration is occurring. In one hand it has been noted that half of ALS patients are insulin-resistant (type 2 diabetes), which is a defect of cellular respiration. Many publications have studied this seemingly paradoxical phenomenon, since the presence of type 2 diabetes seems to have an inverse correlation with ALS[44]. It has been suggested that drugs used to treat type 2 diabetes prevent the occurrence of ALS[45]. An early in-vitro study confirmed the value

---

42   https://www.ncbi.nlm.nih.gov/pubmed/24355598
43   https://www.ncbi.nlm.nih.gov/pmc/articles/PMC4262699/
44   https://www.ncbi.nlm.nih.gov/pubmed/28921834
45   https://www.ncbi.nlm.nih.gov/pubmed/25383557

of one of these drugs[46] but no clinical trials were performed with ACE inhibitors.

On the other hand, genes involved in ALS imply a hyper-metabolism because their expression means that the cell is correcting abnormalities in protein production, which in turn means using more energy.

This hyper-metabolism is not limited to motor neurons, for example it has been shown in patients' muscles.

Steps 5 and 6 could easily be replaced by the proposal of Shin Kwak and his colleagues :

In step 5, cell stress (particularly endoplasmic reticulum and Golgi apparatus) caused by defects in cellular respiration leads to formation of protein granules by delaying their folding in the reticulum endoplasmic and their shipping by the Golgi apparatus.
In step 6, the most fragile cells, the longest motoneurons, which are connected to fast fatigable muscles (those used by athletes), begin to be euthanized by the immune system.

These and other complementary hypotheses will be developed in the following pages.

3.2.1.4. What tell clinical trials ?

Only 1 % of all ALS trials mention "excitotoxicity" in their description. None of them reached phase III.

Among the proposed treatments, the two most serious seem Perampanel and Creatinine. Perampanel like Talampanel, acts as a non-competitive antagonist of the AMPA receptor, a type of ionotropic glutamate receptor in the central nervous system. Perampanel seems having as much dangerous side effects as Talampanel.

---

46 https://www.ncbi.nlm.nih.gov/pubmed/12716021

3.2. Guiding hypotheses in ALS research.

3.2.2. Metabolic hypothesis

Pancreatic endocrine dysfunction has long been suspected of being responsible for the abnormal metabolism of glucose in ALS (Barris 1953, Quick 1969, Mueller and Quick 1970, Gotoh and colleagues, 1972, Koerner 1975, Nagano and colleagues, 1979). It has also been suggested that there is a link between diabetes and Alzheimer's disease[47].

In this hypothesis ALS can occur when a person with a high metabolic rate suddenly experiences an event that alters glucose metabolism, forcing the body to switch to a less efficient metabolism that deprives neurons of energy and causes to develop a muscle loss. Insulin is carried by the blood system and in the elderly, strokes are common. It is thus easy to imagine that a local vascular accident (thrombosis) alters the metabolism of a motor neuron which ends up dying of excitotoxicity.

This hypothesis did not have as strong support as the excitotoxicity hypothesis and it fell into disuse at the turn of the century, but curiously, it is much better founded than others. Indeed, in addition to motor neuron degeneration, ALS is associated with several energy metabolism abnormalities, including weight loss, hypermetabolism and hyperlipidemia. Most of these abnormalities correlate with survival time and clinical evidence confirms a negative contribution of defective energy metabolism to the overall pathogenic process.

This hypothesis is at the origin of clinical trials of IGF which have been successful, but unfortunately not beyond the benefits of Riluzole, while having very important side effects. The causal mechanism is schematically described in next pages and borrows from pathologies such as cerebral infarction.

---

47 https://www.ncbi.nlm.nih.gov/pubmed/31293498

3.2.2.1. ALS patients appear to have been healthy and active people.

In many cases, people with ALS have led healthy, active lives. In fact, it has been shown time and time again that ALS patients have lower disease history rates than the general public[48].

It is well known that a classically « at risk » cardiovascular profile, such as a high body mass index (BMI) or type 2 diabetes mellitus, could protect individuals from ALS by delaying the onset of symptoms and/or slowing the clinical course. Hypertension, hyperlipidemia, arthritis, thyroid diseases, and non-ALS-related neurological conditions are significant factors in delaying the onset of ALS. These conditions were also less prevalent in the ALS population.

On the contrary and equally surprising, a "beneficial" cardiovascular profile, with a low body mass index, a sporting lifestyle and a low level of cholesterol in the blood can increase the risk or worsen the prognosis[49], [50].

In 1978, scientists[51] were surprised to find that insulin was elevated in ALS patients, suggesting insensitivity to insulin. This resulted in a multitude of drug trials with insulin growth factor (IGF-1) variations until 2000. In 1997, a study showed that IGF-1 slows the progression of ALS 26 %[52], which is very similar to current ALS drugs such as Masitinib. One of the many effects of IGF-1 is to increase insulin sensitivity. However, since IGF-1 also has significant side effects, we have not seen any IGF-1 medications.

---

48 https://www.ncbi.nlm.nih.gov/pubmed/25720304/
49 https://www.ncbi.nlm.nih.gov/pmc/articles/PMC6278047
50 https://www.ncbi.nlm.nih.gov/pmc/articles/PMC4810157/
    (An uncommon large study)
51 https://www.ncbi.nlm.nih.gov/pubmed/661736
52 https://n.neurology.org/content/49/6/1621

A 2010 study seems to summarize that of 1978, as it reveals that patients with ALS exhibit abnormal glucose tolerance. Glucose tolerance could be associated with an increase in free fatty acid levels, which is a key determinant of resistance to insuline[53]. However, no suggestion has been made to explain the association between ALS and insulin resistance.

Spinal and bulbar muscular atrophy (SBMA), also known as Kennedy's disease, is a disease quite similar to ALS. In 2017, a SBMA study demonstrated that SBMA patients have insulin resistance[54], which is associated with the severity of the disease.

Previously, it was shown that most neurodegenerative diseases had insulin resistance.

3.2.2.2. Diabetes and neurotrophic factor

Regulating food intake is an important part of maintaining energy homeostasis. Energy homeostasis is controlled by a variety of complex mechanisms, including hormone signaling and multiple molecules. Type 2 diabetes mellitus is a group of metabolic diseases characterized by chronic hyperglycemia. Brain derived neurotrophic factor (BDNF) is a neurotrophin that plays an important role in the maturation, synaptic connection, neuronal repair and plasticity of the central nervous system, as well as in the pathology and treatment of neurological diseases. Despite its name, BDNF is actually found in many tissues and cell types and not just in the brain. BDNF is an important protein in the regulation of dietary intake and body weight control. Several reports have reported an association between plasma BDNF and systemic or peripheral inflammatory conditions, such as acute coronary syndrome and type 2 diabetes mellitus [55].

---

53 https://www.ncbi.nlm.nih.gov/pubmed/20184518
54 https://www.kennedysdisease.org/images/research/
    insulinresistance_nakatsuji2017.pdf

3.2.2.3. Receptors activated by peroxisome proliferators

In the 21st century, the attention of scientists still interested in the metabolic hypothesis of the origin of ALS turned to PPAR agonists.

In eukaryotic cells, mitochondria are the main site of energy production, where ATP is produced via oxidative metabolism. Mitochondrial dysfunction, oxidative stress and neuroinflammation, hallmarks of neurodegeneration, may result from impaired insulin signaling. Insulin-sensitizing drugs such as thiazolidinediones are a new class of synthetic compounds that potentiate the action of insulin in target tissues and act as specific agonists for peroxisome proliferator activated gamma receptor (PPAR-γ). Thus, several PPAR agonists have been proposed as novel and possible therapeutic agents for neurodegenerative disorders.

However, clinical trials with Pioglitazone have been unsuccessful under ALS. Pioglitazone selectively stimulates the nuclear receptor peroxisome proliferator-activated gamma receptor (PPAR-γ) and, to a lesser extent, PPAR-α.

3.2.2.4. What tell clinical trials ?

79 % of all ALS trials mention "metabolism". The same percentage reach phase III. But no studies mention "PPAR" or "peroxisome".

---

55 M. Suwa, H. Kishimoto, Y. Nofuji and colleagues, "Serum brain-derived neurotrophic factor level is increased and associated with obesity in newly diagnosed female patients with type 2 diabetes mellitus," Metabolism, vol. 55, pp. 852–857, 2006.

3.2.3. Endoplasmic reticulum stress

More and more researchers consider that the problem of ALS does not come from a mutated gene, but rather from misfolded proteins.

If there are many types of misfolded proteins that can lead to ALS, then it makes sense to ask how the endoplasmic reticulum behaves during it.

Proteins are used by the cell to process information, transmit energy, ensure the proper functioning of vital services and take charge of functions related to recycling and protection against pathogens. Also a significant part of the cell is used to produce proteins, the protein is then folded into the endoplasmic reticulum and packaged in vesicles by the Golgi apparatus.

However, this line of thought only pushes the cause a little further : if the defect of protein folding is related to the stress of a cell, what makes it become stressed ?

3.2.3.1. Why does the endoplasmic reticulum become stressed ?

The endoplasmic reticulum is responsible for the folding, post-translational modification and trafficking of many transmembrane and secretory proteins. The high rate of protein folding in the endoplasmic reticulum is a burden for organelles and it is essential to prevent protein folding to maintain cellular function. The accumulation of unfolded or misfolded proteins in the endoplasmic reticulum causes endoplasmic reticulum stress. This stress is attenuated by a protective mechanism known as the folded protein response (UPR).

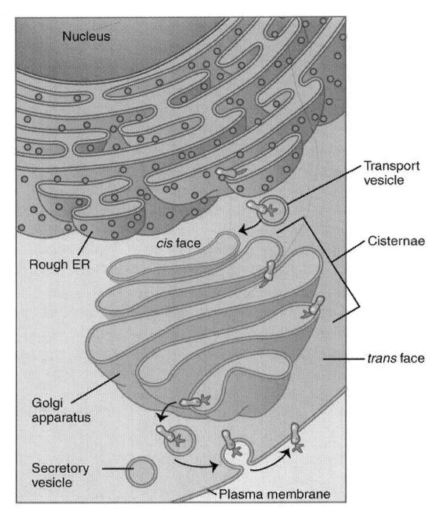

3.2. Guiding hypotheses in ALS research.

The UPR is initially protective by upregulation of specific genes regulated by endoplasmic reticulum stress and inhibition of general protein translation. However, prolonged stress of the endoplasmic reticulum leads to cell death via apoptotic signaling, thus providing a link to neurodegeneration.

Activation of the UPR is one of the first events in motor neurons affected by transgenic rodent models expressing ALS-related mutant superoxide dismutase 1 (SOD1).

Activation of UPR initially results in decreased general protein translation, specific regulation of UPR target genes, such as those encoding endoplasmic reticulum chaperones, and expansion of endoplasmic reticulum volume via increased lipid production. The cell is starved, but it is preferable to being poisoned with deleterious proteins. These are normal transient physiological response mechanisms that, in themselves, are often sufficient to overcome short-term trauma.

However, if homeostasis is not restored, cell death is triggered via apoptotic signaling.

Fragmentation of the Golgi apparatus is a consistent feature in ALS patients and in disease models, and the discovery that Golgi fragmentation is intimately associated with endoplasmic reticulum stress in neurons suggests that these two phenomena may be related in ALS.

Recently, it has been shown that genetic manipulation of endoplasmic reticulum stress in several different SOD1 mouse models modifies the onset and progression of the disease, implicating an active role of the UPR in the mechanisms of the disease. In addition, mutations in V-associated membrane protein associated protein (VAPB), an endoplasmic reticulum transmembrane protein involved in the regulation of endoplasmic reticulum stress, are also the cause of some familial ALS cases.

3.2.3.2. The relationship with Calcium

In 2014, Christopher Miller and his colleagues discovered that the TDP-43 protein of amyotrophic lateral sclerosis could exert its toxic effect by uncoupling the mitochondria and the endoplasmic reticulum. A number of mitochondria are found on the surface of the rough endoplasmic reticulum. Where these two organelles meet, they form structures called mitochondrial endoplasmic reticulum membranes, also called MAMs, and the TDP-43 protein can disrupt this interaction.

Christopher Miller and his colleagues discovered this disruption while they were working on another protein involved in ALS, vesicle-associated membrane protein (VAPB) protein B. They postulated that alterations in MAM could explain many changes in ALS at the cellular level, including calcium dyshomeostasis and mitochondrial diseases.

When the endoplasmic reticulum and the mitochondrial membranes get closer, they build transient bridges, the MAMs. Researchers know little about this association, but MAMs have at least two main functions, says Eric Schon, who believes that MAMs are also involved in Alzheimer's disease. On the one hand, they manage calcium levels as ions move from endoplasmic reticulum to mitochondria. On the other hand, they harbor the synthesis of cholesterol and phospholipids.

Since MAMs regulate calcium homeostasis, De Vos and Stoica hypothesized that TDP-43 could alter calcium levels in mitochondria and cytosol. They suggested that disruption of MAM could lead to a number of problems seen in ALS neurons, including altered calcium homeostasis and mitochondrial lesions, decreased ATP synthesis, and an improper activation of the non-folded protein response of the endoplasmic reticulum.

3.2.3.3. What tell clinical trials ?

No ALS trials mention "endoplasmic reticulum" or "Golgi apparatus".

3.2.4. Reactive astrocytes

This section is also linked to a variant or complement of the excitotoxicity hypothesis. Recent studies have shown that neuro-inflammation and ischemia (hence the link with the hypothesis of excitotoxicity) can cause astrocytes to change their phenotype to two different types of reactive astrocytes, called A1 and A2. Astrocytes, the largest and most numerous glial cells of the central nervous system (CNS), play a variety of important roles in regulating homeostasis, increasing synaptic plasticity, and neuroprotection.

But like many cells, astrocytes can change phenotypes and change roles from support to neurons to their destruction. Indeed, as Diane Re, Virginia Le Verche and Przedborski have shown, astrocytes can participate in the inflammatory response and play a key role in the progression of neurodegenerative diseases. Reactive astrocytes are strongly induced by many pathological conditions in the CNS. The reactivity of astrocytes is initially characterized by a hypertrophy of soma. This same team showed in 2014 that once astrocytes start killing motor neurons, they seem to never stop doing so.

It is also possible that astrocytes are the first to be sick in the etiology of ALS and that the death of neurons is only a consequence. After all neurons can not survive without astrocytes. The pathology of TDP-43 is thus found in both neurons and glia.

There have been several fundamental studies that have shown that the cause of ALS is not in neurons. For example, in 2003, Clement, Don Cleveland, and their colleagues showed that the expression of mutant SOD1 in the glia was sufficient to induce a pathology similar to ALS in mice and that it could accelerate progression.

It is also possible that astrocytes are also victims, like neurons. The work of Yamanaka and colleagues suggests that other cells need to be involved in determining the onset of ALS. What these cells are, is not clear. They exclude however that it is the oligodendrocytes.

However Jeffrey Rothstein and colleagues reported that a cycle of oligodendrocyte death and replacement precedes the onset of motor neuron death and symptoms in model ALS mice. Their publication indicates that motor neurons depend on oligodendrocytes not only for their ionic isolation, but for their very survival. This demonstrates a critical and completely unexpected role for oligodendrocytes. If oligodendrocytes die, progenitor cells can proliferate and replace them. This cycle of degeneration and oligodendrocyte turnover is responsible for relapses and remissions of multiple sclerosis.

ALS researchers have not spent much time thinking about how to help oligodendrocytes support neurons, in contrast to researchers on multiple sclerosis. Anti-inflammatories are well established in the field of multiple sclerosis. Most of the treatment ideas for multiple sclerosis are at preclinical stages. Some of these therapeutic strategies may be beneficial for ALS.

Similarly, previous work has shown that glia[56] and astrocytes[57] have no effect on the timing of onset of symptoms of the disease. Scientists like the Jean-Pierre Julien group in 2005, but also Séverine Boillée of Don Cleveland's group, have suggested that interneurons, myelinating Schwann cells from the periphery and endothelial cells of the vascular system deserved to be studied.

---

56 Jean-Pierre Julien's group had shown in 2005 that glia and even extracellular events influenced the evolution of the disease.

57 In 2007, Damme and Bogaert suggested that by regulating the neuronal expression of GluR2, astrocytes could have another mechanism to protect neurons.

It is also possible that several types of cells are involved in the onset of the disease.

3.2.4.1. Imported inflammation in the CNS

Scientists have known for a long time that when motor neurons begin to fail in people with ALS, the neighboring microglia evolves into an inflammatory state. It happens that cells whose phenotype is close enough, monocytes in the blood do the same.

Pamela Shaw, Weihua Zhao, and Winston Hide of Stanley Appel's lab reported that blood monocytes accelerated the expression of many inflammatory genes in people with ALS. This inflammatory genes expression occurred most dramatically in people with a rapidly progressing form of the disease. What activates these blood monocytes remains unknown.

Damaged motor neurons send signals to immune cells, not just those in the CNS, according to Stanley Appel. There is no doubt that the immune cells of the central nervous system respond vigorously to the degeneration of motor neurons. Imaging of live patients, as well as post mortem analyzes, have proved this. Model animal studies indicate that if immune responses are protective early in the disease, they become destructive thereafter.

Despite activation of these blood cells, the researchers were unable to reliably detect elevated levels of inflammatory cytokines in the blood of ALS patients. However, a study by Christian Lunetta, on which Appel collaborated, reported CRP levels correlated with the severity of functional impairment and, ultimately, survival, in nearly 400 patients with ALS. In addition, a post-hoc analysis of a failure of a Phase II immuno-regulatory NP001 assay revealed that the treatment slows the progression of the disease in patients who started with a higher CRP (Lunetta and colleagues 2017).

Do activated monocytes infiltrate the CNS ? The experiments on parabiosis suggest the opposite, and Appel thinks this is unlikely at the beginning of the disease. Instead, he points to T cells. These cells cross the blood-brain barrier. They can therefore convey information between the two compartments.

3.2.4.2. What tell clinical trials ?

Only 2 % of ALS trials mention "inflammation", which is surprising given most scientists would agree that ALS is associated with some type of inflammation.

3.2.5. Is ALS a neurovascular disease ?

We have seen that the hypothesis of excitotoxicity is inspired by cerebrovascular events. In addition, drugs such as Edaravone have free radical scavenging activity and protect neurons, glial cells and vascular endothelial cells against oxidative stress. Edaravone was first developed for the treatment of acute ischemic stroke.

Scientists were very early interested by a possible alteration of the medullo-spinal barrier as a cause of ALS. Indeed, the analysis of cerebrospinal fluid (CSF) in ALS patients soon revealed the presence of albumin and serum-derived proteins (Annunziata and Volpi 1985, Apostolski and colleagues 1991, Brettschneider and colleagues 2006). The medullo-spinal barrier, like the blood-brain barrier, allows the passage of water, gases and liposoluble small molecules and limits the entry of plasma components, red blood cells and leucocytes into the spinal cord.

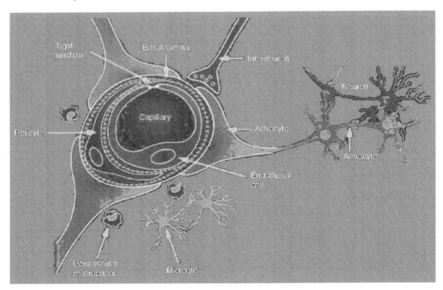

In addition to endothelial cells, the medullo-spinal barrier is composed of the extracellular matrix, astrocytes, neurons, microglia and pericytes.

The endothelial cells and the pericytes are separated by the basement membrane, and at the points of contact the pericytes communicate directly with the endothelial cells.

The pericytes act on the physical stabilization of the blood vessels, the regulation of microcirculation and the capillary blood flow. They affect blood clotting and immune function and can regulate lymphocyte activation, participate in angiogenesis and vasculogenesis.

Yamaneda and his colleagues also showed an increase in microvascular density, a decrease in pericyte coverage, and abnormal angiogenesis in the post-mortem spinal cord.

A higher amount of matrix metalloproteinase 9 (MMP-9), an enzyme responsible for tissue modification (Bell and colleagues, 2012), has been observed in the serum of patients with ALS (Beuche and colleagues, 2000, Demestre and colleagues 2005, Niebroj-Dobosz and colleagues, 2010) and post mortem tissue (Lim, Al, 1996). However, pericytes under stress conditions have been shown to secrete MMP-9, resulting in vascular fragility (Bell et al 2012).

Analysis of post-mortem spinal cord tissue in patients with ALS showed a 54 % reduction in the number of pericytes compared to healthy subjects.

The level of pericyte reduction is correlated with the extent of medullo-spinal barrier damage (Winkler and colleagues, 2013).

As a result of pericyte loss and medullo-spinal barrier degradation, red blood cells can enter the neuronal microenvironment and lyse themselves while releasing hemoglobin. Hemoglobin releases free iron, which can catalyze the formation of radical species, toxic molecules for motor neurons.

Preclinical experiments to recover disrupted medullo-spinal barrier are underway and provide interesting results.

Winkler and his colleagues found that restoring the integrity of the medullo-spinal barrier or chelating iron from blood and antioxidant treatment reduced early motor neuron injury (Winkler and colleagues, 2014). There is an ongoing clinical trial in France of Deferiprone, an iron chelator.

Stanley Appel's team is working[58] on the transplantation of human hematopoietic cells derived from a restricted lineage, such as endothelial progenitor cells, to improve the restoration of the medullo-spinal barrier in ALS.

3.2.5.1. What tell clinical trials ?

There are however less than 2 % of all ALS trials that mention "vascular" and less than 1 % mention "blood-brain barrier".

---

58 https://www.ncbi.nlm.nih.gov/pubmed/30918315

3.2.6. Possibility of enteroviral infection

There is a strange coincidence in ALS, one of the roles of the TDP-43 protein is to mitigate HIV infection. Another interesting fact is that inflammation happens in the CNS during ALS. The immune system is designed to target « no-self » biological materia. So what is the pathogen that the immune system is trying to attack in ALS ? These questions are also asked for other neurodegenerative diseases, such as Alzheimer's disease, for which the bacterium p. Gingivalis is seriously incriminated.

A potential role of enteroviruses in ALS has been proposed for decades because of their ability to target motor neurons and the analogy with post-polio ALS syndrome. Many clinical studies have been conducted to detect enteroviruses in the tissues of patients with ALS. However, the available data are controversial and inconclusive.

Three studies reported an incidence of enterovirus genome detection of between 60 % and 88 % in the spinal cord / brain of patients with ALS compared to 0 % to 14 % in control groups (Woodall and colleagues 1994, Berger and colleagues 2000, Giraud and colleagues, 2001).

In addition, analysis of cerebrospinal fluid revealed enterovirus detection in 14.5 % of 242 ALS patients and 7.6 % of 354 controls (Vandenberghe and colleagues, 2010). However, three other studies failed to detect enterovirus RNA in the spinal cord/brain of patients with ALS or controls (Swanson and colleagues, 1995, Walker and colleagues, 2001, Nix and colleagues colleagues, 2004).

The discrepancies between these studies are probably due to methodological differences and the sensitivity/specificity of viral genome detection. In addition, the stage of the disease at the time of sample collection may also be critical for viral detection, as viruses can be detected or active only in certain phases of the disease or only in a subset of patients.

Studies involving a population-based retrospective cohort may provide a means to better understand the links between enterovirus infection and subsequent ALS. But the most common symptoms of enterovirus infections are flu-like symptoms. Those symptoms are often overlooked until more disastrous consequences occur. Thus, existing clinical data on enteroviral infections may not accurately reflect the actual prevalence of infection.

Overall, with these limitations, it would be very difficult to come up with a compelling strategy to firmly establish the link between enterovirus infection and ALS in humans.

3.2.6.1. What tell clinical trials ?

No ALS trials mention "enteroviral". A related study is about « Post-polio syndrome ».

3.2.7. What about latent viruses in DNA ?

3.2.7.1. HIV-1

There is little difference in practice between a viral infection, a mutated gene and the genome of a virus contained in our DNA. Indeed, in these various examples, the patient's DNA is modified with respect to the "standard" genome.

About 8 % of the mass of the human genome comes directly or indirectly from retroviral sequences. In one way or another, evolution was not strong enough to remove them or their contribution was innocuous or even positive.

It was proposed for the first time in the 1970 s that retroviruses may play a role in the pathogenesis of ALS. It is known that a small percentage of people infected with human immunodeficiency virus-1 (HIV-1) or human T-cell leukemia virus (HTLV-1) will develop ALS-like syndromes. Although HTLV-1-associated SLS syndrome has several features that distinguish it from classical ALS, HIV-infected patients may develop neurological manifestations similar to classical ALS. However those symptoms occur at a younger age. and some patients can show dramatic improvement when they receive antiretroviral therapy. And indeed, as one of the roles of the TDP-43 protein is to attenuate HIV infections, a mutated TDP-43 protein would be unable to protect against a viral infection.

However, most patients with a probable or definitive diagnosis of ALS show no evidence of HIV-1 or HTLV-1 infection.

3.2.7.2. HERV

In contrast, recent reports have shown a stronger interest for association of HERV with ALS, as analysis of serum samples, and post-mortem brain tissue in a number of patients with classical ALS, have revealed a significant increase in HERV-K compared to the controls. These results suggest that endogenous retroviral elements are sometimes involved in the pathophysiology of ALS, but there is no indication that they are the main cause of the syndrome.

Recently, a number of experiments have implicated HERV envelope protein (HML-2 Env) as contributing to the neurodegeneration of ALS. It has been reported that HML-2 Env was expressed in the cortical and spinal neurons of patients with ALS. But overall, the contribution of HERV viruses to ALS has not been definitively proven.

3.2.7.3. Triumeq : An interesting clinical trial

In 2016, Triumeq, an antiretroviral therapy was tested in clinical trial. Patients were observed during a 10-week lead-in period before receiving Triumeq treatment for 24 weeks at four specialist ALS centers. The primary outcomes were safety and tolerability. Secondary outcomes included HERV-K expression levels, urinary p75ECD levels, neurophysiological parameters, and clinical indicators.

The trial was registered as NCT02868580.

40 patients with ALS received Triumeq and 35 completed treatment. There were no drug-related serious adverse events ; one patient was withdrawn from the study due to a drug-associated increase in liver enzymes.

A favorable response on HERV-K expression levels was observed, accompanied by a decline in ALSFRS-R progression rate of 21.8 %. This is nearly the same amount reached by most successful ALS drugs. One patient died five months after stopping treatment, while five were expected to have died during the treatment period.

A phase 3 trial will be deployed to assess the effect of Triumeq on overall survival and disease progression.

3.2.7.4. What tell clinical trials ?

There are nearly 0.5 % of all ALS trials that mention "virus".

3.2.8. An overly neglected hypothesis : Bacterial infection

The craze for neurogenetics over the last two decades has diverted attention away from the environmental causes of sporadic ALS.

There is also a problem of methodology : scientists consider neurons to be perfect cells, but aging cells look like old boats whose hulls are weighed down by mollusks, cells are parasitized by fungi and bacteria. For example, it is now thought that amyloid aggregates in Alzheimer's would be defense mechanisms against bacteria that also form dental plaques.

This idea that cells are not like in textbooks, is difficult to integrate into the routine of science.

Over the past two decades, Alzheimer's studies have focused on the damaging functions of β-amyloid, with less emphasis on its physiological roles : protection against infection and cancer, repair of the blood-brain barrier, and synaptic maintenance (Brothers and colleagues, 2018).

The presence of β-amyloid in various tissues and organs of older individuals and patients with Alzheimer's disease has acquired a new meaning in light of this biomolecule functioning as an antimicrobial peptide (Joachim and colleagues, 1989). For example, new studies have detected microorganisms in the tissues of older individuals, including liver, skeletal muscle, and brain. This suggests that an increased microbial load causes higher synthesis of β-amyloid (Lluch and colleagues his colleagues, 2015).

In addition, preclinical studies have reported an increase in antimicrobial peptides in senescent tissues as a function of age, implying that these defense peptides may be directly proportional to the bacterial burden (Dinakaran and colleagues, 2014).

Interestingly, many studies over the past decade have linked tissue pathogens to chronic diseases, such as cancer, stroke, type 2 diabetes (T2DM) and Alzheimer's disease, probably involving intestinal microbes transferred into their body. etiology (Elkind and colleagues, 2009, Dapito and colleagues, 2012, Sato J. and colleagues, 2014).

On contrary a phase III clinical trial of Ceftriaxone, an antibiotic used for the treatment of a number of bacterial infections, did not provide any improvement to the ALS patients.

3.2.8.1. BMAA, symbiotic cyanobacteria

But for now, the only case where a bacterium could be linked to ALS occurred 50 years ago. Endemic ALS outbreaks on the island of Guam were 100 times larger than average. Studies in Guam have suggested that ALS, Parkinson's disease and dementia are caused by the non-protein, neurotoxic amino acid beta-methylamino-L-alanine (BMAA) present in Cycas micronesica seeds, a tree plant.

BMAAs are produced by symbiotic cyanobacteria in cycad roots, where the concentration of protein-bound BMAA in seeds and flour is high.

Perhaps the most interesting is that BMAA has been found in the brain tissue of some North American patients who died of Alzheimer's disease.

Caller and colleagues (2009) noted the existence of a group of 9 cases of ALS in the northeastern United States in a town near a lake containing both Cyanobacteria Microcystis and Anabaena sp, two known genera of cyanobacteria. for their ability to produce BMAA.

As cyanobacteria are ubiquitous in the world, it was been noted that it is possible that all humans are exposed to low levels of BMAA cyanobacteria. This hypothesis has been popularized in the public domain through leading scientific journals (Discover Magazine (McAuliffe 2011), The Asian Scientist (Lim 2012) and Scientific American (Eplett 2015).

This awareness has led to studies on its presence in food and dietary supplements. However, despite the many studies on this topic, no one has found a link between ALS and BMAA. A very detailed study [59] examined the history of the relationship between BMAA and ALS and concluded that there was no strong relationship between the two.

3.2.8.2. Lyme disease

Apart from the case of BMAA, it is not possible to find a consensus on a link between other bacteria and ALS, including for Lyme disease. Associations between Lyme disease (Borrelia burgdorferi) and certain neurodegenerative diseases have been proposed, but the elements supporting an association are lacking. There is no geographic correlation in the United States between Lyme disease cases and deaths from Alzheimer's disease, Amyotrophic Lateral Sclerosis (ALS), Multiple Sclerosis (MS), or Parkinson disease[60].

3.2.8.3. What tell clinical trials ?

There are nearly 1.5 % of all ALS trials that mention "bacterial".

---

59   https://www.ncbi.nlm.nih.gov/pmc/articles/PMC6503681/
60   https://www.ncbi.nlm.nih.gov/pubmed/26488307

3.2.9. Fungal infection or sample contamination ?

Alonso and his colleagues have published a series of 4 reports showing a possible link between a fungal infection and Alzheimer's disease. They showed fungal antigens and DNA corresponding to many fungi in the cerebrospinal fluid of 5 ALS patients, compared with 3 controls.

A subsequent study of brain specimens from 11 ALS patients using immunohistochemistry identified fungal structures (ie, yeast and hyphae[61]) in the spinal cord, medulla and motor cortex (Alonso and colleagues, 2017).

A recent report has applied a metagenomic sequencing approach to RNA isolated from lumbar motor neurons in 11 ALS and 8 control patients, in addition to the frontal cortex DNA of 209 Alzheimer's patients, and including 192 control neurons from the NCBI Sequence Read Archive (SRA) for a comparative study (Keith and Mitchell, 2017). Although no particular fungus has been described, fungi accounted for 0.0004 % and 0.001 % of metagenomic sequences, respectively, for Alzheimer's disease and ALS. But it could also be a contamination error or even a methodology error as detection of fungal infections have low sensitivity when 0.001 % would imply an extremely high sensitivity.

However, there are very few studies on the subject and most of them come from the same team, that has obtained the same results for several other neurodegenerative diseases. Caution is therefore required.

---

61 Hyphen is a filamentous vegetative element, often with several cellular nuclei (multinuclear), characteristic of fungi, certain algae and certain plant protists. It may be several centimeters long but only a few microns in diameter and therefore, in its isolated state, invisible to the naked eye. These filaments become visible when they are gathered in sufficiently large cords ; we then speak of mycelium.

3.2.9.1. What tell clinical trials ?

No ALS trials mention "fungal".

3.2.10. Intracellular transport problems

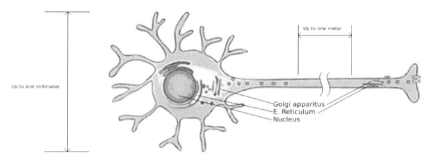

This hypothesis probably supplements the hypothesis of excitotoxicity, because it adds another factor explaining how difficult it is for neurons to have a viable metabolism. It consists of the idea that the transport of materials and information between the soma and the end of a motor neuron is particularly dangerous. In fact one might wonder if a motor neuron is not just a kind of pump with a long pipe, because a motor neuron needs to be surrounded by several other kinds of cells in order to survive. This makes it a very different cell from other types of cells.

Motor neurons differ from other neurons in that their soma are unusually large, with long axons up to 1 m long in an adult human. These axons require the reception of membrane and cytoskeletal proteins, neurotransmitter receptors and lipids from the body of the neuron.

These components must be transported from the endoplasmic reticulum/ Golgi apparatus into the cell body for long distances along the axon. Proteins are also synthesized via axonal ribosomes and mRNAs, which greatly facilitates local protein synthesis.

In neurons, the Golgi apparatus is involved in the fast flow and in the orthograde, retrograde and transsynaptic transports of several macromolecules. Therefore, it is reasonable to propose that a fragmentation of the Golgi apparatus is associated with an alteration of the transport and processing functions of the macromolecules.

3.2.10.1. Fragmentation of the Golgi apparatus

The Golgi apparatus acts as a dispensing station in which newly synthesized proteins and lipids in the endoplasmic reticulum are transported to the endosomal system, secretory granules or plasma membrane. Although it is a very dynamic organelle, the Golgi normally retains a characteristic morphology, consisting of stacks of flattened membranes known as cisterns and associated vesicles. The piles of Golgi cisterns are interconnected laterally by tubules, forming a ribbon network.

In 1990 and 1993, the year of the discovery of SOD1, Mourelatos and his colleagues published an article that seems very advanced in retrospect, because it deals with degradations in the organelles of neurons and this subject is now strongly linked to proteinopathies. Unfortunately, the study included only four patients, and the discovery of SOD1 in the same year certainly overshadowed it. The title was « *The Golgi apparatus of motor neurons in amyotrophic lateral sclerosis* ».

In 1992, another study[62]revealed the same degradation of the Golgi apparatus.

Studies have confirmed fragmentation of the Golgi apparatus in 10-50 % of sporadic patients and up to 70 % of motor neurons in ALS patients with SOD1, FUS or Optineurin mutations. It is interesting to note that Golgi fragmentation is larger in larger human motor neurons, such as those in the cerebral cortex (Fujita and colleagues, 1999) and the anterior

---

62   https://www.ncbi.nlm.nih.gov/pubmed/1546747

horn (Fujita and colleagues, 2000). which suggests that they are particularly vulnerable to perturbations of Golgi function.

Golgi fragmentation is also present in the cells of the anterior horn of the spine in sporadic ALS patients with poor cytoplasmic localization of healthy TDP-43, implying a link between the pathologies linked to TDP-43 and those of the Golgi apparatus. This is still considered valid in 2019 [63], [64].

3.2.10.2. What tell clinical trials ?

There are nearly 11 % of all ALS trials that mention "transport". 2 % reached phase III.

63 https://www.ncbi.nlm.nih.gov/pubmed/30721407
64 https://www.ncbi.nlm.nih.gov/pubmed/26696811

3.3. Chronology of the major stages of ALS research.

1972 : Neuronal cytoplasmic inclusions containing RNA in ALS.

It may seem strange and somewhat absurd to learn that it was discovered a long time ago that ALS is characterized by neuronal cytoplasmic inclusions, then it was forgotten in the wake of the genetic fervor, then rediscovered only recently. American authors[65] of this 1972 study indicate that these inclusions are not observed in sporadic ALS in adults and differ from those associated with other motor neuron diseases. They only observed two juvenile cases of ALS, found protein inclusions in the cytoplasm, because of this and as no one had previously reported this sort of thing about ALS in adults, they suggested that sporadic juvenile ALS is a distinct entity and not simply an extension of the sporadic disease of the adult.

But a few years later, Japanese researchers make the same observation again[66]. A curious case is an article by French scientists who seems to have encountered in 1987, a case of ALS and FTD with cytoplasmic inclusions[67]. This is reminiscent of TDP-43. Nearly 100 articles have been devoted to the presence of granules in ALS cases and to the fragmentation of the endoplasmic reticulum and the Golgi apparatus by Okamoto and his colleagues from 1980[68].

---

65   https://jamanetwork.com/journals/jamaneurology/article-abstract/571659
66   https://www.ncbi.nlm.nih.gov/pubmed/216220
67   Motor neuron disease, parkinsonism and dementia
Report of a case with diffuse Lewy body-like intracytoplasmic inclusions
M.B. Delisle, P. Gorce, E. Hirseh, J.J. Hauw, A. Rascol, and H. Bouissou
Acta Neuropathol (Berl) (1987) 75:104-108
https://doi.org/10.1007/BF00686799
68   https://www.ncbi.nlm.nih.gov/pubmed/6251694

3.3. Chronology of the major stages of ALS research.

Some studies report the same findings in 1989, about ubiquitinated inclusions[69] and every year since, there is at least one article on this subject until 2006. A few articles per year is absolutely negligible in regard of the number of articles per year on ALS (500 per year in the last decade of the last century, and now 1500 per year).

And the number of articles has never really exploded on the subject of protein aggregates in ALS, there are now at most 20 articles per year and in 2019 there are always more articles on SOD1[70] (2 % of all cases of ALS) only on inclusions involving TDP-43[71] (95 % of all cases).

It seems odd that one of the central topics in ALS is not the subject of many publications reflecting an active research.

---

69 https://www.ncbi.nlm.nih.gov/pubmed/2484732
70 https://www.ncbi.nlm.nih.gov/pubmed/?term=SOD1+
    +amyotrophic+lateral+sclerosis
    3913 articles
71 https://www.ncbi.nlm.nih.gov/pubmed/?term=TDP-
    43+amyotrophic+lateral+sclerosis
    1684 articles

1993 : SOD1 mutations are correlated with ALS[72].

This discovery comes at a time when molecular biology is becoming increasingly important in publications, laboratory creations and job offers. The consensus is then that molecular biology has incredible power of explanation and facility to create ad hoc treatments through relatively simple genetic therapies. It is therefore a tool to allow the rapid creation of patents and wealth. This craze was similar to the one we saw recently for Crispr-cas9.

In the early 80 s, there was a lot of research to try to highlight if SOD1 was involved in the Down syndrome.[73], [74] SOD1 is indeed on chromosome 21, as is the APP gene, which may participates in the appearance of amyloid plaques of Alzheimer's disease and DSCR1 which is the gene involved in Down's disease.

As soon as Daniel Rosen and Teepu Siddique published the first article in 1993 about the discovery of the link between mutations of SOD1 and ALS, Nature published an enthusiastic commentary, much more forward-looking than the cautious article in Rosen and Siddique, under the title "*Did radical strike Lou Gehrig?*". This made a bizarre connection between what cosmetics advertising was showing on TV screens to one of the most frightening diseases. The same commentary also introduced the term "exitotoxicity".

SOD1 is one of three superoxide dismutases responsible for the destruction of free superoxide radicals in the body. It is encoded by the SOD1 gene. SOD1, given its role as an antioxidant, has helped promote the idea that reactive oxygen

---

72 Mutations in copper/Zn superoxide dismutase gene are associated with familial amyotrophic lateral sclerosis.
Rosen DR, Siddique T, and al.
https://www.ncbi.nlm.nih.gov/pubmed/8446170
73 https://www.ncbi.nlm.nih.gov/pubmed/6232420
74 https://www.ncbi.nlm.nih.gov/pubmed/3036686

species are at the origin of ALS. The rational was easy to understand : Mutation of SOD1 would lose this antioxidant function and so little by little, motor neurons would die. The mutation introduced a "*loss of function*".

Reactive oxygen species (ROS), such as peroxides and free radicals, are the highly reactive products of many normal cellular processes, including mitochondrial reactions that produce the metabolism of ATP and oxygen. Examples of ROS include hydroxyl radical OH, H2O2 and superoxide (O2). Some ROS are important for certain cellular functions, such as cell signaling processes and immune responses against foreign substances. Free radicals are reactive because they contain unpaired free electrons ; they can easily oxidize other molecules in the cell, causing cell damage and even cell death. Free radicals are thought to play a role in many destructive processes from the body, from cancer to coronary artery disease.

In this article Rosen and Siddique, are much more reasonable than Nature's comment, they explain that it is not clear why a SOD1 dysfunction would only affect the motor neurons. This in itself would hint that the problem is not of genetic origin. Rosen and Siddique also indicate that it is curious that the found mutations may explain the inheritance of familial ALS, as the loss of function is recessive rather than dominant.

They also make a somewhat bizarre suggestion about a therapeutic intervention that will never be tried : To introduce unmutated SOD1 into the central nervous system of patients with a SOD1 mutation. While it is in line with the loss of function idea, it is hard to see any medical value in introducing unmutated SOD1 the cerebro-spinal fluid, not in cells. This would require genetic therapies, something clearly out of scope for a treatment in 1993.

This article, and the publicity given to it by the scientific press, has diverted for almost 20 years, the ALS research away of

3.3. Chronology of the major stages of ALS research.

misfolded protein granules, which dates back to the 1980 s and is today the consensual explanation. This article has been cited 1135 times in 2019, a large number for the field of ALS research.

This explanation has unfortunately been extended by other scientists to sporadic cases of ALS, even though, as early as 1998, SOD1 protein was found to create misfolded and poorly localized proteins. This explanation was eroded from 2006 when the discovery of TDP-43 involvement in 95 % of ALS cases and 2011 with the discovery of C9orf72 as the leading cause of familial ALS.

It is not sure that this article would receive today the same enthusiastic welcome, first the substance of the article is based on a correlation between 13 families that had a genome different from that of healthy individuals. It is never mentioned how many individuals this concerns. Not only is this a small, statistically insignificant group, but there is no attempt in the article to try to reject the hypothesis.

But if you ask a professional today what is the main gene involved in ALS, unfortunately there is a good chance that he will answer instantly « **SOD1** ».

3.3. Chronology of the major stages of ALS research.

1998 : Treatment of aberrant RNAs in ALS[75]:

The excitotoxicity hypothesis has been modeled on the fact that acute elevations of glutamate induce neuronal damage in conditions such as stroke, status epilepticus, and neurological trauma.

High concentrations of extracellular glutamate may occur when presynaptic terminal release is increased or when synaptic cleft recapture is insufficient. This re-absorption is provided by the glutamate transporters present in neurons and astrocytes.

The most important glutamate transporter is by far EAAT2.

High concentrations of glutamate may also occur if the intracellular glutamate content is released by the injured neurons. This release may result in death of surrounding neurons and may therefore be involved in the spread of neurodegeneration.

It is therefore important to know if the EAAT2 glutamate transporter is present in sufficient quantity in the case of ALS.

That year, scientists found that about 60 % to 70 % of the 30 patients with sporadic ALS lost between 30 % and 95 % of the EAAT2 transporter protein of astroglial glutamate in the motor cortex and spinal cord.

Rothstein et colleagues report the presence of aberrant RNA in 65 % of sporadic ALS cases based on 30 patient reviews. Aberrant RNAs were not present in 40 control patients with other neurodegenerative diseases. The researchers said the loss of motoneurons is due to aberrant mRNA and it was prescient.

75 Aberrant RNA Processing in a Neurodegenerative Disease : the Cause for Absent EAAT2, a Glutamate Transporter, in Amyotrophic Lateral Sclerosis Chien-Liang Glenn Lin, Lynn A. Bristol and al.
https://www.cell.com/neuron/fulltext/S0896-6273(00)80997-6

3.3. Chronology of the major stages of ALS research.

EAAT2 is the major transporter that removes the excitatory neurotransmitter glutamate from the extracellular space in the central nervous system synapses. This transporter is mainly located on astrocytes. Glutamate clearance is necessary for proper synaptic activation and the prevention of neuronal damage due to excessive activation of glutamate receptors. EAAT2 is responsible for more than 90 % of the reuptake of glutamate in the brain.

So it was natural to think that an excessive activation of glutamate receptors could have been at work.

They find a lack of EAAT2 compared to normal in patients with ALS, this lack is not due to a lack of production, nor a loss of function due to a mutation, so for them it is due to defective transcription during the production of the protein (splicing) and rapid degradation of these defective proteins by the quality control mechanisms.

A defect in the splicing machine (not in the gene) leads to the use of inappropriate 5 'and 3' splice sites. This results in missing or additional abnormal transcripts and is an apparently new concept in the pathogenesis of the disease.

Curiously, the researchers say that the signs of poor protein translation are specific to ALS. But indeed as we have seen that the UPR mechanism is probably active in ALS, so protein production is slow down and protein aggregate.

The scientists also claimed that these findings suggested that EAAT2 loss was the cause of ALS. However, their article provides no justification for this assertion.

Several abnormal EAAT2 mRNAs have been identified in the affected areas of ALS patients. Aberrant mRNAs were very abundant and were found only in affected areas of ALS patients, but not in other areas of the brain. They have not been found in non-neurological diseases or other diseases.

They were also detectable in the cerebrospinal fluid of live ALS patients at the onset of their illness.

Other researchers have wondered[76] why aberrant RNA treatment occurs only in pre-mRNA EAAT2, and why only in the motor cortex and spinal cord ? Moreover, the reason why such a mechanism should specifically affect EAAT2 mRNAs while leaving transcripts coding for other unaffected proteins remains a mystery to them.

In the following years Rothstein will abandon the idea that glutamate is at the root of ALS. He said in 2005 before a Ceftriaxone phase II trial : *"Because ceftriaxone only protects against glutamate damage, just one problem in ALS, it's not surprising that the mice eventually succumbed to weakness and paralysis despite treatment »*.

The clinical trial had reached Phase III, when organizers decided to stop everything because it did not seem like the drug was effective.

---

76 https://www.cell.com/neuron/fulltext/S0896-6273(00)80979-4

1998 : Doubts arise over the theory of oxidative stress for ALS[77].

The discovery of mutations in the enzyme superoxide dismutase (SOD1) in 1993 suggested that ALS occurs when the defective enzyme allows superoxide radicals to accumulate to damaging levels and kill motor neurons, thereby causing paralysis.

Discoveries reported in 1998, however, cast doubt on this idea. L.I. Bruijn and his colleagues decided to test this theory by studying the effects of eliminating or increasing normal SOD1 levels in mice. They found that, contrary to what the theory predicts, the manipulation of SOD1 levels had no effect on the disease course. They also find aggregates of SOD1 in the cytoplasm.

This discovery casts doubt on the idea that nerve cell death in ALS results from oxidative stress related to abnormal SOD1 levels. This research suggests that drugs designed to eliminate oxygen radicals are unlikely to help patients with ALS SOD1, contrary to the prognostic by Rosen and Siddique in 1993.

This paper has been cited 258 times, which is a record for ALS-related publications. Usually "good" papers are cited only about twenty times because of the small number of researchers involved in ALS research.

So we are at the end of 1998, 21 years ago, and this article tells us that the oxidative stress hypothesis that was developed after the discovery of SOD1 mutations in ALS in 1993 is false. In addition, the same year, we learned that ALS is a disease related to the aberrant treatment of mRNA. So why

---

77 Aggregation and motor neuron toxicity of an ALS-linked SOD1 mutant
    independent from wild-type SOD1.
Bruijn LI, Houseweart MK and al.
http://www.ncbi.nlm.nih.gov/pubmed/9743498

will the next 10 years be devoted to models based on SOD1 mutations ?

What influence did this paper have ?

Although the exact toxicity of SOD1 mutations remains poorly understood, this paper was important in building a consensus that SOD1 toxicity emerges via a gain in toxic function and not a loss of function which is associated with excitotoxicity.

In a sense, Biogen's ASO BIIB067 (ISIS-SOD1Rx) is the culmination of this line of research.

2002 : How does the SOD1 mutation cause ALS?[78]?

In 2002, it had been known for 4 years that the development of familial ALS of type SOD1 did not depend on the level of activity of the SOD1 enzyme, but rather on a gain of dominant function. In fact, the modifications of the expression of the SOD1 enzyme by overexpression or targeted deletion do not show any effect on the evolution of the disease in the mutant SOD1 mouse. Since the enzymatic activity of SOD1 is not involved in the disease process, what is the causal agent of this gain of function ?

The functions of a protein are essentially associated with its three-dimensional form, so it was natural to look for whether the mutated proteins have a three-dimensional shape different from the wild-type SOD1 protein. This article from 2002 does not achieve this goal, but it reinforces the idea that SOD1 mutations cause protein conformational abnormalities.

Anfinsen's dogma says that the three-dimensional shape of a molecule is linked to a minimal energy (Gibbs free energy) and that proteins would oscillate around this position thanks to their thermal energy. But in living beings, proteins are produced in a linear form by ribosomes, it is the passage in the endoplasmic reticulum that "folds" a protein,

The correct folding of newly produced proteins is made possible by several chaperone proteins of the endoplasmic reticulum. Only correctly folded proteins are transported from the rough endoplasmic reticulum to the Golgi apparatus. Disturbances in redox regulation, calcium, lack of glucose, viral infection or protein overexpression can lead to an endoplasmic reticulum stress response, a state in which protein folding

---

78 Common denominator of copper/Zn superoxide dismutase mutants associated with amyotrophic lateral sclerosis : decreased stability of the apo state.
Lindberg MJ, Tibell L, Oliveberg M.
http://www.ncbi.nlm.nih.gov/pubmed/12482932

slows down, resulting in increased unfolded proteins. This stress is a potential cause of damage in hypoxia / ischemia, insulin resistance and other disorders.

More than 100 point mutations of SOD1 have been associated with ALS. However, these mutations are dispersed in the protein and provide no clear functional or structural clues to the mechanism of the underlying disease. Mutations only marginally affect the stability of the native protein

Mikael Oliveberg and his colleagues found that SOD1, without a metal ion, had a less stable form than the wild-type protein. Their results suggest that destabilization of the immature protein may be a contributing factor to the progression of ALS. This article has been cited 64 times.

In 2017, another article[79] in bioinformatics resulted in the same result.

In fact it seems that the destabilization of a protein is a common phenomenon that was already known in 2002. But this destabilization of the three-dimensional shape of SOD1 had not been previously associated with ALS.

However knowing that a protein shape is not stable, does not tell anything about the event that makes it unstable. In 2008 it was found that defects in endoplasmic reticulum or Golgi may cause protein conformational changes that are associated with ALS[80].

---

79   https://www.ncbi.nlm.nih.gov/pmc/articles/PMC5498623/
80   https://www.ncbi.nlm.nih.gov/pubmed/18440237

2003 : Do SOD1 mutations interfere with protein folding?[81]?

We are now in 2003, 5 years after the discovery that mutations of SOD1 are associated with ALS. More than 100 point mutations of SOD1 are now associated with ALS.

The reduced stability of ALS-related mutations has, in the past, led some scientists to believe that the early events of the pathogenesis leading to ALS involve the aggregation of proteins.

In 2003, inclusion-body-like aggregates were already found in human ALS patients, and transgenic mice expressing mutant SOD1 produced inclusion bodies in motor neurons and astrocytes related to a pathology similar to ALS. Other scientists have shown the ability of different mutant SOD1 enzymes to undergo ordered aggregation in vitro, and their tendency to form solid but transparent gels.

Additional support for the misfolded hypothesis is in how ALS begins and progresses. Neurodegeneration begins locally and spreads from a segment of myotome[82] to the neighboring segment. This domino-like spread of the pathology has already been considered a sign of a viral infection accompanying the disease.

This article by Stathopulos, Meiering and their colleagues convinced ALS researchers that the gain of toxic function, for many familial mutant SODs associated with ALS, is a consequence of protein destabilization. Protein destabilization in turn leads to increase in aggregations of cytotoxic proteins.

Macromolecular aggregate assemblies typically occur locally and sometimes after a considerable latency period. Once a seeding aggregate is formed, however, it can rapidly catalyze

---

81   https://www.ncbi.nlm.nih.gov/pubmed/12773627
82   Myotome : The group of muscles innervated by a single spinal nerve.

further aggregation invasively, which is consistent with the pathological development of ALS.

This article is cited 65 times, a good score, had a measurable impact on subsequent research. A first aspect is that it contributed to reinforce the idea that there is a gain and not a loss of function in the cases of the SOD1 mutations. This was not necessarily intuitive for the scientists of the field.

Another aspect brought by this article is that SOD1 pathology is not necessarily limited to family cases. The reasoning that SOD1 also concerns sporadic cases is that problems related to misfolded and poorly localized proteins are less due to a genetic aspect than to a problem of RNA processing. Sandrine Da Cruz from Don Cleveland's laboratory[83] shown that misfolded SOD1 protein is easily detectable in patient samples with SOD1 mutations, but is below detectable limits in spinal cord and cortex tissues from SOD1 patients with sporadic or non-SOD1 ALS. The lack of accumulation of misfolded SOD1 leads them to conclude that the misfolding of SOD1 is not a major component of sporadic ALS. But that did not convince some in the ALS [84], research community, despite the notoriety of Don Cleveland's lab.

This article also draws attention to the instability of some forms of protein, so it has been cited in studies[85] examining the curious links between cancer and neurodegeneration.

In fact, over-regulated genes in cancer are often under-regulated in neurodegenerative disorders and vice versa. The fact that apparently unrelated diseases share functional pathways suggests a link between their etiopathogenesis and the properties of the molecules involved. Are there any specific

83 Misfolded SOD1 is not a primary component of sporadic ALS
https://www.ncbi.nlm.nih.gov/pmc/articles/PMC5472502/
84 https://www.ncbi.nlm.nih.gov/pmc/articles/PMC6094144/
85Neurodegeneration   and   Cancer :   Where   the   Disorder   Prevails
https://www.ncbi.nlm.nih.gov/pmc/articles/PMC4615981/

3.3. Chronology of the major stages of ALS research.

characteristics that explain the exclusive association of proteins to cancer or neurodegeneration ?

2003 : Hopes in neurotrophic factors[86].

There are several ways to mitigate the effects of a disease, one of which is to suppress the root cause (for example, by killing one pathogen with antibiotics), the other to help the body to adapt to the stressful situation. Neurotrophic (nourishing) factors are molecules that help neuronal cells to cope with stress, for example, by helping them draw more energy from their environment.

Neurotrophic factors (NTF) are a family of biomolecules, almost all of which are peptides or small proteins. Most NTFs exert their trophic effects on neurons by transmitting signals via tyrosine kinases[87]. In the mature nervous system, they promote neuronal survival, induce synaptic plasticity and modulate the formation of long-term memories. Neurotrophic factors also promote the initial growth and development of neurons in the central nervous system and the peripheral nervous system, and are able to regenerate damaged neurons in specimens and animal models. Some neurotrophic factors are also released by the target tissue to guide the growth of developing axons. Most neurotrophic factors belong to one of three families :

- neurotrophins,

- ligands of the family of neurotrophic factors derived from the glial cell line (GFL),

- neuropoietic cytokines.

---

86 https://www.ncbi.nlm.nih.gov/pubmed/12907804

87 Tyrosine kinases are a subgroup of the larger class of protein kinases that attach phosphate groups to other amino acids (serine and threonine). Phosphorylation of proteins by kinases is an important mechanism in communicating signals within a cell (signal transduction) and regulating cellular activity, such as cell division. It functions as an "on" or "off" switch in many cellular functions. A number of viruses target tyrosine kinase function during infection.

3.3. Chronology of the major stages of ALS research.

Adeno-associated viruses (AAV) were used in 2003 for some time, to administer genetic therapies. Unresolved problems remained at that time, particularly for neurodegenerative diseases, because of the blood-brain and medullo-spinal barriers that filter large molecules, and drugs, in order to protect the central nervous system.

Genetic therapies aim to permanently correct genetic abnormalities in DNA. In ALS, the most common motivation is to be able to continually generate neutrophic factors in the CNS, but how to override the blood-brain or medullo-spinal barrier ?

To deliver these viral loads within the blood-brain barrier, Brian Kaspar and his colleagues used an innovative approach based on a particularly useful property of adeno-associated viruses (AAV).

Some viruses, during the few million years of existence of primates, have developed a strategy to invade their nervous system. AAVs can migrate from a muscle to the neuromuscular junction, then to the axon and eventually reach the neuronal nucleus for gene therapy. This displacement from the end to the nucleus of the neuron is called : Retrograde transport. Kaspar and colleagues used these viruses properties, injecting AAV into the respiratory and motor motor muscles, to deliver retrograde neurotrophic factors, including insulin-dependent growth factor-1 (IGF-1) and growth factor derived from the glial cell line (GDNF), in the CNS of mice with ALS.

It's a bit similar to what Nurown does, except that it's much simpler (no indirect route via MSC stem cells, no periodic intrathecal injection) and more efficient. One can only wonder why this therapy was not developed for humans.

2003 : How the disease spreads from cell to cell[88].

An article written by Clement from Don Cleveland's laboratory shown the predominant influence of non-neuronal cells on the pathogenesis of ALS. The progression of ALS is still a little mysterious, even if explanations have already been proposed. The article simply explains that since non-neuronal cells are connected to multiple neurons, a pathogen on a neuron can migrate to an astrocyte, and from there to another neuron, and so on. All other explanations including a prion effect, seems a bit more awkward.

Glial cells and damaged neurons must work together to cause the disease. Motor neuron toxicity has been shown to require damage from mutant SOD1 acting in non-neuronal cells. This is consistent with the failure of SOD1 mutant expression in single cell type experiments to study induction of motor neuron degeneration. It is also compatible with the failure to accelerate the progression of ALS by increasing levels of SOD1 G93A in neurons.

Indeed, death of the motor neuron could in principle be caused solely by external causes, such as lesions on several types of adjacent cells such as interneurons, astrocytes and microglia.

Clement says that it is wrong to think that SOD1 mutations on motor neurons are responsible for the disease, because cells in the neuron environment also influence the course of the disease.

Although glial cells have strong similarities with neurons since they can be mutated from one type of cell to another, this calls into question two almost dogmatic aspects of ALS research. One of these is the theory of excitotoxicity. Excitotoxicity hypothesis seems weakened as it is specific to neurons.

---

88   https://www.ncbi.nlm.nih.gov/pubmed/14526083

3.3. Chronology of the major stages of ALS research.

The other aspect is even more serious : If the environment is critical for ALS, it greatly diminishes the quasi-dogma that mutated genes are responsible for familial ALS and this opens the door to theories of inflammation, proteinopathies or even cancer-like processes.

As a single gene could no more be held responsible for ALS, the response of the scientists was to multiply the number of genes involved in ALS.

As one might expect, this article has been cited 287 times, a record for research on ALS !

In a way, this article has encouraged the search for treatment based on neurotrophic factors like Nurown, because if the motor neuron environment is decisive and if we do not know why the motor neurons are dying, then on a purely pragmatic approach it is better to help indiscriminately all cells of the CNS to have a better live.

2003 : ALS is a distal axonopathy[89]

Here is probably the strangest scientific article about ALS. But is is one of the most cited : 400 times in 2019. In this book, it is surpassed only by the SOD1 and TDP-43 discovery articles.

Fischer and colleagues started with the question of where motor neuron dysfunction begins : within the motor neuron cell body, within the motor axon, or even at the level of the neuro-muscular junction ?

Human studies of ALS at that time, did not provided an answer to this question, and no data were available correlating weakness or death with loss of spinal motor neurons.

In order to better understand the progression of disease in the SOD1 G93A mutant mouse, the authors undertook a systematic pathological study of these animals at multiple time points along the course of disease.

They quantified the numbers of spinal motor neurons, axons in the nerve roots, and the degree of denervation at neuromuscular junctions, providing a sequential view of motor neuron pathology in these animals.

Their findings demonstrate that before any loss of motor neurons, there is a severe loss of ventral root motor axons and significant denervation at corresponding neuromuscular junctions.

Progression of abnormalities was from distal to proximal, indicating a « dying back » pathophysiology.

In addition, they had the opportunity to study at autopsy a patient with sporadic ALS who died early and unexpectedly. His pathology also suggested a pattern of disease similar to the findings in mice.

---

89   https://www.ncbi.nlm.nih.gov/pubmed/14736504

3.3. Chronology of the major stages of ALS research.

Treatments to rescue motor neurons according to the cell death model of motor neuron pathology have shown only limited success in mouse models as well as in humans.

By separating the motor neuron from its target muscle, axonal degeneration may be the more important contributor to the progressive deterioration of motor function in ALS, therefore representing a very important and neglected therapeutic target.

Furthermore, if cell body degeneration is relatively late compared to axonal degeneration, early intervention at the first sign of motor symptoms could potentially prevent the subsequent irreversible loss of motor neurons.

Another teams had the same finding in 2006[90], in 2013[91], by two independent teams in 2016[92] [93] and by two other teams in 2018[94] [95]. Some those articles are specially important because they studied humans, not mice.

---

90   https://www.ncbi.nlm.nih.gov/pubmed/16928866

91   https://www.ncbi.nlm.nih.gov/pmc/articles/PMC3869683/

92   https://www.ncbi.nlm.nih.gov/pubmed/27038603/

93   https://www.ncbi.nlm.nih.gov/pubmed/26592719/

94   https://www.ncbi.nlm.nih.gov/pmc/articles/PMC6234026/

95   https://www.ncbi.nlm.nih.gov/pubmed/30203787

2005 : Theories of gliosis[96].

Two years have passed, here we are in 2005. About 200 minor articles on SOD1 have been published during these two years, without any significant progress.

Clement and many prestigious colleagues, including Jean-Pierre Julien, discovered two years ago that the expression of a protein by a mutant SOD1 neuron does not cause ALS. In 2005, Jean-Pierre Julien and his colleagues, go further and suggest that mutant SOD1 protein in the extracellular medium, secreted by spinal cord cells, induces microgliosis and triggers neuronal death. It's an interesting complement to Clement's discovery. Scientists in 2005, were still thinking that SOD1, which is associated with only 2 % of ALS cases, had some relation with the other cases, and that by studying SOD1, they could uncover what was causing the other 98 % cases.

Granines (chromogranins or secretogranins) are acidic proteins and are present in the secretory granules of a wide variety of endocrine and neuroendocrine cells. The granins function as pro-hormones, giving rise to a series of peptide fragments for which autocrine, paracrine and endocrine activities have been demonstrated in-vitro and in vivo, and they also have an antibiotic activity. The intracellular biochemistry of granins includes the binding of Ca2+, ATP and catecholamines (epinephrine, norepinephrine) to the hormone-related vesicle nucleus. Since 1994, it has been known[97] that chromogranin A is expressed in central nervous system lesions in patients with neurological diseases.

Japanese researchers have shown[98] that chromogranins A and B can interact with mutant SOD1 protein.

---

96 http://www.ncbi.nlm.nih.gov/pubmed/16369483
97 https://www.ncbi.nlm.nih.gov/pubmed/8041489
98 https://www.ncbi.nlm.nih.gov/pubmed/18567360

3.3. Chronology of the major stages of ALS research.

Secretion of mutant SOD1 may represent a toxic pathway consistent with the non-autonomous nature of ALS. In 2005 Jean-Pierre Julien and his colleagues will investigate the idea that SOD1 proteins of the wild-type and mutant type can be secreted by non-classical secretory pathways, that is to say outside the cell. They would linked those secretory pathways to chromogranins.

Unlike chromogranins, SOD1 is a cytosolic protein and is synthesized in free ribosomes. Mutant SOD1 had a distribution pattern similar to chromogranin. This colocalization was observed in the rough endoplasmic reticulum, transport vesicles and granule-like structures. In contrast, the naturally occurring SOD1 protein was mainly localized in cytosol and sometimes in mitochondria and luminal structures, including smooth and rough endoplasmic reticulum.

Chromogranin-mediated mutant SOD1 secretion is deleterious because extracellular mutant SOD1 proteins cause gliosis and death of embryonic motoneurons in mixed culture.

Unlike secreted mutated SOD1, extracellular wild-type SOD1 probably has protective properties. Their data suggest that the wild-type extracellular SOD1 protein suppresses extracellular inflammation, perhaps through an antioxidant effect.

Researchers consider interneurons to be important contributors to the secretion of chromogranins and mutant SOD1 complexes near motor neurons.

In this model, it is the extracellular mutant SOD1 located near motor neurons that would increase the risk of motor neuron damage. It is very different from the already proposed models where it is either toxicity or loss of function in mutated SOD1, inside the cell, that were supposed to cause the disease.

Although interneurons and motoneurons are the predominant source of extracellular mutant SOD1 mediated by chromogranin interactions, mutant SOD1 protein secreted by

3.3. Chronology of the major stages of ALS research.

other pathways from other cells such as microglia and astrocytes could also contribute to pathogenesis.

3.3. Chronology of the major stages of ALS research.

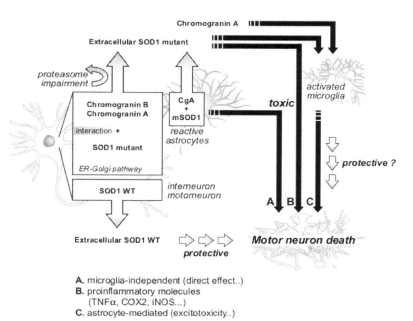

A. microglia-independent (direct effect..)
B. proinflammatory molecules
   (TNFα, COX2, iNOS...)
C. astrocyte-mediated (excitotoxicity..)

Source : Chromogranin-mediated secretion of mutant superoxide dismutase proteins linked to amyotrophic lateral sclerosis. Urushitani M, Sik A, Sakurai T, Nukina N, Takahashi R, Julien JP.

This article shows that scientists started to feel constrained by the techniques of molecular biology and they looked at other technologies, in fact the researchers here pay great attention to the localization of molecules, and this implies the use of sophisticated microscopes.

It is also an article a bit disturbing because chromogranins belong to the neuro-endocrine system. Why do they appear when there is mutant SOD1 protein in the inter-cellular space ? Is it chromogranins who created it ? Chromogranin expression is related to diabetes and cancer. They are indeed expressed by neuroendocrine tumors. We are very far from the genetic disease that Siddique and Rosen had thought of in 1993.

3.3. Chronology of the major stages of ALS research.

2006 : TDP-43 is correlated with ALS[99].

In 2006, something important is happening for ALS researchers. Until the mid-2000 s, the cause of most non-communicable diseases such as cancer or ALS was thought to be genetic. It was a concept that had been passionately promoted by researchers who said in the last decade of the last century, that we would be able to treat cancer with genetics. Much more soberly Craig Venter, president of Celera Genomics, one of two teams which analyzed the human genome, recalled in 2001 that « *We simply do not have enough genes for this idea of biological determinism to be correct* ».

At that time, it was therefore difficult for a researcher to make assumptions about other disease mechanisms than genetic mutations, without risking to jeopardize their career. In another degenerative disease, Alzheimer, researchers on hyper phosphorylated proteins have been referred to as "Tauists" by "Baptists". The "Baptists" being the good guys, supporters of a genetic origin of this disease (mutations in APP gene). It has not escaped anyone that in the United States the Baptist faith is widespread and that "Tauism" for the phosphorylation[100] of Tau protein, is pronounced in English as "Taoism" the Chinese religion, and one of main promoters of the Tau hypothesis, was Virginia Lee, who was born in China…

Since SOD1 is a very potent antioxidant in cells, a mutated SOD1 should be flawed and unable to protect the cell (loss of function). So there had to be one or more other genes for the 98 % of cases other than those where SOD1 is involved. For

---

99 http://www.ncbi.nlm.nih.gov/pubmed/17023659

100 Protein phosphorylation is one of the most important and frequent regulatory mechanisms. Phosphorylation is catalyzed by various specific protein kinases, while phosphatases are dephosphorylated. Kinases and phosphatases are generally regulated by external signals, such as hormones, cytokines and other growth factors, as well as intracellular calcium changes.

example, in 2006 a team led by Siddique thought to be on the trail of a common gene between family ALS and FTD[101].

In 2006, it was discovered[102] by Virginia Lee's laboratory that a protein is associated with ALS and that this protein is considerably more prevalent in the pathology of ALS than mutated SOD1 proteins.

So it is a paradigm change : It is a non-mutated protein which is deleterious in most cases of ALS.

In a sense, this is a big step forward, because so far most sporadic cases (90 % of all cases) were explained with the hypothesis of excitotoxicity and scientists knew that this hypothesis was wrong.[103] The discovery of the association of the TDP-43 protein with most cases of ALS is therefore welcome.

But this raised important questions about how this misplaced and misfolded protein appears in sporadic ALS and other neurodegenerative diseases. Not all scientists were convinced that an unmutated protein is at the root of the disease.

For researchers from other fields of neurodegenerative disease, this was great news. TDP-43 joined the club of neurodegenerative (non-mutated) Alzheimer's, and Parkinson's / Lewy body dementia. The discovery of the influence of TDP-43 in ALS therefore has a unifying aspect of enormous

---

101C. Vance, A. Al-Chalabi, D. Ruddy, B.N. Smith, X. Hu, J. Sreedharan, T. Siddique, H.J. Schelhaas, B. Kusters, D. Troost, F. Baas, V. de Jong, C.E. Shaw,
Familial amyotrophic lateral sclerosis with frontotemporal dementia is linked to a locus on chromosome 9p13.
Brain 129 (2006) 868–875.

102 A Japanese team was also close to make this discovery :
https://www.ncbi.nlm.nih.gov/pubmed/17084815
103 For example, scientists discovered in 2018 that hypoexcitability precedes denervation in large fast-twitch motor units in two unrelated mouse models of ALS.
http://www.ncbi.nlm.nih.gov/pubmed/29580378

significance. But a few years later we will also discover mutated versions of the protein TDP-43 in a few cases of ALS, as we have seen that mutated SOD1 produced unfolded and mislocated proteins.

Not Mutated TDP-43 :

About 95 % of patients with TDP-43 positive aggregates have no mutation in this pathogen[104]. These aggregates consist of full-length, phosphorylated and aberrantly ubiquitinated TDP-43 as well as 35- and 25-kDa C-terminal fragments of the protein.

Mutated TDP-43 :

The mutated TDP-43 protein accounts for 3 % of familial cases and 1.5 % of sporadic cases of ALS[105] (Lagier-Tourenne et Cleveland, 2009)

---

104 https://www.ncbi.nlm.nih.gov/pubmed/25487060/
105 https://www.ncbi.nlm.nih.gov/pubmed/19303844/

3.3. Chronology of the major stages of ALS research.

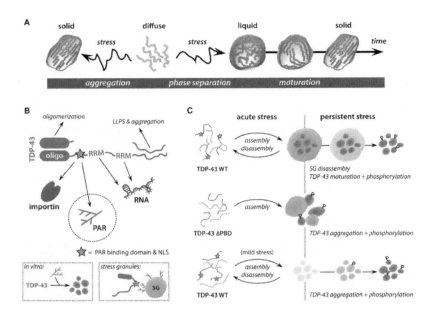

The Road to TDP-43 Aggregation
https://www.ncbi.nlm.nih.gov/pubmed/30193092

In 2019, this paper had been cited 1548 times, considerably more than most ALS articles and even more than the 1993 Rosen and Siddique article, that had twice as long time to capture citations.

2008 : A link between an abnormal cell cycle and TDP-43[106]

Motor neurons were thought to not divide. Once they reach the end of neurodevelopment, they would survive until the death of their host. Their cell cycle is forever stopped, however this is not a rule shared by all types of neurons, for example there is what is called restorative neurogenesis after trauma and also during neurogenesis in the hippocampus. The other cells of the central nervous system divide in a classical way.

Some articles have shown that motor neurons may try to resume the cell cycle in the case of neurodegenerative diseases. This article from 2008, links TDP-43 to the cell cycle.

Outside periods of cell division, the cells are in a state of rest called the G0 state. The eukaryotic cell cycle comprises four distinct states : the G1 state, the S state (synthesis), the G2 state (the set of those three states is called interphase) and the M state (mitosis and cytokinesis).

The activation of each phase depends on the progression and completion of the previous one, and control points are used to check if it is possible to move safely to the next stage.

Nonproliferative cells in multicellular eukaryotes return to the resting G0 state from G1 at the end of neurodevelopment and may remain at rest for long periods, possibly indefinitely (as is often the case for neurons). This is very common for fully differentiated cells.

Cellular senescence occurs in response to DNA damage and external stress and is usually a G1 arrest. Some cells semi-permanently enter the G0 state and are considered as post-mitotic cells, for example certain cells of the liver, kidneys and stomach. Many cells do not enter the G0 state and continue to

---

106 https://www.ncbi.nlm.nih.gov/pmc/articles/PMC2268791/

divide throughout the life of an organism, for example, epithelial cells.

The possibility of a return to the cell cycle was very early, abundantly cited with regard to Alzheimer's disease[107]. In 2007 there was even a review about this topic that was cited 158 times[108]. This review aimed at stimulating the idea that cell cycle regulation is actually a constant problem for mature neurons. The authors illustrate that, far from being permanently postmitotic, adult neurons must continuously hold their cell cycle in check. This perspective stems from the finding that cell cycle control can fail in "postmitotic" neurons. Their conclusion was that the price of failure is high and the death of neurons in many diseases may be an inexorable consequence of the re-initiation of the cell cycle in an adult neuron.

In an in-vitro model of Alzheimer's disease of adult neuronal culture, it has been shown that treatment of a neuron with beta-amyloids forces the onset of a cell cycle. However, instead of complete cell division, the neuronal cell cycle was interrupted and neurodegeneration ensued[109].

Researchers[110] have depleted TDP-43 expression by RNA interference (RNAi) to identify transcripts regulated by TDP-43. Their results indicate that cyclin-dependent kinase 6 (Cdk6) is a target of TDP-43 regulation and suggests that TDP-43 inhibits Cdk6 expression. Simultaneously, they found that inhibition of TDP-43 alters cell cycle distribution and induces apoptosis.

In mammalian cells, the cell cycle is activated by CDK6 at the beginning of G1 through interactions with cyclins D1, D2 and D3. There are many changes in the expression of genes that are regulated by this enzyme. Once the complex is formed, the

---

107 https://www.ncbi.nlm.nih.gov/pubmed/15039034/
108 https://www.ncbi.nlm.nih.gov/pubmed/17453017/
109 https://www.ncbi.nlm.nih.gov/pmc/articles/PMC6407038/
110 https://www.ncbi.nlm.nih.gov/pmc/articles/PMC2268791/

3.3. Chronology of the major stages of ALS research.

C-CDK6 enzymatic complex phosphorylates the pRb protein. After its phosphorylation, pRb releases its binding partner, E2F, a transcription activator, which in turn activates DNA replication. The CDK6 complex provides a switching point to initiate division by responding to external signals, such as mitogens and growth factors.

It is therefore conceivable that a lack of TDP-43 in the nucleus may let motor neurons begin a cell cycle that is unlikely to succeed.

This was confirmed[111] in 2016. Youhna M. Ayala, Tom Misteli, and Francisco E. Baralle point to the apparent relationship between TDP-43 phosphorylation, cytosolic TDP-43 accumulation, and cell cycle regulatory proteins. Their data show that the increased proliferative activity and CDK6 levels induced by Progranulin deficiency are accompanied by a cytosolic accumulation of TDP-43.

Their results also indicate that the well-known nuclear effect of TDP-43, inducing repression of CDK6 expression, is blocked in Progranulin deficient lymphoblasts.

---

111 https://molecularneurodegeneration.biomedcentral.com/articles/10.1186/s13024-016-0102-7

2008 : Mutations in TARDP 1 [112] and irrational stubbornness.

In 2008, three years after the discovery that TDP-43 was implicated in most cases of ALS (sporadic and familial) and FTD, it is discovered that there are mutations in TDP-43 in both sporadic and familial ALS. Soon, many more TDP-43 mutations will be found. But this search for TDP-43 mutations reveals also a great psychological difficulty among scientists, to accept a non-genetic origin of the TDP-43 form of ALS.

In 2006, at the discovery of TDP-43's involvement in ALS and FTD, scientists had said that a toxic TDP-43 without mutations in the TARDP gene would be difficult to explain, it was a bit of a residue of the war between *Tauists* and *Baptists*.

Here is how these scientists reasoned : A non communicable disease is necessarily of genetic origin, so if one finds a mutation on TDP-43, it is that mutation which is the cause of ALS. There was an unrestrained search for TDP-43 mutations and this article is historically the first of a long series, as if it were necessary to correct a profound anomaly.

We know now, in 2019, that other genes involved in ALS would be found later, but in overall mutated genes would cover only 10 % of all ALS cases.

But in their seminal article Virginia Lee's group has never mentioned that TDP-43 mutations were the cause of ALS. And any publication that would like to find a relationship between a mutation of TDP-43 and ALS, should explain why this mutation is not inheritable, since in 95 % of cases the ALS is not inherited. This is quite possible, as is the case for cancer where most cases are sporadic mutations, but most scientists did not consider this possibility for ALS.

---

112 https://www.ncbi.nlm.nih.gov/pubmed/18309045

3.3. Chronology of the major stages of ALS research.

The abstract of this article, opens the hostilities with an acerbic « *The function of TDP-43 in the nervous system is uncertain, and a mechanistic role in neurodegeneration remains speculative* » which implicitly denies the contribution of the group of Virginia Lee. The authors proceed by suggesting that the mutations found are the cause of ALS for both familial and sporadic forms.

It would be extraordinary if it were true, but the article is an epitome of risky extrapolations. The article in question, however, was cited **764** times in mid-2019. Normally this should indicate that it is of **extraordinary importance**, but in fact it just identifies a few of the mutations in TDP-43 which are now known to be several tens, and these are **very rare** mutations among sporadic ALS cases. It should have been a minor article, interesting for historical reasons, but nothing more.

A similar example is published[113] in 2008, with a provocative title "*TDP-43 **is not** a common cause of sporadic amyotrophic lateral sclerosis*". This is apparently a rebuttal of TDP-43's involvement in ALS, but in fact the article does not demonstrate that, but rather "*Our data indicates that genetic variation in TARDBP is not a common cause of sporadic ALS in North America*". Which, moreover, refutes the article that is the subject of this section, and rather reinforces the 2006 article on TDP-43, but the title has nothing to do with what is found and seems to have originated from a kind of mental slip.

---

113 https://www.ncbi.nlm.nih.gov/pubmed/18545701

2008 : Endoplasmic reticulum stress and induction of the unfolded protein response in ALS[114].

Fragmentation of the Golgi apparatus and morphological changes to the ER have been described in SOD1 mice since 1992 (Gonatas and colleagues, 1992), but also in sALS patients (Mourelatos and colleagues, 1993).

The deleterious role of TDP-43 in ALS was discovered two years before 2008, and introduced the idea that protein folding was one of the major problems of ALS. So as mutations in SOD1 account for only 2 % of total ALS, so what makes those protein to be misfolded in the other cases ? It is quite natural to look again in the endoplasmic reticulum.

This article, that was heavily cited (116 times), show that a full UPR, including induction of stress sensor kinases, chaperones and apoptotic mediators, is also present in spinal cords of human patients with sporadic disease.

Furthermore, the UPR chaperone protein disulphide isomerase (PDI) was found present in CSF and was aggregated and widely distributed throughout the motor neurons of these patients.

The authors also show positive regulation of UPR before the onset of symptoms in SOD1 rodents, implying that incorrect protein folding plays an important role in the disease. So this study offers new insights into pathogenesis, placing ER stress onto a generic pathophysiology for ALS.

While the significance of inclusions in disease is still not fully understood in 2008, most ALS scientists have accepted an association of those cytoplasmic inclusions with ALS pathogenesis.

The UPR signalling system is triggered when misfolded proteins accumulate within the endoplasmic reticulum (ER) (Kaufman, 2002).

114 https://www.ncbi.nlm.nih.gov/pubmed/18440237

3.3. Chronology of the major stages of ALS research.

The three major sensors of the UPR, IRE1, ATF6 and PERK, mediate a down-regulation of protein synthesis and an up-regulation of genes encoding chaperones, such as the immunoglobulin binding protein (BiP), and protein disulphide isomerase (PDI).

Although cyto-protective initially, when prolonged, the UPR triggers apoptosis by several ER stress-specific cell death signals.

Pharmacological inhibition of PDI increased the number of inclusions present. This suggests that PDI protects against their formation.

Hence, in this study the authors asked whether the UPR and PDI are induced in sporadic ALS.

They demonstrate up-regulation of the full spectrum of UPR markers in lumbar cord tissue from human sALS patients, implying that ER stress is common to all ALS.

PDI was also found in CSF and anterior horn cells, where it was widely distributed and aggregated, suggesting an association with intracellular inclusions.

2008 : The origin of ALS is not in motor neurons[115].

The Cleveland team, one of the few labs that has long been working on ALS, wanted to determine if the onset of ALS involved only motor neurons, or if other types of cells could be implicated. In fact, previous years have repeatedly indicated that the origin of ALS was not in motor neurons. This is essentially the favorite thesis of Séverine Boillée, who was at that time, a member of the Cleveland team. Séverine Boillée is in 2019 at the Brain and Spinal Cord Institute (ICM) in France.

To determine if the onset of ALS involved only motor neurons, Cleveland, Goldstein and their colleagues used chimeric animals in which all motoneurons express the mutant SOD1 protein (G37R mutation), while the other neurons and non-neuronal cells are a mixture of mutated cells generating the mutated protein and of wild-type cells. This generated two sets, one where both neurons and non-neuronal cells express mutant SOD1, and the other (which could be further subdivided) where only neurons express mutant SOD1.

If the onset of the disease is simply determined by the expression of SOD1 in the motoneurons, then all the different chimeras must show the appearance of the disease at the same age. In most of these chimeras, the presence of healthy glial cells significantly delayed the onset of motor neuron degeneration, increasing disease-free life by 50 %.

So, something other than motor neurons had to determine the onset of ALS. The Cleveland team ruled out oligodendrocytes because there were no wild-type oligodendrocytes in the chimeras to protect motor neurons. Similarly, previous work has shown that microglia and astrocytes have no effect on the onset of the disease.

The scientists then suggested that interneurons (such as the Jean-Pierre Julien group in 2005), myelinating Schwann cells of

---

115 https://www.ncbi.nlm.nih.gov/pmc/articles/PMC2396671

3.3. Chronology of the major stages of ALS research.

the peripheral nervous system and endothelial cells of the vascular system deserved to be studied. They wrote, "*There is an accumulation of evidence supporting the hypothesis that it is the presence of mutated SOD1 linked to ALS in several cell types that, together with damage directly into motor neurons, leads appearance of non-autonomic motor neurodegeneration of the cells*".

2009 : FUS is correlated with ALS.

In 2009, two separate research groups [116] [117] analyzed unrelated families with an ALS phenotype and found 14 mutations in the FUS gene.

FUS appears very rapidly at sites where DNA destruction occurs, suggesting that the role of FUS is to orchestrate DNA repair as a result of any alteration. The N-terminus of the FUS protein appears to be involved in transcriptional activation, while the C-terminus is involved in protein and RNA binding. Once again a protein found implicated in ALS, has a strong link with cancer diseases.

After the 2006 paradigm change of the discovery that a non-mutated protein (TDP-43) is the major factor causing sporadic ALS, FUS is causing scientists to reluctantly abandon their expensive SOD1 and excitotoxicity, and to think that the metabolism of RNA could play a fundamental role in the viability of the neuron. At the same time, there are differences in pathology between FUS mutations and TDP-43 protein disorders.

The cells of patients with FUS mutations do not contain aggregated TDP-43 granules, unlike the majority of sporadic cases of ALS, although they include ubiquitin inclusions in the motoneuron nucleus. The researchers then suggest that the mechanisms of FUS and TDP-43 may be distinct, in a narrative effort to return to the known terrain of genetic mutations, but in 2019 we know that the biological roles played by FUS and TDP-43 are very related[118].

Both TDP-43 and FUS/TLS have been associated with multiple nuclear and cytoplasmic steps of RNA processing.

---

116 https://www.ncbi.nlm.nih.gov/pubmed/19251627/
117 https://www.ncbi.nlm.nih.gov/pubmed/19251628/
118 https://www.ncbi.nlm.nih.gov/pmc/articles/PMC3586380/

3.3. Chronology of the major stages of ALS research.

Comprehensive maps of TDP-43-binding sites in RNAs of mouse or diseased human CNS have been determined.

Reducing TDP-43 expression in the adult nervous system alters pre-mRNA splicing of more than 900 genes.

This reveals an essential role for TDP-43 in sustaining the levels of RNAs derived from very long intron-containing pre-mRNAs.

Those RNAs are important for neuronal function, some of which are reduced in human disease.

Using similar high-throughput sequencing and computational approaches, scientists identified ~5,500 RNA targets of FUS/TLS in both mouse and human brain. The expression levels of 610 genes were dependent on FUS/TLS, and only 112 of the genes were also dependent on TDP-43.

Systematic comparison between the TDP-43– and FUS/TLS-dependent targets identified RNAs with exceptionally long introns and multiple binding sites for both TDP-43 and FUS/TLS.

Depletion of FUS/TLS or TDP-43 in human neurons differentiated from pluripotent stem cells confirmed the downregulation of long intron–containing TDP-43 and FUS/TLS targets.

Several of these common targets are substantially reduced at the protein level in affected post-mortem neurons of patients with sporadic ALS, thereby identifying a common pathogenic pathway in motor neurons from the misregulation of either TDP-43 or FUS/TLS.

2009 : First animal model for studying the TDP-43 inclusions in ALS[119].

Since the discovery of the TDP-43 protein three years ago in 2006, many laboratories have struggled to obtain correct level expression of the TDP-43 protein in mouse models. Up to 2009, in most attempts, the overexpression of the wild-type TDP-43 almost completely suppresses the targeted neurons and was accompanied by astrogliosis and microgliosis causing neurodegeneration.

It should also be noted that as usual there is a logical paradox in wanting to model a largely unknown disease with a genetic modification that is deterministic. First, because our knowledge may be false, for example, if the disease does not have its origin in motor neurons (as proposed many times), it is useless to want to make an animal model that only concerns motor neurons.

In addition the goal that only motor neurones, not other neurons, should degenerate, and should fail only at an old age, is very difficult to attain. The very fact that the first TDP-43 animal model was difficult to create is very telling.

Designing animal models is not deterministic, probably many genetic animals are created, and if one of the animals develops symptoms resembling those of patients, then the scientists clone or reproduce this line. Here we are not yet at this stage, for each mouse it will still be necessary to inject the genetic modification.

Another paradox, commonly practiced in ALS research, is that a human gene is introduced into an animal. Indeed, many human genes are different from genes in other animals. This is the case with TDP-43, of which 10 % of the sequence is different between humans and the mouse[120]. If we want the

119 https://www.ncbi.nlm.nih.gov/pubmed/19223871
120 https://www.uniprot.org/uniprot/Q13148#similar_proteins

results of experiments on mice to be transposable in humans, we have to introduce a human gene into the model animal.

Jason Tatom and his colleagues injected an adeno-associated viral vector (AAV) carrying the wild-type human TARDBP gene into the substantia nigra of rats. The animals then expressed approximately three times the normal amount of TDP-43 in the midbrain and developed some features of the human disease TDP-43. In particular, whereas TDP-43 is a nuclear protein, in this model animal, it is found in the cytoplasm in about 1 % of the transduced cells[121]. Excess TDP-43 was toxic to dopaminergic neurons.

However, having created a TDP-43 rodent model that requires genetic modification for each individual, is not as convenient as a rodent model with stable germline transmission (having a hereditary disease). This allows scientists to order TDP-43 mouse models from their usual suppliers.

---

121 Transduction is the process by which DNA is transferred from one bacterium to another by a virus.

2009 : Zinc and protein aggregates in the case of SOD1[122].

In 2009, it has been known for more than 10 years that SOD1 protein aggregates in granules in the cytoplasm. This aggregation of proteins is really one of the few features common to all forms of ALS, but also to other neurodegenerative diseases. Nordlund, Oliveberg and their colleagues were therefore very interested in knowing what makes these proteins more likely to produce aggregates instead of being ubiquitinated (marked for recycling) and thus recycled into the cytoplasm.

They were also more likely to study SOD1, perhaps because their lab had invested much more in this protein, than in other proteins that are much more common but more recently discovered, such as TDP-43. This is unfortunate because it is unlikely that the lessons learned from the SOD1 study can be transferred to TDP-43.

Patients know empirically that modulating their intakes of copper or zinc, can influence the spread of the disease, and we will see later that this has been validated at the medical level. It is therefore interesting to understand what roles these metals play in ALS.

In 2002, Mikael Oliveberg and his colleagues had already discovered that all mutants of SOD1 had one thing in common : the protein alone, without its active site metal ions, is less stable than the wild-type protein. An unstable protein can change its shape, that is to say, have a very different biological behavior.

The researchers thought that destabilization of the immature protein could be a contributing factor to the progression of ALS. The authors of the article in this section, then, suggest that SOD1 is a highly conserved ancient protein and could be a

122 https://www.ncbi.nlm.nih.gov/pubmed/19497878

kind of molecular dinosaur. This molecule can be so specialized that any mutation imbalances it.

The structural integrity of the SOD1 enzyme is essentially based on the correct coordination of copper and zinc. The loss of these cofactors not only promotes aggregation of SOD1 in vitro, but also appears to be an essential prerequisite for pathogenic aliasing in amyotrophic lateral sclerosis.

SOD1 copper is functionally necessary for the enzyme to neutralize free radicals, but zinc appears to play a more structural role. The zinc (Zn) site on this protein is considered to be the major modulator of SOD1 protein stability and ALS intensity. The results highlight a critical role for the native zinc site in controlling SOD1 folding and show that even subtle modifications of the metallic elements of the sequence can confer on the wild-type protein the same structural properties as the mutations causing ALS.

The SOD1 molecule thus seems to result from a compromise between the optimization of its functional and structural characteristics.

This article is minor compared to others, but it is clear that it marks a change in mentalities. The fact that it is not an US laboratory that is at the origin, is also symptomatic, a less famous laboratory will be more likely to adopt new ideas.

2009 : Neural stem cells provide growth factors[123].

Researchers have long wanted to provide growth factors to tissues damaged by ALS, but a viable ALS treatment must be delivered behind the blood-brain or medullo-spinal barrier, which is an obstacle to any therapy.

Previous attempts at gene therapy by Brian Kaspar's team took place in 2003. Gene therapy was injected into the respiratory and motor muscles of the motor limbs and benefited from the fact that the axon of a motor neuron crosses the medullo-spinal barrier. This made it possible to circumvent this barrier by migrating the viral load from the periphery of the motor neuron to the central nucleus where the gene therapy was to be delivered. But the effectiveness of this therapy, certainly inventive, was very limited.

Manzinni and Mandon's team, had been pioneer in 2003 in the use of mesenchymal cells in the treatment of ALS. Here too the efficiency was very limited.

Hwang, Kim and their colleagues described in 2009 how they designed neural stem cells to deliver vascular endothelial growth factor (VEGF) in the spinal cord of ALS model mice.

The researchers transplanted VEGF overexpressing stem cells intrathecally. At least some of these cells then migrated to the gray matter of the spinal cord. This was a major advance over many techniques providing growth factors only at the injection site.

A stem cell is a non-specialized cell that can divide without limit as needed and can, under specific conditions, differentiate into specialized cells. They can also generate new stem cells.

Stem cells include embryonic stem cells from the embryo, fetal stem cells from the fetus, and stem cells from adults. One type

---

123 http://www.ncbi.nlm.nih.gov/pubmed/19626053

of adult stem cell is the epithelial stem cell, which gives rise to keratinocytes in the multiple layers of epithelial cells of the epidermis of the skin. The adult bone marrow has three types of stem cells :

- hematopoietic stem cells, which give rise to the red blood cells, white blood cells and platelets,

- the endothelial stem cells, that creates the types of endothelial cells lining the blood and lymphatic vessels,

- mesenchymal stem cells, which is at the origin of different types of muscle cells.

When a stem cell differentiates, it can undergo significant changes in size, shape, metabolic activity, and overall function. To induce a stem cell to differentiate into a specialized form and function, it is sufficient to manipulate the genes and therefore the expression of proteins. The main mechanism by which genes are turned on or off is through transcription factors. A transcription factor is part of a class of proteins that bind to specific genes in the DNA molecule and promote or inhibit their transcription.

Transcription factors are proteins that affect the functioning of RNA polymerase. RNA polymerase is an enzyme complex responsible for the synthesis of RNA from a DNA template.

Due to their ability to divide and differentiate into specialized cells, stem cells are a potential treatment for diseases such as ALS which is characterized by failing cells. However, many obstacles must be overcome for the application of stem cell therapy.

For a long time, scientists used embryonic stem cells, which was a problem because of the rejection of these cells by the patient's immune system, as well as for ethical reasons.

3.3. Chronology of the major stages of ALS research.

Adult stem cells isolated from a patient are not considered foreign by the body, but their degree of differentiation is limited.

Researchers have recently developed induced pluripotent stem cells (iPSCs) from adult stem cells. These cells are genetically reprogrammed multipotent adult cells that function as embryonic stem cells ; they are capable of generating characteristic cells of the three germ layers.

Induced pluripotent stem cells are considered a promising advance in the field because their use avoids the legal, ethical and immunological pitfalls of embryonic stem cells.

This article, little cited in relation to its importance, is the first that uses stem cells delivering neurotrophic factors for the treatment of ALS.

2009 : About axonal transport mechanisms[124].

It is not known why motor neurons are specifically targeted in ALS and why not all motor neurons are simultaneously affected. While upper motor neurons and lower motor neurons are involved, some subtypes of lower motor neurons are relatively resistant to neurodegeneration. Indeed, some motor neurons are spared until the final stage of the disease, such as oculomotor neurons and Onuf nuclei, and patients retain a visual, sexual and normal bladder function throughout the evolution of the disease. sickness.

Resistant motor neurons differ significantly from anatomically and functionally vulnerable motor neurons. Surprisingly, there are also differences in vulnerability between the motor neurons of the spine, because those that are part of the fastest motor units degenerate before those of the slower motor units, thus adding additional complexity to the question of the vulnerability of the motor neurons.

Axonal transport defects may be an important factor underlying the selective vulnerability of motor neurons. An abnormal accumulation of phosphorylated neurofilaments, mitochondria and lysosomes in the proximal axon of large motor neurons and axonal spheroids is indeed present in patients with ALS.

Retrograde axonal transport (from the axon to the center of the neuronal cell) slows down in motor neurons in animal models of amyotrophic lateral sclerosis, depriving the cell body of neurotrophic factors from the extracellular media. But according to the researchers in this section, the real problem seems to be that when the retrograde carriers fed dynein finally reach the cell body, they are not the neurotrophins they deliver, but signals of stress that causes apoptosis.

---

124 http://www.ncbi.nlm.nih.gov/pubmed/19657041
http://www.ncbi.nlm.nih.gov/pubmed/19651777
http://www.ncbi.nlm.nih.gov/pubmed/19635794

3.3. Chronology of the major stages of ALS research.

Researchers Eran Perlson, Erika Holzbaur and their colleagues show that slowing down retrograde signaling only leads to slight degeneration and can not explain the etiology of ALS.

On the other hand, they show by co-cultures of motoneurones and glial cells expressing the mutant SOD1 protein in compartmentalized chambers, that the inhibition of the retrograde stress signaling is sufficient to block the activation of the cellular stress pathways and rescue motor neurons from mSOD1-induced toxicity.

Eran Perlson, Erika Holzbaur and their colleagues suggest that transported proteins are key to the rapid decline of ALS. For these researchers, the cellular environment contributes significantly to cell death, resulting in a change in the balance between survival and death receptors.

This article provides additional support for the non-autonomous ALS theory of cells, that changes in motor neurons have the ability to cause cell death. But it adds that this death is accelerated by interactions with surrounding non-neuronal cells also undergoing a cellular stress.

2010 : Something is hiding in chromosome 9[125]!

Finland has the highest incidence of ALS outside some Pacific islands. The country's genetic bottlenecks in its past (because of dramatic reduction in the number of people that can reproduce) have made its citizens genetically more homogeneous than in most other countries.

In 2010 Hannu Laaksovirta, Terhi Peuralinna and Jennifer Schymick took DNA from 405 people with ALS and 497 control cases. They found a strong association between SNPs of the 9p21 locus and the occurrence of ALS, this 9p21 locus was totally unknown to the ALS field at the time. It must be said, however, that chromosome 9 is the site of numerous genetic abnormalities related to the central nervous system[126].

People with ALS, linked to 9p21, included 44 people with a family history of ALS, as well as 58 people whose illness was apparently sporadic.

Sporadic cases are not necessarily cases that are not inherited. Patients with sporadic cases may have a parent with the deleterious mutation but who has been fortunate in not getting sick or who has not lived long enough to develop the symptoms. It is called incomplete penetrance.

Simultaneously in 2010, a British group, led by Aleksey Shatunov and Ammar Al-Chalabi, conducted a similar study with 599 patients and 4144 controls. Next, they collected data on all previous ALS GWAS they were able to collect, for a total of 4312 patients and 8425 controls. Like the Finnish team, they found it odd that the only locus that reached statistical significance was 9p21 while SOD1 is on chromosome 21 and TARDBP (TDP-43) on chromosome 1.

---

125 http://www.ncbi.nlm.nih.gov/pubmed/20801717
http://www.ncbi.nlm.nih.gov/pubmed/20801718
http://www.ncbi.nlm.nih.gov/pubmed/20801719
126 https://en.wikipedia.org/wiki/Chromosome_9#Diseases_and_disorders

3.3. Chronology of the major stages of ALS research.

The region of interest centered on 9p21, contains three known genes and none of them is involved, even by far, in neurodegenerative diseases.

The British authors set out several reasons why they did not find a gene (or more exactly, a locus), including one that was premonitory. For them the mutation they were looking for had to be in an unknown gene[127] or in an exon.

Proteins are expressed by genes, but unlike Crick and Watson's minimalist and highly aesthetic vision of 60 years ago, the mechanism of protein expression is extraordinarily complex. Non-contiguous areas of the DNA ("enhancer" and "silencer") participate in the creation of the mRNA, but also undergo modifications of expression by proteins. The mRNA that is copied from a subset of DNA is actually a kind of conditional collage of different areas of the DNA. These areas are called exons, those that apparently do not contribute are called introns. We now know that introns too, indirectly contribute to the expression of proteins. The process is called gene splicing and allows the DNA to produce much times more proteins than there are loci (genes).

---

127 The notion of gene is a convenient approximation, today we speak of locus.

2011 : At last C9orf72[128]!

In 2011 and to continue the work of the previous year, a consortium was set up between Finland, the United States and England to further explore this intriguing situation in 9p21.

The disorders of repeated nucleotide expansion, also known as microsatellite expansion disorders, are caused by genetic change within a single gene in which a repetitive nucleotide sequence, typically 3 to 10 nucleotides, spans a large number of copies. The vast majority of these diseases are hereditary due to a gain in function for the expanded allele.

Identifying trinucleotide repeats has led to a better understanding of a complex set of hereditary neurological diseases.

The first disease to be identified in the early 1990 s was the fragile X syndrome, which has since been mapped in the long arm of the X chromosome. There are 230 to 4000 CGG repeats in the gene that causes the syndrome. Fragile X in these patients, compared to 60 to 230 carriers and 5 to 54 replicates in unaffected individuals.

The second, a disease linked to the triplet DNA repetition, the fragile X-E syndrome, was also identified on the X chromosome, but was found to be the result of a repeat of GCC nucleotides.

As amino acid motif repetition diseases have been discovered, several categories have been established for grouping them according to similar characteristics.

- Category I includes Huntington's disease (HD) and spinocerebellar ataxias caused by repeated "CAG" expansion in specific protein-encoding gene sections.

---

128 http://www.ncbi.nlm.nih.gov/pubmed/21944779
http://www.ncbi.nlm.nih.gov/pubmed/21944778

- Category II expansions tend to be more phenotypically diverse, with heterogeneous expansions generally of low amplitude, but also present in gene exons.

- Category III includes Fragile X syndrome, myotonic dystrophy, two spinocerebellar ataxias, juvenile myoclonic epilepsy, and Friedreich's ataxia.

Numerous linkage analyzes and genome-wide association studies (GWAS) had shown the previous year that the p-arm of the ninth chromosome harbored a genetic factor related to familial and sporadic ALS. But what had prevented progress was that many scientists considered the apparently non-Mendelian inheritance of a microsatellite marker to be a methodological error.

Mariely DeJesus-Hernandez, Ian Mackenzie and Rosa Rademakers realized that the missing variant was not detected because it had to be a deletion sequence or some kind of PCR[129] resistant sequence.

The researchers therefore designed a PCR protocol around a primer that bound to the repeat sequence. Since the hexamer primer could bind anywhere in the repeats, the technique did not amplify a single full-length expansion, but a whole range of fragments. From this amplified DNA band, it became apparent that people with ALS had a very wide repetition section.

The researchers estimated that 700 to 1,600 repetitions were present in family members with ALS or FTD, which was new for two reasons: Not only was a nucleotide repetition associated with ALS, but this repetition was also present in the FTD.

---

129 Polymerase chain reaction is a method of molecular biology of in-vitro gene amplification. It makes it possible to duplicate in large numbers a known DNA or RNA sequence, from a small quantity (of the order of a few picograms) of nucleic acid and specific primers consisting of oligonucleotides of synthetic 20 to 25 nucleotides. It is thus possible, for example, to detect the presence of HIV or to measure a viral load. However, it is not reliable for some sample sources.

3.3. Chronology of the major stages of ALS research.

With regard to the Traynor team in the United States, the researchers focused on a Welsh family and a Dutch family hit by both ALS and FTD. After a first failure, the team collected DNA samples from a few members of this family and isolated the ninth chromosome DNA in order not to have to search the entire genome. They sequenced 300 independent sequences of the entire chromosome, but in a specific region of the chromosome, the coverage rate of the sequencing fell to only twice as if the "read" from the sequencer were of very different natures at this location.

The DNA molecule is much larger than the capabilities of the sequencers. It is therefore necessary to cut the genome into fragments and to sequence each of these fragments. Fragments may partially overlap to define so-called "contig" regions of sequences. To say that the fragments overlap, means that they have at least one common part. But if we find many identical fragments, without partial recovery, we can not reconstruct the genome.

Looking at the sequences themselves, the researchers realized that the blocking point consisted of a whole series of repetitions of GGGGCC in C9orf72. Like the Mayo group, they had to design an ad hoc PCR test to be able to identify the repeats.

Alan Renton, Elisa Majounie, Raphael Gibbs and Jennifer Schymick from Traynor's team then focused on a Finnish population with this new test. Among their collaborators in this region were Pentti Tienari and Hannu Laaksovirta. In a cohort of 402 people with ALS, expansion accounted for 46 % of familial cases and 21 % of sporadic cases. In addition to a common SOD1 D90A mutation in Scandinavia, the C9orf72 variant accounted for the majority of ALS cases in Finland.

The team also looked at 75 Finns with FTDs, 29 % of which had very many nucleotide triplet repeats on C9ORF72.

3.3. Chronology of the major stages of ALS research.

When Traynor's team examined 238 people with familial ALS in North America, Germany, and Italy, "*my jaw dropped, because every other sample had this type of expansion.* » « *I never thought I would see the day that a mutation would explain so many cases of familial ALS.*"

2012 : Genetic overlap between spinocerebellar ataxia and ALS[130].

There is significant genetic overlap[131] between neurodegenerative diseases such as spinocerebellar ataxia, hereditary spastic paraplegia, ALS, and frontotemporal dementia. Since the TDP-43 pathology is found in a number of neurodegenerative diseases, this has broad implications. The discovery of C9orf72's involvement in ALS has probably inspired researchers to re-examine the potential existence of links between ataxia and ALS. Indeed, in one case as in the other, there are repeats of amino acid motifs[132].

Spinocerebellar ataxias are a group of neurodegenerative diseases that are highly heterogeneous both clinically and genetically and often fatal. They are characterized by a cerebellar syndrome that results in particular disorders of walking and balance. Some cases of ataxia have been misdiagnosed as familial ALS cases. Mutations in ATXN2, the gene that generates the Ataxin-2 protein, cause spinocerebellar ataxia type 2 (SCA2).

Ataxin-2 protein is involved in the regulation of mRNA translation through its interactions with the poly (A) binding protein. It also participates in the formation of stress granules and P-bodies, which also play a role in the regulation of RNA.

Researchers at Aaron Gitler's laboratory had already discovered that the Ataxin-2 gene between codons 27 and 33 of glutamine was a risk factor for ALS. Most people have 22 or 23 repetitions on this gene. Curiously, having more than 34 repetitions leads to a higher probability not of ALS, but of another disease, spinocerebellar ataxia.

---

130 http://www.ncbi.nlm.nih.gov/pubmed/22764223
131 These violent repeats have violent extends
https://www.ncbi.nlm.nih.gov/pmc/articles/PMC6089690/
132 Mais pas sur les mêmes gènes, et dans un cas sur des introns, et dans l'autre sur des extrons.

3.3. Chronology of the major stages of ALS research.

The pathogenic TDP-43 protein present in the cytoplasmic stress granules tends to be both fragmented and phosphorylated. Hart and Gitler expected the additional pattern repeats to improve the Ataxin-2/TDP-43 interaction, effectively trapping TDP-43 in stress granules and promoting the onset and progression of the disease.

Hart and Gitler were convinced that the additional repeats could enhance the Ataxin-2-TDP-43 interaction, by more effectively trapping TDP-43 in the stress granules.

Hart tested the hypothesis on three types of cells. He transfected them with Ataxin-2 totaling 22, 31 or 39 replicates.

The simple addition of Ataxin-2, regardless of the size of the repeats, had no effect on TDP-43. To force TDP-43 to migrate into cytoplasmic stress granules, Hart then stressed the cells. Intermediate-length repeats approximately doubled the concentration of pathogenic TDP-43 relative to Ataxin-2 with longer or shorter repeat sequences.

Since only fragmented TDP-43 was phosphorylated, Hart suspected that **cleavage would precede** and could even favor phosphate acquisition. This led Hart to use antibodies specific for activated caspases. Caspases are a sign of ongoing apoptosis. Cells with mid-length ataxin repeats, **those associated with ALS**, then showed the presence of caspase-3, cells expressing longer or shorter versions did not.

It appears that the medium length repeats somehow lower the stress threshold of the cell, which makes it prone to activate caspase and to place TDP-43 in stress granules.

Treatment of cells with a caspase inhibitor reduced the accumulation of phosphorylated fragments of TDP-43, suggesting that caspase activation occurs upstream of TDP-43 aggregation.

The scientists suggested that since caspase inhibitors are effective in reducing pathological changes in TDP-43, this pathway could be pursued as a therapeutic target for ALS. However this is an awkward proposal, apoptose is a mechanism that deactivates dysfunctioning cells so it is hard to see how letting a dysfunctioning cell to live, would enhance patient's health.

There is however a **gold nugget in this article**, it is that a mildly stressed cell develop a TDP-43 pathology.

2013 : Association between obesity and ALS[133]

The purpose of this study was to investigate the association between body fat and the risk of amyotrophic lateral sclerosis (ALS) with an appropriate prospective study protocol.

The European Foresight Survey on Cancer and Nutrition (EPIC) covered more than 500,000 people in 10 Western European countries.

What the study suggests is contrary to public health recommendations : There is a reduced risk of death for ALS patients who have a level of body fat that for healthy people would be judged to be too high.

Underweight women have a significantly higher risk of dying from ALS compared to those who are of normal weight ; on the contrary, too high waist circumference was associated with a decreased risk of death from ALS in women.

Although in the EPIC cohort, there are not enough underweight men to draw a conclusion, the increase in BMI appears to be also associated with a reduced risk of death from ALS in men.

The association of decreased risk of ALS with increased body fat may also be due to preclinical metabolic impairment. Altered energy metabolism is observed in patients with ALS, resulting in weight loss and body fat as the disease progresses. This has been attributed to hypermetabolism with increased energy expenditure throughout the progression of the disease. This happens specially with ALS patients with genetic forms of the disease.

It could be argued that these results describe a presymptomatic phase, more than a risk factor for the disease. If this were the case, one would expect, on average, to reduce BMI and SMR with the number of years of follow-up among ALS cases ; however, this has not been observed.

___

133 https://www.ncbi.nlm.nih.gov/pmc/articles/PMC3598455/

3.3. Chronology of the major stages of ALS research.

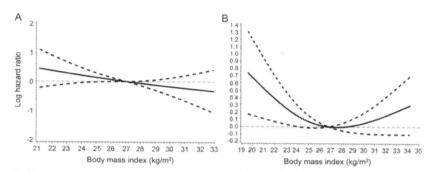

Spline regression curves of body mass index in relation to amyotrophic lateral sclerosis mortality in men (A) and women (B)

Source : https://www.ncbi.nlm.nih.gov/pmc/articles/PMC3598455/

Two types of conclusions could be drawn, one classic, corroborated by numerous studies, that having an overweight (but not obesity) is a favorable factor. The other conclusion is more hypothetical ; it is that active and lean people are more likely to develop ALS than other people. This could explain why many athletes seem to have been victims of ALS.

2013 : Oligodendrocytes fail very early in ALS[134].

ALS researchers may have spent less time than multiple sclerosis researchers thinking about how to help oligodendrocytes provide metabolic support to neurons. The use of anti-inflammatories is a well-established practice in the field of multiple sclerosis.

A single oligodendrocyte can extend its processes to 50 motor neuron axons, enveloping about 1 µm of myelin sheath around each axon. Each oligodendrocyte forms a segment of myelin for several adjacent axons.

In the spinal cord of amyotrophic lateral sclerosis (ALS) mice, oligodendrocytes negatively regulate transporters that transfer glycolytic substrates to neurons. Oligodendrocyte progenitors show increased proliferation and differentiation, although the cause of these oligodendrocyte changes is unknown.

Dwight Bergles and colleagues found that extensive degeneration of oligodendrocyte gray matter[135], is formed in the spinal cord of SOD1 (G93A) ALS mice prior to the onset of the disease. Although new oligodendrocytes are formed, they fail to mature, resulting in progressive demyelination. The researchers also found that oligodendrocyte dysfunction was also prevalent in human ALS, as demyelination of the gray matter were observed in the motor cortex and spinal cord of patients with ALS.

The role of white matter in the degeneration of motor neuron axons is well established, but the damage to myelin in the gray matter is a new concept, said coauthor Jeffrey Rothstein.

134 http://www.ncbi.nlm.nih.gov/pubmed/23542689
135 The gray matter is the part of the tissues of the central nervous system composed essentially of the cell bodies and the dendritic tree of neurons as well as certain glial cells. Under the microscope, the gray substance appears darker than the rest of the nerve tissue. The rest of the nerve tissue is called the white substance, and it consists essentially of the whitish-colored, myelin-sheathed bundles of axonal fibers.

3.3. Chronology of the major stages of ALS research.

Selective removal of mutant SOD1, oligodendrocytes significantly delays the onset of the disease and prolongs its survival. It suggests that ALS-related genes increase motor neuron vulnerability and accelerate disease by directly altering oligodendrocyte function.

Several researchers have recounted before 2013 that oligodendrocytes might be important in ALS pathology, some as early as 2005 like Jean-Pierre Julien group without much information to support this hunch. This article confirms those early proposals.

This article is also important because oligodendrocytes as well as astrocytes (or Schwann cells in SNPs) have been proposed as vectors of the spread of the disease, because of the interconnection that they realize between the neurons.

2013 : Is Antisense Oligonucleotide Therapy Safe ?[136]

Antisense therapies have been slow to appear. The Phase I clinical trial on the SOD1Rx results announced in 2013 represents an achievement for antisense RNA therapy as well as for the mode of administration. Scientists had to infuse antisense oligonucleotides into the cerebrospinal fluid of patients because the compounds did not cross the blood-brain barrier.

Twenty-one participants, all with the SOD1 mutation, well tolerated intrathecal SOD1Rx infusions. The main adverse effects were pain and headache, probably due to lumbar puncture rather than the drug itself. In addition, the concentration of oligonucleotides in the cerebrospinal fluid of the participants increased after treatment, and was then rapidly eliminated, according to predictions based on monkey studies.

Part of the success of Ionis Pharmaceuticals, the company that did this test, came from the chemical modification of oligonucleotides to make them last longer in the body and bind more closely to target RNAs. SOD1Rx, like Kynamro, incorporates 2'-O-methoxyethyl sugars. This modification is typical of the second generation of Isis oligonucleotide chemistry, but the company has developed other options.

This therapy, now known as Tofersen (formerly known as IONIS-SOD1Rx and BIIB067), has successfully completed Phase I and II in many centers around the world. The therapy was developed as part of a collaboration between Ionis Pharmaceuticals and Biogen, but is now only developed by Biogen.

If the last phase III clinical trial, due to be completed in May 2020, is positive, this would be an important step in the fight against ALS.

---

136 http://www.ncbi.nlm.nih.gov/pubmed/23541756

3.3. Chronology of the major stages of ALS research.

2014 : Sequential Pathology Diagram of TDP-43 in the FTD and Alzheimer[137].

TDP-43 and FTD

Johannes Brettschneider, Kelly Del Tredici, and David Irwin examined 39 cases of Frontal Behavioral Dementia (FTD) to define a pattern of sequential pathology. In the least complicated cases, inclusions of TDP-43 occur in the basal forebrain. In the next step, proteinopathy progresses to the prefrontal region. In the third pattern defined by the group, the pathology of TDP-43 also occurred in the brain stem, motor cortex and gray matter of the spinal cord. In the most severe cases, it also affected the occipital areas.

Overall, the pathology of FTLD progresses from the front of the brain to the back. This contrasts with the staging system of ALS, which starts in the motor cortex at the apex (the top) of the brain and moves downward and forward. « The propagation mechanisms could be very similar, but the initial focus of the pathology seems to be different between ALS and FTLD," Brettschneider said.

TDP-43 and Alzheimer

In 2014, Keith Josephs, Dickson and their colleagues identified the pathology of the TDP-43 protein in 195 cases in 342 autopsies of Alzheimer patients. This large proportion suggests that TDP-43 inclusions occur in more than half of Alzheimer's patients. However, in 2019, only one-third of Alzheimer's cases are thought to have a TDP-43 pathology.

Scientists have established that there is a five-step progression of the inclusion pathology of TDP-43 in granules. The progression can be divided into five distinct topographic stages, supported by correlations with clinical features and

---

137 http://www.ncbi.nlm.nih.gov/pubmed/24240737
http://www.ncbi.nlm.nih.gov/pubmed/24407427

neuroimaging, beginning with amygdala[138], then in the entorhinal cortex[139] and subiculum[140], followed by the dentate gyrus and occipitotemporal cortex. then by the lower temporal cortex. In the final stage, the middle frontal cortex and basal ganglia are also affected. Pathology moves from amygdala to control areas from memory to the cortex. This path differs from the routes taken by the Aβ and tau proteins. In particular, amyloid does not occur in the amygdala.

This staging system seems to support the "dying forward" hypothesis. It may be more correlated with the bulbar form of ALS, which is characterized by a rapid progression, and also with FTD. In particular C9ORF72 carriers have a higher incidence of bulbar onset disease[141], as well as FTD and sometimes Parkinson.

---

138 A formation of almond-shaped gray matter in the anterior position of the temporal lobe.

139 In the medial temporal lobe, two important cortical regions can be found below the hippocampus. These are the cortex and the parahippocampal cortex.

140 The subiculum is the lower part of the hippocampal formation.

141 https://www.ncbi.nlm.nih.gov/pmc/articles/PMC3925297/

3.3. Chronology of the major stages of ALS research.

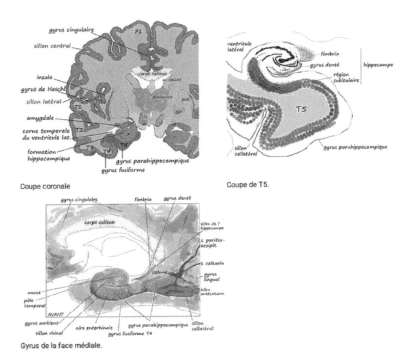

Coupe coronale

Coupe de T5.

Gyrus de la face médiale.

Source Wikipedia

3.3. Chronology of the major stages of ALS research.

2014 : A cytoplasmic role for TDP-43[142].

In ALS, hyperphosphorated and poorly conformed fragments of TDP-43 are aggregated into cytoplasmic granules. Researchers have often wondered if it was by accident, or if it corresponded to a real strategy of the cell, as it is the case for stress granules.

Nael Alami, Rebecca Smith, and colleagues undertook to investigate this issue by comparing the behavior of wild-type and mutant versions of the human protein in fly, mouse, and patient cells.

In fly motor neurons and mouse primary cortical neurons, the researchers fluorescently labeled the over-expressed human TDP-43 protein or one of two mutant forms : M337V and A315T.

Most of the naturally occurring TDP-43 proteins remained in the nucleus, although a steady stream of cytoplasmic granules containing the protein extended to the tip of the axon.

In contrast, mutant forms of the protein have accumulated in and around the cell body. Very little protein, moved far along the axon. Live imaging revealed that the granules containing the mutant TDP-43 protein moved less rapidly on the axon than the wild-type form did. The forward movement was particularly slow, and a high percentage of the pellets actually declined. Interestingly, mitochondria moved equally in the axon in all mice, suggesting that mutants of TDP-43 do not interfere with axonal transport in general, but only with granules.

Compared to the wild-type, the granules containing the mutant TDP-43 protein linked to ALS have indeed been transported less efficiently ; their movements were interrupted more often, with breaks, which made the movements more retrograde. This alteration of the anterograde movement of the mutant TDP-43

---

142 http://www.ncbi.nlm.nih.gov/pubmed/24507191

granules explains their reduced ability to reach the distal axons and the neuromuscular junction.

RNA binding proteins are critical to the maintenance of the transcriptome via controlled regulation of RNA processing and transport. Alterations of these proteins impact multiple steps of the RNA life cycle resulting in various molecular phenotypes such as aberrant RNA splicing, transport, and stability. Disruption of RNA binding proteins and widespread RNA processing defects are increasingly recognized as critical determinants of neurological diseases.

This article presents one the mechanisms that are now recognized to converge toward altered neuronal function highlighting the susceptibility of neurons to deleterious changes in RNA expression and the central role of RNA binding proteins in preserving neuronal integrity.

2014 : Embrouillamini about astrocytes [143].

This article is a UFO in the world of ALS research. Although highly cited, he rejects a number of works that seemed well established, yet it not itself very fruitful. It highlights the inconsistency of the results not only between researchers, but also often with themselves.

In 2014, we knew for a long time that the origin of ALS was not in motor neurons, but in other cells. But 8 years after the discovery of TDP-43 and 3 years after the discovery of C9orf72, most knowledge about the mechanisms of motor neuron degeneration in ALS still came from studies on SOD1-type mouse models. A clear conclusion from these studies was that non-neuronal cells play a critical role in the neurodegeneration related to SOD1 mutations. Indeed, the presence of healthy glial cells significantly delayed the onset of motor neuron degeneration, increasing the life without disease by 50 %.

Since the work of Jean-Pierre Julien's group in 2005, it has been suggested several times that interneurons, myelinating Schwann cells of the peripheral nervous system and endothelial cells of the vascular system could be at the origin of ALS.

But other studies have suggested instead that astrocytes could cause spontaneous degeneration of motor neurons. For example, in 2003, researchers led by Don Cleveland of the University of California at San Diego involved astrocytes in motor neuron death, showing that administering SOD1 to these non-neuronal cells still resulted in motor neuron disease.

In order to determine whether astrocytes from ALS patients can kill motoneurons independently without being exposed to SOD1, the Przedborski group decides to study the mix of different types of cells after they have been exposed to ALS, without prejudging of what causes ALS. For that they decide to

---

143 http://www.ncbi.nlm.nih.gov/pubmed/24508385

design "their" in-vitro model of ALS. This well-cited article (100 times), however, contradicts many other studies.

Diane Re and Virginia Le Verche isolate astrocytes derived from post mortem motor cortex and spinal cord tissue from six ALS patients and 15 controls. They realize after a month of culture, that astrocytes have dominated other cultures. The researchers then mixed these astrocytes with motor neurons derived from human embryonic stem cells. While neurons thrived when co-occurring with non-ALS control astrocytes, their numbers began to fall after only four days of culture with ALS. All this clearly shows that astrocytes in patients with ALS specifically kill motor neurons, unlike control astrocytes.

However, other types of neurons than the motor neurons were resistant to the deleterious signals delivered by the astrocyte ALS, and the fibroblasts of ALS patients also did not destroy the motoneurons, indicating that the **toxic relationship was specific to astrocyte and motor neurons**.

To determine the role of SOD1 the researchers inhibited the expression of this protein in astrocytes using four small hairpin RNAs. Their results indicate that **neither SOD1 nor TDP-43 contribute to sALS astrocyte toxicity !**

These results contradict a study conducted by a team of Brian Kaspar, who showed that astrocytes derived from neural progenitor cells taken from patients with ALS needed SOD1 to destroy motor neurons, even though patients with ALS had no mutation of this gene (Haidet-Phillips and colleagues, 2011). But in 2014, in the same issue as the publication of the Przedborski group, the Haidet-Phillips group publishes an article[144] that is very similar to that of the Przedborski group, except that it incriminates NF-κB and therefore a mechanism of apoptosis rather than necroptosis, but in any case SOD1 is no longer supposed to be the primary cause of ALS.

---

144 https://www.ncbi.nlm.nih.gov/pmc/articles/PMC3978641/

3.3. Chronology of the major stages of ALS research.

For this team, the inactivation of SOD1 in human astrocytes of patients with ALS does not preserve the motoneurons. How ALS astrocytes become toxic remains completely obscure. No known ALS-related mutations were identified in their samples and yet the toxic phenotype persisted even after several passages of adult astrocytes in culture. The authors suggest that necroptosis is the dominant mode of cell death in their in-vitro model of ALS.

In 2019 it is difficult to say who is right between all these contradictory studies.

Apoptosis and necroptosis are major mechanisms of cell death that usually result in opposite immune responses. Apoptotic death usually leads to immunologically silent responses, while death by necroptosis releases molecules that promote inflammation, a process called necrosis.

In 2015 Brian Kaspar published a review criticizing the mix of different cells in the same container, such as that of the Przedborski group, while recognizing that the impact of glial cells on neurological diseases had become evident. An article in 2016[145] seems to support the thesis of this article. Another article of 2016[146], with as co-author Don Cleveland notes the controversy but does not take part. An article in 2017, also with co-author Don Cleveland, seems to support the thesis of this article. Although little cited (19 times) this article seems to have tried to solve the controversy with new methods and

---

145 https://www.ncbi.nlm.nih.gov/pubmed/27795420

146 « *A crucial unsettled controversy remains as to whether toxicity from sporadic ALS-derived astrocytes is or is not mediated by changes in SOD1.* » https://www.ncbi.nlm.nih.gov/pmc/articles/PMC5585017/

materials[147]. An article[148] about Alzheimer's finds a correlation between Braak's staging and the markers of necroptosis.

An article from 2018[149], by one of the authors, implicitly criticizes the methodology used in its own article of 2014 !

In a 2019 article from the same Przedborski laboratory, little progress seems to have been made to identify the cause of motor neuron death, although necroptosis, whatever it really means, is always asserted to be probably the cause of death. the death of motor neurons.

---

147 « *Here we have undertaken large-scale, unbiased analyses for accumulation of misfolded SOD1 in tissue samples from over 50 high quality human ALS autopsies using immunofluorescence/immunohistochemistry and immunoprecipitation with seven different monoclonal and polyclonal antibodies raised by independent investigators against differing epitopes exposed only in misfolded human SOD1.* »

148 http://www.ncbi.nlm.nih.gov/pubmed/28758999

149 https://www.ncbi.nlm.nih.gov/pubmed/29559895

2014 : More information on C9orf72 repetitions[150].

Jiou Wang and his colleagues report that year, that during the transcript, the stranded sense of the six-letter rehearsal twists on itself, leaving the opposite strand free. The antisense strand then binds to nascent C9orf72 mRNA and the RNA-DNA hybrid disrupts normal transcription.

They propose a molecular cascade ranging from abnormalities of the structures of DNA to the pathology of the patient.

When strands of a DNA helix, separate during processes such as transcription, the RNA can bind, but generally only transiently. The researchers thought that a more stable bind could derail the transcription of C9orf72. Indeed, when they added an enzyme digesting RNA-DNA hybrids to the in-vitro expression system, the number of complete transcripts increased while those that were incomplete were reduced to nil.

What proteins could RNA bind to ? A rolling RNA test isolated 288 candidates. One of these was nucleolin, a protein that helps synthesize and assemble ribosomes within the nucleolus, a small nucleus sphere dedicated to this purpose. In cells of patients with repeated C9orf72 expansion, nucleolin spreads throughout the nucleus. These cells, derived from a patient, also succumbed more easily to stress.

That year, several documents indicated a new direction for understanding this vast array of neurological diseases. A common feature may be the formation of these RNA-DNA duplexes which then activate the cellular signaling pathways that ultimately control the expression of genes associated with nucleotide repetition.

---

150 http://www.ncbi.nlm.nih.gov/pubmed/24598541
http://www.ncbi.nlm.nih.gov/pubmed/24598546

2014 : Potential role of TDP-43 in the modulation of endoplasmic-mitochondrial reticulum association and intracellular calcium signaling[151].

Mitochondria and endoplasmic reticulum (ER) are essential organelles in eukaryotic cells, which play a key role in various biological pathways. Mitochondria are responsible for the production of ATP, the maintenance of Ca2+ homeostasis and the regulation of apoptosis, while the endoplasmic reticulum is involved in protein folding, lipid metabolism, and homeostasis of Ca2+. These organelles have their own functions, but they also communicate through the endoplasmic reticulum membrane. The endoplasmic reticulum membrane is associated with mitochondria (MAM) to provide another level of regulation in energy production, lipid processes, Ca2+ buffer and apoptosis. As a result, MAM defects impair cell survival and death.

Several recent studies have linked the toxicity of the TDP-43 protein with damage to the mitochondrial stress signaling pathways[152], [153], [154], [155] and the endoplasmic reticulum[156], [157], [158].

These different results suggest that the endoplasmic-mitochondrial reticulum axis could be disrupted by the TDP-43 protein.

Mitochondria and the endoplasmic reticulum form close structural associations that facilitate a number of cellular functions. However, the mechanisms by which regions of the

151 http://www.ncbi.nlm.nih.gov/pubmed/24893131
152 https://www.ncbi.nlm.nih.gov/pubmed/20702714/
153 https://www.ncbi.nlm.nih.gov/pubmed/20736350/
154 https://www.ncbi.nlm.nih.gov/pubmed/23827948/
155 https://www.ncbi.nlm.nih.gov/pubmed/21471218/
156 https://www.ncbi.nlm.nih.gov/pubmed/24312274/
157 https://www.ncbi.nlm.nih.gov/pubmed/22970712/
158 https://www.ncbi.nlm.nih.gov/pubmed/22057717/

3.3. Chronology of the major stages of ALS research.

endoplasmic reticulum were attached to mitochondria were not well known at the time. The disruption of associations between the endoplasmic reticulum and mitochondria is related to several neurodegenerative diseases.

Radu Stoica and Kurt De Vos, show that the resident endoplasmic reticulum resident protein VAPB interacts with the protein 51 interacting with the mitochondrial protein tyrosine phosphatase (PTPIP51) to regulate endoplasmic reticulum-mitochondrial associations.

Further Radu Stoica and Kurt De Vos demonstrate that TDP-43 disrupts the interactions between the endoplasmic reticulum and the mitochondria and that this is associated with a disruption of the VAPB/PTPIP51 interaction and Ca2+ cellular homeostasis.

Finally, Radu Stoica and Kurt De Vos report that the overexpression of TDP-43 led to the activation of glycogen synthase kinase-3β (GSK-3β) and that GSK-3β regulated the VAPB-PTPIP51 interaction.

The thesis of this article is probably consensual in 2019. 2014 was a pivotal year for research, where the gain or loss of function via a mutation, seem to have less supporters than previously.

2014 : A yeast chaperone protein dissolves protein aggregates[159].

Protein misfolding is now implicated in many fatal neurodegenerative diseases, including amyotrophic lateral sclerosis (ALS) and Parkinson's disease (PD). No therapy has so far reversed these protein folding events.

Jackrel and Shorter wanted to use Hsp104, a yeast protein, to target misfolded conformers for reactivation. Hsp104 solubilizes the disordered aggregates and amyloid of yeast cells, but has limited activity against the proteins of human neurodegenerative diseases.

Jackrel and Shorter previously developed variants of Hsp104 that suppress aggregation, proteotoxicity, and re-establish appropriate localization of ALS and PD proteins in yeast cells, and attenuate neurodegeneration in an animal model of Parkinson's disease..

In this paper, Jackrel and Shorter have established that potentiated Hsp104 variants have high substrate specificity and, in yeast, suppress the toxicity and aggregation induced by TDP-43, FUS and α-synuclein. wild-type, as well as mutant missense versions of these proteins that cause neurodegenerative disorders. The potentiated Hsp104 variants also rescue the toxicity and aggregation of TAF15 but not EWSR1, two prion-like RNA binding proteins that are linked to the development of ALS and frontotemporal dementia.

A small molecule, Arimoclomol, is a potent activator of HSF1 that also amplifies the expressions Hsp70 and Hsp90. Arimoclomol showed an HSF1-induced reduction in overall concentrations of TDP-43. Arimoclomol has also shown promising results in phase II trials on ALS and is currently (2019) in phase III.

---

159 http://www.ncbi.nlm.nih.gov/pubmed/25062688

2015 : Where does ALS begin ? Importance of the cortical component of motor neuron circuits[160].

Pyramidal neurons in the motor cortex V-layer (LVPN) regulate voluntary muscle control and selectively degenerate (with lower motor neurons) in amyotrophic lateral sclerosis.

Using innovative methods and microscopes, on brain slices, the authors characterized the earliest morphological and electrophysiological perturbations, pyramidal neurons of the V-layer of the motor cortex, in SOD1 (G93A) mice. Apical dendritic regression occurred from postnatal day P28, dendritic spine loss from P21, and an increase in EPSC frequency from P21 in LVPNs.

These results suggest that the death of corticospinal neurons in the SOD1 G93A model of ALS is preceded by presymptomatic cellular alterations that may cause extensive disturbances of the neural network of the motor cortex.

The authors note, however, that the presence of direct corticospinal inputs in motor neurons differs markedly from one species to another. Indeed primates (including humans) have varying direct control levels, ranging from strong muscles for the hands, to weak muscles for the proximal limbs. In contrast, direct functional corticospinal inputs in the motor neurons of the lower limbs are lacking in mice, although there is some morphological evidence of direct corticospinal contacts on mouse lumbar motor neurons.

Despite these species differences, the authors believe that they demonstrated that morphological and functional changes in LVPNs mouse models occur before or are synchronous with the loss of motor neurons. This suggests that direct

---

160 http://www.ncbi.nlm.nih.gov/pubmed/25589758

3.3. Chronology of the major stages of ALS research.

corticospinal connections may be less important in pathogenesis. of ALS than previously thought.

This article returns to the debate on the first anatomical site that ALS strikes. This remains a subject of intense debate even today. Although Charcot proposed for the first time the primacy of higher motor neurons in the pathogenesis of ALS, and this has been theorized in the hypothesis of central degeneration, other hypotheses have instead negated the primacy of cortical dysfunction.

This article takes an extreme position, that degeneration begins in the cortex, and during neurogenesis.

2015 : Neurons can give rise to extra axons when TDP-43 is eliminated[161].

As the pathological aggregates of TDP-43 are located in the cytoplasm, Virginia Lee's team decided to study more precisely the consequences of this abnormal location. The team used genetic engineering technologies to implant a human gene into a mouse (this is called by the ugly name of a humanized mouse). This human gene has itself been modified by suppressing the nuclear localization sequence of the human gene protein.

This gene will therefore produce TDP-43 protein in the cytoplasm of mouse cells. Adam Walker used a neurofilament heavy chain promoter, active in all neurons, to drive transgene expression. An element of response to tetracycline ensured that the gene would remain inactive and that the mice would develop normally as long as their diet contained the doxycycline inhibitor.

When the mice reached the age of about five weeks, the researchers changed their diet by removing the doxycycline[162] and observed the course of the disease. The mice then developed TDP-43 inclusions in the spinal cord and brain. In addition, the animals' brains narrowed and their motor neurons retracted from the muscles and died. The animals also presented progressive neuronal motor disease. They developed leg tremors and lost the ability to grasp a wire or balance on a rotating rod. They lost weight and died about 10 weeks after stopping a doxycycline-based diet. Lee believes that the disease results from a decrease in the expression of

---

161 http://www.ncbi.nlm.nih.gov/pubmed/26197969
http://www.ncbi.nlm.nih.gov/pubmed/26437864

162 Tetracycline-Controlled Transcriptional Activation is a method of inducible gene expression where transcription is reversibly turned on or off in the presence of the antibiotic tetracycline or one of its derivatives (e.g. doxycycline).

3.3. Chronology of the major stages of ALS research.

the TDP-43 protein, that disappeared one week after the activation of the transgene.

When Walker and his colleagues reintroduced doxycycline into the diet of other transgenic mice which had been without doxycycline for six weeks (the equivalent of several human years), it rendered the gene inactive (the gene was designed this way). A week later, the animals began to be more dexterous, they gained weight and lived a normal life.

Aggregates of TDP-43 began to disappear within two weeks with the inactivating gene and they completely disappeared after three months. The cortical and motor neurons stopped degenerating. Even more, the remaining neurons seemed to take over from those who had died.

Six weeks later, the diet including doxycycline doubled the percentage of neuromuscular junctions innervated by motor neurons. The researchers assumed that the motor neurons still present were able to take over from those who had weakened while the transgene TDP-43 was over-expressed.

Although it is a transgenic mouse and the article does not refer to any treatment, it is very encouraging to know that motor neurons can recover from the toxicity of TDP-43 protein for patients with ALS, since TDP-43 type pathologies represent more than 90 % of ALS forms.

2015 : First overview of gene therapy for SMA[163].

SMA, an autosomal recessive disorder, results from missense mutations or deletion of the SMN1 gene for one of its subtypes. Other genes are involved in other subtypes of SMA. The SMN1 gene encodes for the protein named *"survival of the motor neuron"*. SMN1 processes mRNAs and, for unknown reasons, motor neurons are particularly vulnerable when they contain two bad copies of the SMN1 gene.

Kaspar and his colleagues used the harmless AAV9 adeno-associated virus to transmit a functional SMN1 gene to motor neurons. Different types of AAV, with different capsid[164] structures, target different types of cells and AAV9 is able to cross the blood-brain barrier.

Once it has found its target cells, the virus slides its genetic material into the nucleus, where it remains as an extra-chromosomal DNA fragment. This DNA persists, so a treatment should theoretically provide the SMN protein for a lifetime.

Brian Kaspar sold the exploitation rights to AveXis Inc., a gene therapy company that is now owned by Novartis. As usual, the drug has been renamed several times and is now called Zolgensma.

Zolgensma is the subject of controversy, first its price makes it one of the most expensive drugs in the world ($ 2,125 million), while this therapy can be produced by any good laboratory for internal use, for a few thousand dollars. Another controversy is that it appears that AveXis employees falsified data to facilitate the marketing authorization process. Brian Kaspar, was AveXis chief scientific officer, and his brother Allan Kaspar

---

163 http://www.ncbi.nlm.nih.gov/pubmed/20190738
http://www.ncbi.nlm.nih.gov/pubmed/20212484
164 A capsid is the protein shell of a virus.

was senior vice president of R&D. They leaved AveXis in early May 2019[165].

165 https://www.fiercepharma.com/pharma/novartis-avexis-shifted-top-scientific-leadership-before-zolgensma-data-scandal-erupted

2016 : Does the scavenger of free radicals Edaravone slows ALS progression?[166]

Also known as MCI-186, Edaravone is a drug originally developed by Mitsubishi Pharma Corporation. It was approved in Japan for stroke treatment in 2002, followed by China and India, where generic versions of the drug are also available. Doctors prescribe it to eliminate free radicals and protect neurons after a cerebral infarction. This small organic compound neutralizes peroxidic lipid radicals and peroxynitrite, thus preventing damage to the blood vessels and neurons of the brain (Yoshida and colleagues 2006, Fujisawa and colleagues, 2015).

Abe and his colleagues wondered whether this would also protect motor neurons from ALS. In rodent models, it slows down progression and preserves motor neuron populations (Ikeda and Iwasaki 2015, Ito and colleagues 2008, Aoki and colleagues 2011).

It was approved for ALS in the US in 2017 based on a small randomized controlled trial of people with early-stage ALS in Japan who had been given the drug for six months. It had failed two previous trials in patients at different stages of ALS.

---

166 http://www.ncbi.nlm.nih.gov/pubmed/25286015

2016 : Stem cells in support and controversy (Nurown)[167].

In 2016 a clinical trial of phase I/II has just been performed on Nurown. BrainStorm Cell Therapeutics' researchers believe that stem cell therapy has slowed the progression of the disease. However, they can not prove to the authorities that the treatment has worked, because it is a trial of few patients, open and uncontrolled.

An open trial is a type of clinical trial in which no information is concealed from trial participants. This contrasts with a blind experience where information is concealed to reduce bias. Open trials may be appropriate for comparing two very similar treatments to determine which one is most effective. Open trials may also be uncontrolled, ie without a placebo group.

BrainStorm extracted mesenchymal stem cells (MSCs) from each participant in the clinical trial, and treated them with three growth factors : a basic fibroblast growth factor, a growth factor platelet derivative and a β1 heregulin. These three factors allowed to change the phenotype of MSC to a phenotype resembling that of neural stem cells. The cells were then reinjected. Brainstorm calls this new type of cell, MSC-NTF.

In this phase I/II clinical trial, designed to test the safety of MSC-NTFs in 24 people with ALS, half of the participants received an intramuscular injection, with 1 million cells injected into 24 sites in the biceps and the right triceps. The other half of the participants received intrathecal infusions directly into the spinal cord, with a dose of one million stem cells per kilogram of body weight.

---

167 https://www.alzforum.org/news/research-news/supportive-stem-cells-safe-als

3.3. Chronology of the major stages of ALS research.

As preliminary results showed that the drug was relatively well tolerated, the investigators then converted their trial into a phase IIa, escalating dose study.

The last four patients received a dose of 2 million cells per kilogram intrathecally, plus two injections of 1 million cells intramuscularly. Treatment with this larger dose did not endanger patients either.

There was no control group and anyway, the study was too small to prove any effectiveness.

A scientist who has also studied this type of gene therapy, Clive Svendsen, questioned this analysis of individual efficacy. « ALS is not a linear disease," he said, so that one person can have more or less rapid progression. Although his reasoning is not very clear, he also suggests that BrainStorm deliberately embellished the effectiveness of the treatment to attract investors.

2016 : Copper to the rescue in ALS[168].

CCS is a metalloprotein responsible for the contribution of copper to the protein SOD1 so that it can exert its protective action.

The expression of SOD1 is not modified by the availability of copper but by the ability of the CCS gene to deliver copper. It has been demonstrated that mice with mutations in the CCS gene show symptoms similar to ALS.

It has been known for several decades that Cu(II)ATSM belongs to a class of molecules with anti-inflammatory and antioxidant effects.

Scientists in the Beckman group were studying transgenic mice with a double mutation, SOD1 and CCS. They decided to try the compound Cu(II)ATSM in a transgenic mouse, unable to stand up and close to the end of its short lifespan.

The researchers dissolved Cu(II)ATSM in dimethylsulfoxide and spread it on the neck of the little animal, where it was quickly absorbed through the skin. A few hours later, the mouse had become able to move. Incidentally **two important things** could be inferred from that fact. First, the disease, at least in those mice, is mainly in the axon of lower motor neurons. Second, it was possible for the mice to recuperate motricity, so the lower motor neurons were not dead.

As a result of various experiments on these transgenic mice with a double mutation (SOD1 and CCS), the researchers show that with continuous treatment, the mice can live 18 months, that is to say almost half of the average life of non-transgenic laboratory mice, instead of dying after three months.

« The biggest surprise is that these mice are almost cured. I have never seen that, « commented Fernando Vieira of the ALS

---

168 http://www.ncbi.nlm.nih.gov/pubmed/26826269

3.3. Chronology of the major stages of ALS research.

Therapy Development Institute (ALS TDI). Moreover the press has been dithyrambic about Cu(II)ATSM.

Obviously it is easy to imagine that this could be a very good drug for ALS patients with SOD1 and CCS mutated, but treatments that work on mice rarely work on humans.

The article itself does not adopt the neutral form that is usual in the scientific literature, for example it refers to the million Dollars offered as part of Prize4Life, as if it suggested that it deserves it. He also says that in twenty years, no pharmaceutical agent has extended the life of more than a few weeks while Riluzole prolongs the life of several months.

It is also unclear how this research is new except marginally. When reading it, we do not learn anything about the mechanisms by which Cu(II)ATSM has a beneficial effect on ALS. Articles from 2011 and 2013 already showed the benefits of Cu(II)ATSM for ALS[169] [170] and articles from 1994 indicated its interest in ischemia. In fact Cu(II)ATSM belongs to a class of molecules that have been identified very early[171] as being useful in SOD1-related diseases.

In addition, mutations of SOD1 are only present in a fraction of people with the disease. « *I'm not sure that this will have an impact on sporadic diseases* » said Lucie Bruijn of the ALS Association. The same is true of Jeffrey Rothstein, another prominent ALS scientist.

Bruijn noted that Cu(II)ATSM-based therapy worked best in mice overexpressing both mSOD1 and CCS, and weakly in animals overexpressing only mSOD1. Beckman and colleagues argued that transgenic mice were more reflective of the SOD1/CCS ratio in humans than mice only overexpressing mutated SOD1.

---

169 https://www.ncbi.nlm.nih.gov/pmc/articles/PMC3243559/
170 https://www.ncbi.nlm.nih.gov/pubmed/23952668/
171 https://www.ncbi.nlm.nih.gov/pubmed/10399024

3.3. Chronology of the major stages of ALS research.

Beckman said that if Cu(II)ATSM proved to be safe and effective, he considered that it could become a prophylactic drug that a person with a SOD1 mutation could take for decades.

This treatment, targeting up to 2 % of ALS patients (those with both SOD1 and CCS mutations), generated a great deal of interest in the ALS community, even though most ALS patients could not benefit from ALS. Unscrupulous people promote the complex in order to sell it (or a counterfeit compound) illegally to desperate people.

2016 : Astrocytes attack motor neurons in two stages[172]

The major histocompatibility complex (MHC) is a set of genes that encode cell surface proteins. The main function of MHC molecules is to bind to pathogen-derived antigens and display them on the surface of cells so that the appropriate T-cells can recognize them and destroy them.

By interacting with CD8 molecules on the surface of cytotoxic T cells, MHC class I is involved in the destruction of infected or malignant host cells. It is called "cell-mediated-immunity".

By interacting with CD4 molecules on the surfaces of helper T cells, class II MHC induces the establishment of specific immunity (also known as acquired immunity or adaptive immunity).

ALS is thought to be a disease characterized by prolonged astrogliosis, with microglial activation and infiltration of immune cells derived from blood in the spinal cord, which may have an essential function during the course of the disease course.

An intriguing hypothesis suggests that the evolution of the adaptive immune system may have coincided with the development of the neural crest and the tissues derived from it. In these terms, the adaptive immune system can be an evolutionary emanation of the vertebrate nervous system.

Under normal conditions, MHC I is little or not expressed in mature neuronal cells, but its expression increases considerably after viral or parasitic infection, exposure to cytokines. In addition, MHC I is activated in progressive degeneration.

Spinal motoneurons from transgenic mice bearing the SOD1 G93A mutated gene markedly activate the expression of

172 http://www.ncbi.nlm.nih.gov/pubmed/26928464

several MHC I-associated molecules at the onset and during progression of the disease. The mechanism triggering this response and its local consequences are not yet clearly defined. It remains to be seen whether MHC I expression by motor neurons is closely related to direct communication with invading immune cells (CD8+ T cells) or whether other mechanisms may affect the viability of motoneurons independently of the immune system.

Brian Kaspar and his colleagues wondered how MHC class I could affect motor neurons and astrocytes.

First, they compared MHC class I levels in the spinal cord of people who died of ALS with those of healthy people. They also examined the spinal cord of mice expressing the SOD1 gene of mutant human ALS. They were struck by the lack of MHC class I in motor neurons from deceased ALS patients or in mouse model SOD1 mutated motor neurons.

SungWon Song and Carlos Miranda then report that astrocytes first weaken neurons by telling them to stop making MHC Class I proteins, and then they destroy them.

The researchers wondered whether motor neurons banished only MHC class I or whether astrocytes were involved. They derived motoneurons from wild-type mouse stem cells and mSOD1-expressing mice. Both produced similar amounts of MHC class I. When the researchers added mSOD1-expressing mouse astrocytes, the expression of MHC class I neurons fell. The same thing happened when astrocyte conditioned nutrients were added to motor neuron cultures without astrocytes. The results suggested that astrocytes secrete a signal for neurons to remove their MHC class I.

The researchers hypothesized that MHC class I loss made neurons vulnerable to astrocyte attacks. To test this, they over-expressed MHC class I molecules in mouse motoneurons before adding mSOD1 astrocytes. It was surprisingly protective. They had the same experience with motor neurons

3.3. Chronology of the major stages of ALS research.

derived from stem cells from six different people with ALS. In all cases, the additional MHC class I protected neurons from the toxic effects of human astrocytes from ALS.

Astrocytes must have a MHC class I sensor to determine whether or not to attack motor neurons. According to co-author Christopher Walker, a possible candidate would be what is known as killer inhibitory receptors. Normally expressed on natural killer cells (NK), these proteins allow the immune system to determine whether a target cell is a friend or an enemy. If the NK cells find the MHC Class I to bind, they leave the cells alone. If they do not find one, they attack.

Astrocytes do not normally express these receptors, but Kaspar and his colleagues claim to have found them in astrocytes located in the spinal cord of mSOD1 mice and on the surface of mSOD1 astrocytes used in their co-cultures.

2016 : A promising antisense therapy for C9orf72[173].

Expansions[174] of C9orf72 hexanucleotides are the most common genetic cause of amyotrophic lateral sclerosis and familial frontotemporal dementia.

In 2016, Jie Jiang, Qiang Zhu and Tania Gendron generated three types of genetically modified mice in order to evaluate the impact of the number of repetitions. In one of the three mouse types RNAs had up to 450 GGGGCC repeats and in the other two types of mice, either a single allele where C9orf72 was inactivated or C9orf72 was inactivated in both alleles.

In mice with a 50 % reduction in C9orf72 (a single inactivated allele), there was no ALS-related disease, whereas the total absence of C9orf72 produced splenomegaly, enlarged lymph nodes, and mild deficits in social interactions. What is normal, the genes all have utility, to suppress their expression makes lose a biological function.

In mice with overexpression of C9orf72, hexanucleotide extensions resulted in accumulation of RNA and dipeptide-repeating proteins that were dependent on age, repetition length, and expression level. All this was accompanied by loss of hippocampal neurons, anxiety, and impaired cognitive function.

Single-dose antisense oligonucleotide (ASO) injection targets RNAs containing repeats but preserves C9orf72-encoding mRNA levels. Those ASO injection resulted in long-lasting reduction of dipeptide repeat RNA and protein granules, as well as an improvement in behavioral deficits.

These efforts establish the feasibility of ASO-mediated treatment. Such therapy, BIIB078 by Biogen, is in a phase III clinical trial in 2019.

---

173 http://www.ncbi.nlm.nih.gov/pubmed/27112497
174 Cet expression a le même sens que « répétition de nucléotides »

3.3. Chronology of the major stages of ALS research.

2016 : Propagation of TDP-43 [175].

How does ALS begin in a person ? We have discussed this topic several times, in 2019 it is still unsolved. Regularly a study appears which condones, one or the other contradictory hypotheses, of which the principal ones are *"dying forward"*[176] *"dying back"*.

Scientists led by Virginia Lee and Trojanowski have recently proposed four neuropathological stages of TDP-43 pathology in ALS[177], patients, based on the affected areas in people with increasing pathological burden. This staging is clearly under the *"dying forward"* umbrella. There are two other staging schemes for TDP-43 pathology.

Glenda Halliday thinks that to apply these staging schemes for TDP-43 pathology, the clinical phenotype must be known beforehand, which is undermining the potential predictive value of the pathological examination.

She noted that data from human post-mortem studies support the concept that protein spreads from the periphery to higher motor neurons, or even the cortex, with distinct patterns for different diseases. This concept is clearly under the *"dying back"* umbrella.

Halliday and his colleagues then developed a scheme to differentiate neuropathological FTD from ALS based on deposits in the anterior cingulate cortex and the hypoglossal nucleus[178]. These studies highlight the varied patterns of spread of each disease.

In the FTD, lesions begin in the frontal regions and move up into the brain, whereas in ALS, inclusions first appear in the

175 https://www.alzforum.org/news/conference-coverage/new-data-reinforces-concept-protein-propagation
176 En Anglais : *Forward dying et backward dying.*
177 http://www.ncbi.nlm.nih.gov/pubmed/23686809
178 http://www.ncbi.nlm.nih.gov/pubmed/26231953

motor cortex and then descend to the anterior and posterior regions of the brain. This staging has also been replicated by other groups[179], [180]. The evidence supports the idea that misfolded proteins propagate along axons, she noted.

However this staging concept does not seem to have spread in the scientific or medical community.

---

179 http://www.ncbi.nlm.nih.gov/pubmed/26216351
180 http://www.ncbi.nlm.nih.gov/pubmed/27338935

2016 : Repetition of dipeptides (DPR)[181], [182].

Although a healthy person has between 2 and 23 repeats of the GGGGCC hexanucleotide sequence in his C9orf72 gene, people with ALS or FTD can have hundreds or even thousands of them. These sequences are then translated in the **sense** and **antisense** directions to give five different dipeptide repeats (DPR).

Protein tandem repeats, are well known because of C9orf72 repeats. But actually they are ubiquitous, one third of human proteins have such repeats. A well-known example of proteins with tandem repeats is collagen. But sometimes they happen because of "*slippage* "during DNA replication and they cause human diseases such as fragile X syndrome, several spinocerebellar ataxias, myotonic dystrophy, ALS and Friedreich's ataxia. Those errors may explain why proteins such as TDP-43 and FUS are associated with ALS, as they are involved in RNA processing. Reparation of those errors consume more energy than usual, which might explain why ALS patients have a high metabolism.

Taylor and McKnight both wanted to understand how these dipeptides repeats could harm neurons So both of them did some screening tests to find the proteins with which the peptides interacted.

Nearly 70 % of these DPRs, which included TDP-43, FUS, hnRNPA1, and hnRNPA2B1 proteins related to ALS, contained low complexity domains (LCDs).

The researchers then looked at how the DPRs had affected different membrane-free organelles. A common theme emerged : Since arginine-rich repeats interacted strongly with LCD-containing proteins in each organelle, they essentially "gelled" the organelles.

---

181 https://www.ncbi.nlm.nih.gov/pubmed/27768896
182 https://www.ncbi.nlm.nih.gov/pubmed/27768897

This essentially stopped the movement of proteins in and out of the structure.

This, in turn, deprived the cell of rRNA, which remained trapped in the granule component of the nucleolus. The researchers reported a similar gelling phenomenon in stress granules. They also detected GR/PR[183] peptides in other membraneless nuclear organelles, including nuclear specks. Nuclear specks are enriched in splicing and transcription factors, as well as in Cajal bodies.

Liquid phase separations that form membrane-free organelles are highly regulated and tunable processes. For each factor that promotes assembly, another promotes disassembly. It may be possible to would exploit those antagonistic relationships in future ALS or FTD therapies.

---

183 DPR proteins (glycine-arginine [GR], proline-arginine [PR], glycine-alanine [GA], glycine-proline [GP], and proline-alanine [PA]) are found in both the nucleus and the cytoplasm of C9ORF72 patient tissues, including brain and spinal cord, as well as in patient induced pluripotent stem cell (iPSC)-derived motor neurons. Of the DPR proteins, GR and PR are toxic in human.

2017 : Imported inflammation in the CNS[184].

Researchers led by Stanley Appel reported that blood monocytes accelerated the expression of many inflammatory genes in people with ALS, and this happened dramatically in people whose form of the disease progressed rapidly. We do not know why these genes are expressed and why their activation accelerates neuroinflammation in the central nervous system in one way or another.

Recent evidence suggests that this inflammatory response extends beyond CNS[185]: Appel's Lab has reported T-cell dysfunction regulating inflammation in people with ALS

At least one characteristic of systemic inflammation, C-reactive protein (CRP), has been detected in the blood of patients with ALS. A study by Christian Lunetta, on which Stanley Appel collaborated, reported CRP levels correlated with the severity of functional impairment and, ultimately, survival among nearly 400 patients with ALS. In addition, a post-hoc analysis of a failure of a Phase II immuno-regulatory NP001 assay revealed that treatment slowed the progression of the disease in patients who started with elevated CRP[186].

Do activated monocytes infiltrate the CNS ? The experiments on parabiosis suggest the opposite, and Appel thinks that is unlikely at the beginning of the disease. Instead, it points T cells. They cross the blood-brain barrier and react and activate monocytes and microglia. They can therefore serve as an intermediary between the two compartments.

Johnathan Cooper-Knock, who led a recent study linking the inflammation of both microglia and peripheral cells to the progression of ALS, said that Appel's findings were timely.

---

184 http://www.ncbi.nlm.nih.gov/pubmed/28437540
185 SNC : Système Nerveux Central
186 http://www.ncbi.nlm.nih.gov/pubmed/28384752

3.3. Chronology of the major stages of ALS research.

Cooper-Knock also found that high IL-8 predicted the rate of decline.

In 2019, Appel designs a therapy for ALS based on Treg cells.

2017 : A gene therapy targeting SOD1 wins the Prize4Life

In the years prior to 2017, continuous infusion of antisense oligonucleotides (ASOs) into brain ventricles has been reported as a promising approach to induce significant inhibition of SOD1 in SOD1 G93A rats.

A Phase I clinical study using intrathecally administered ASOs in patients has revealed the absence of serious adverse events, highlighting the feasibility of this strategy in humans.

These and other AAV studies have provided encouraging therapeutic results and potential for translation into drugs. However, these approaches only led to an incomplete rescue.

The team of Martine Barkats and Maria Grazia Biferi at the Institute of Myology in Paris, had developed in previous years a strategy for SMA, using AAV viral vectors that after an injection, target the central nervous system (CNS) : the brain, spinal cord and, above all, motor neurons. This gene therapy was incorporated in the following years into Zolgensma gene therapy.

Maria Grazia Biferi and her colleagues have therefore sought to transpose this strategy to ALS. An AAV vector was chosen that could reach the CNS in the SOD1 form of ALS. This protein is over-expressed and accumulates in the cell, where it is toxic. Different strategies have been tested to increase survival.

Silencing of transcriptional SOD1 can be achieved by skipping a constitutive SOD1 exon (exon skipping) using ASOs complementary to the primary transcription splicing regulatory elements. The resulting deleted mRNA, containing a premature termination codon, is then degraded by the endogenous cellular surveillance disintegration pathway.

Maria Grazia Biferi and her colleagues reported in 2017 the high therapeutic potential of this exon skipping strategy in

3.3. Chronology of the major stages of ALS research.

newborn and adult SOD1 G93A mutant mice using ASO against mutant human SOD1 inserted into an AAV10 virus load.

Researchers at the Institute of Myology have combined two methods of vector delivery that also target peripheral organs : systemic and intracerebroventricular. They administered this treatment to newborn mice and achieved excellent results with a survival rate close to 100 %. In adult SOD mice, the survival rate was increased by more than 50 %.

This gene therapy approach induced an efficient hSOD1 exon skip into the spinal cord, resulting in a significant reduction in hSOD1 mRNA and protein levels. The survival of SOD1 G93A mice was prolonged, with a mean increase in life expectancy of 92 % and 58 % for mice injected at birth or at age 50 days, respectively. The onset of the disease was also delayed by 95 and 63 days, respectively, compared to untreated mice. Finally, the administration of the AAV10-U7-hSOD1 has prevented weight loss and preserved the motor skills and strength of the skeletal muscles.

A US laboratory (ALS TDI) repeated the experiments with their vectors and obtained the same results, thus validating their protocol.

The laboratory of Martine Barkats and Maria Grazia Biferi received the $1 million, Prize4Life award for a treatment of ALS.

2018 : Motor neurons become hypoexcitable just before degenerating[187].

ALS research has always been tainted with obsolete paradigms and inadequate animal models that are still used because they are very inexpensive and easy to manage. One consequence is that even after tens of thousands of reports, we still know very little about human ALS. Here is an example of research that contradicts one of ALS's major misconceptions. In mid-2019, this article has been cited only 6 times. This is a very low score, even considering the fact that it is very recent, however we find it very interesting.

Glutamate-mediated excitotoxicity has been proposed early as a potential mechanism for motor neuron degeneration in ALS (Rothstein and colleagues, 1990). According to this hypothesis, an elevation of intracellular calcium by a repetitive reaction or by calcium permeable glutamate receptors is harmful and would trigger their death by apoptosis.

Calcium-related apoptosis death is particularly likely in motor neurons because of their limited ability to absorb calcium. In the context of the hypothesis of excitotoxicity, it has been suggested that the intrinsic hyperexcitability of motoneurons could in itself contribute to excitotoxic stress. A chronically hyperexcited motoneuron would trigger more peaks in response to a given synaptic input and, as a result, more calcium ions would flow into the cytoplasm, ultimately resulting in death.

However, a work[188] in 2014 had already invalidated this concept (still widespread in 2019). For the authors of this study that was cited 36 times, motor neurons do not develop hyperexcitability at the disease stages just prior to denervation of neuromuscular junctions. Instead, homeostatic processes

---

187 http://www.ncbi.nlm.nih.gov/pubmed/29580378
188 https://www.ncbi.nlm.nih.gov/pmc/articles/PMC3979619/

maintain excitability in most cells and, in a large subpopulation, homeostasis fails and is replaced by hypoexcitability.

Marin Manuel and colleagues reported that in mouse models of amyotrophic lateral sclerosis, some of these neurons lose their ability to react just before they degenerate. These motor neurons are the ones that innervate the largest and most powerful muscle fibers, which are known to die first in ALS.

Their findings suggest that, rather than becoming hyperexcitable, as many previous studies have suggested, motor neurons in ALS become hypoexcitable just before they disappear.

Drug manufacturers are designing compounds that reduce neuronal activity in patients with ALS, such as Riluzole. This strategy followed the research that, in the early stages of the disease, neurons in the motor cortex are hyperactive, requiring lower electrical currents to trigger action potentials (Vucic and colleagues, 2008).

In contrast, others reported that motor neurons derived from induced pluripotent stem cells from patients with ALS were hyperexcitable at the beginning of the culture, but then became hypoexcitable (Wainger and colleagues, 2014).

For his part, Manuel's group found that just before the onset of symptoms, a subset of motor neurons in the spinal cord appeared to be hypoactive in SOD1 mice with the G93A mutation. These neurons have failed to respond repeatedly in response to sustained stimulus (Delestrée and colleagues, 2014). However, it was unclear whether these hypoactive neurons were on the verge of degeneration.

To remedy this, Maria de Lourdes Martinez-Silva and her colleagues, took advantage of a well-known phenomenon of ALS : large fast-twitch motor units are the first to degenerate. These units include a single motor neuron that controls several fast-twitch fibers that contract quickly and powerfully, but are easily fatigued.

When such a motor neuron begins to degenerate, its axonal endings disconnect from the muscle fibers, resulting in muscle weakness and possibly atrophy. Medium-sized motor units also contract quickly but they do not tire very quickly, then they degenerate. Small motor units, made of slow-twitch fibers that contract slowly and weakly but never tire, succumb last.

The researchers developed a protocol developed to stimulate individual motor neurons in the mouse's spinal cord, record electrical impulses, and also measure the resulting muscle contractions at the ankle of mice. This allowed them to determine simultaneously whether this motor neuron was hypoactive and what type of motor unit it belonged, based on contractile properties such as contraction amplitude, contraction time, and fatigue resistance.

The researchers examined SOD1-G93A mice aged 40 to 60 days, while they still had intact neuromuscular junctions. From electrical recordings of 80 motoneurons in SOD1-G93A mice and 63 motoneurons in wild-type mice, the researchers found that most of these motoneurons created an action potential in response to a single electrical impulse. However, 21 % of motoneurons in SOD1-G93A mice failed to trigger repeatedly in response to incessant control, whereas in wild-types only 6 % were struck in this way.

In SOD1-G93A mice, these hypoactive neurons are connected to about 40 % of rapidly fatigable motor units and none of the slow contraction units. They innervent 20 % of fatigable motor units of average size, but only the largest units of this class.

The results suggest that hypoexcitable motor neurons are connected to the most vulnerable motor units, which degenerate earlier in the disease. The researchers replicated these findings in FUS-P525L knock-in mice, an animal model which develops motor symptoms more slowly than the SOD1 model. At the age of six months, just before the expected onset of symptoms, some of their motor neurons innervating the largest and most vulnerable motor units were hypoexcitable.

The results suggest that just before degeneration, motor neurons lose their ability to react repetitively, while responding normally to an initial electrical impulse. Interestingly, researchers also found that hypoexcitable neurons were slightly less polarized on average.

The debate on hyperexcitability versus hypoexcitability can be partially semantic. Clifford Woolf of the Boston Children's Hospital suggested that this slight depolarization could be interpreted as hyperexcitability. With a membrane potential closer to the threshold required to trigger an action potential, voltage-dependent phenomena, such as calcium influx, could occur more easily and cause neurotoxicity. However, he recognizes that the absence of repetitive reactions suggests hypoexcitability.

In patients with ALS, researchers usually stimulate the soma of the neuron and measure the results as muscle contractions. According to this measure, slightly depolarized motoneurons might appear hyper-excitable because their ability to respond to a pulse repeatedly is not tested.

Gareth Miles raised a similar point. « *Human studies are largely based on peripheral axonal recordings and there are a lot of different things going on in soma*," he said.

Manuel's team responds that as its researchers measured the result of repetitive neural discharges in the soma, these measurements are not distorted by events taking place further downstream.

Previously, Miles reported that during their hypoexcitable phase, iPSC-derived motoneurons had slightly depolarized membrane potential (Devlin and colleagues, 2015). He thinks that Manuel's data is consistent with the idea that a hypoexcitable phase precedes degeneration.

On the one hand, in a physiological context, the lower motoneurons receive the inputs of the upper motoneurons, and not the electrical pulses of a machine. In addition, many other cells in the motor cortex and spinal cord, including inhibitory interneurons and glia, contribute to the final axonal flow that reaches the muscle tissue, he said.

The main conclusion of these experiments is that fast motor neurons become less sensitive to repetitive stimulation, ie they become hypoexcitable, shortly before the symptoms of ALS appear in the mouse, whereas the neuromuscular junctions are still intact. However, slow motor neurons remain unchanged.

These results were replicated in unrelated genetic models of ALS in mice[189] during the development and formation of synapses in upper motor neurons *in vitro*.

---

189 https://www.ncbi.nlm.nih.gov/pmc/articles/PMC6550035/

2018 : The endoplasmic reticulum stress promotes the aggregation of the wild-type SOD1 protein [190].

Can stress on the internal mechanisms of the cell lead to ALS ? Many ALS patients have been saying for a long time that their illness "started" with a serious injury or infection.

Researchers led by Claudio Hetz report in 2018 that in animals expressing the wild-type version of the human SOD1 protein, large aggregates of oxidized SOD1 accumulate with age. The stress of the endoplasmic reticulum accelerates the process and astrogliosis appears thereafter, from this moment the motor neurons begin to die and the first symptoms of ALS appear. All of this adds to the growing evidence that age-related chronic endoplasmic reticulum stress is a critical player in the disease.

To fold back correctly, the SOD1 protein undergoes a series of post-translational modifications first. These include the insertion of zinc and copper ions, disulfide bond formation and homodimerization. The complexity of this operation could explain that any of the 150 mutations could destabilize SOD1, leading to an aberrant aggregation and eventually to ALS.

Although these poorly aggregated forms are a hallmark of SOD1 protein, at least two studies have reported misfolded forms of protein in sporadic cases of the disease (Forsberg and colleagues, 2010). A study led by Robert Brown and Daryl Bosco used antibodies specific to different conformations of SOD1 and demonstrated small oligomeric species in ALS tissues. However, other researchers have not detected aggregates of wild-type SOD1 in ALS tissues (Da Cruz and colleagues, 2017).

Nevertheless, in order to study a potential mechanism of SOD1 aggregation of wild-type, Danilo Medinas and his colleagues began by following the appearance of different species of

---

190 http://www.ncbi.nlm.nih.gov/pubmed/30038021

aggregates in transgenic mice. The researchers isolated spinal cord tissue from young (4 months old), middle (8 months old) and older (16 months old) SOD1-WT mice, which over-express the wild-type human protein.

Where in the cell did these aggregates begin to form ? Using cell fractionation experiments, the researchers found them in the cytosol, nucleus and endoplasmic reticulum.

While disulfide-dependent chemical species predominated in all cell compartments, they were the only species in the endoplasmic reticulum. This suggests that the environment of the endoplasmic reticulum strongly favors the oxidation and potentially the aggregation of SOD1.

To see if he could mimic this stress associated with aging of the endoplasmic reticulum in younger mice, Medinas injected animals three months old three times a week for five weeks with low doses of tunicamycin. Tunicamycin is an inhibitor of N-glycosylation. Tunicamycin caused an accumulation of unfolded proteins in the endoplasmic reticulum lumen.

This diet induced an increase in stress genes in the endoplasmic reticulum and resulted in the formation of large aggregates of oxidized SOD1. However, a single high dose of tunicamycin was unable to create this stress and aggregates, suggesting that a state of chronic stress, similar to that seen in older animals, was necessary to promote SOD1 aggregation.

Overall, the results suggest that endoplasmic reticulum stress, worsens with age, promotes oxidation, incorrect folding, and aggregation of SOD1 protein. In addition, the aggregated SOD1 protein promotes greater stress of the endoplasmic reticulum, leading to a vicious circle that can activate harmful astrocyte responses.

2018 : Could the next ALS drug be... a cancer drug[191]?

In 95 % of ALS patients, TDP-43 is absent from the nucleus and forms aggregates of phosphorylated proteins in the cytoplasm of affected neurons and glia. It has been known since 2003 that there is a link between PARP and ALS[192]. These enzymes form a family of 17 members. They are found in the cell nucleus. Their main function is to report single-stranded DNA to the enzymatic system responsible for restoring double-stranded DNA.

In 2014, it was suggested that FUS as PARP, were components of the cellular response to DNA damage, and defects in this response (such as mutations) could contribute to ALS[193].

Recently, the response to DNA damage (DDR) has been shown to be induced by the repeated expansion of C9orf72 in amyotrophic lateral sclerosis[194]. Thus, the expression of PARP in ALS could be a consequence of a defense mechanism.

On the contrary, this study proposes that the expression of PARP may interfere with another defense mechanism (stress granules) and creates TDP-43 toxic aggregates, because this study has identified the core TDP-43 protein as a liaison to the PAR. Although this study has attracted attention because it proposes to use existing anticancer drugs to resolve TDP-43, it is very preliminary because it has been tested only on a small number of flies and only in vitro.

It is unclear if PARP inhibitors are destroying existing aggregates of TDP-43 in neurons, in addition to preventing the formation of new aggregates. Moreover, it is unclear whether this strategy could only be beneficial for the TDP-43 forms of

---

191 https://www.ncbi.nlm.nih.gov/pubmed/30100264
192 https://www.ncbi.nlm.nih.gov/pubmed/12528821
193 https://www.ncbi.nlm.nih.gov/pubmed/24049082
194 https://www.ncbi.nlm.nih.gov/pubmed/28481984

the disease. For example, some scientists have suggested that it would be beneficial to stimulate, not inhibit, PARP activity in FUS ALS. The idea is to give these enzymes more time to repair breaks in DNA in ALS neurons. In fact, treatment with veliparib, a PARP 1/2 inhibitor, can lead to poor localization and aggregation of FUS in the cytosol of cells in culture, thus contributing to cytotoxicity.

Many questions remain :

- This research does not explain the localized onset or the observed spread in ALS.

- We do not know why PARP activity is high in ALS. This could reinforce another stress, if PARP is inhibited.

- It will be important to determine if this strategy works in the mammalian models of the disease, as flies are very different from mammalian life forms.

- It is unclear if PARP inhibitors are destroying existing aggregates of TDP-43 in neurons, in addition to preventing the formation of new aggregates. This is important because, since the neurons of people with ALS already have the TDP-43 pathology, PARP inhibitors would be useless.

- Moreover, it is unclear whether this strategy could be beneficial for positive forms of TDP-43 disease. For example, some scientists have suggested that it would be beneficial to stimulate, not inhibit, PARP activity in FUS ALS. The idea is to give these enzymes more time to repair breaks in DNA in ALS neurons. Indeed, treatment with vagiparib, a PARP 1/2 inhibitor, may result in poor localization and aggregation of FUS in the cytosol of cells in culture, contributing to cytotoxicity.

- In addition, the PARP-1 inhibitor 5-iodo-6-amino-1,2-benzopyrone did not provide any benefit in a murine model of SOD1 ALS.

3.3. Chronology of the major stages of ALS research.

- Neurologists are concerned about the long-term use of these drugs in the treatment of chronic neurodegenerative diseases such as ALS. Interfering with the long-term process of DNA repair would be dangerous for cells that reproduce rapidly.

- It may be more appropriate to use tankyrase inhibitors (PARP5) instead of PARP1/2 because these enzymes probably do not participate in the DNA repair process, making them potentially safer. Several highly selective PARP5 inhibitors are under development for cancer, but none has been clinically tested.

2019 : TDP-43 forms cytoplasmic droplets independently of stress granules[195].

Although the cytoplasmic aggregation of TDP-43 is a pathological feature of amyotrophic lateral sclerosis and frontotemporal dementia, the way in which aggregates are formed and what determines their nuclear clearance has not been determined. There is a lot of work on a liquid-liquid phase separation (LLPS) of TDP-43, in the nuclei of several cell types.

Fatima Gasset-Rosa of Don Cleveland's team wanted to examine the endogenous TDP-43 protein using high-resolution microscopy in various somatic cell types, including mouse and human neurons. In each of them, she found that the normal TDP-43 protein formed droplets in the nucleus that merged and separated dynamically, exchanging rapidly with the TDP-43 protein in the nucleoplasm. This suggests that dynamic liquid-liquid phase separation (LLPS) is a physiological part of the function of the TDP-43 protein in the nucleus.

However, if the researchers treat human neuroblastoma cells with TDP-43 or FUS fibrils, TDP-43 is removed from the nucleus and accumulates as liquid droplets in the cytoplasm. The same droplets are formed if the researchers over-express TDP-43 in the cytoplasm. These membrane-less organelles were also dynamic, easily exchanging their TDP-43 with the one around them.

The results demonstrate that, independently of the stress granules, the TDP-43 protein phase changes into the cytoplasm in response to various stressors. Those phase changes can interfere with the nucleocytoplasmic transport and siphon the TDP-43 protein. nuclear, resulting in cell death.

This suggests that the cytoplasmic TDP-43 droplets may be toxic, without the need for them to be in the form of solid aggregates, as was commonly believed.

---

195 http://www.ncbi.nlm.nih.gov/pubmed/30853299

3.3. Chronology of the major stages of ALS research.

The results support the idea that droplets of liquid TDP-43 are formed in the early stages of the disease, then produce gels or solids when the pathology worsens, suggested Gasset-Rosa. « *This process may be essential to understand the emergence of the pathology of the TDP-43 protein.* »

3.3. Chronology of the major stages of ALS research.

4. Clinical considerations

4.1. Lack of markers of progression

4.1.1. Pragmatic models for stratifying progression

When conducting a clinical trial, there is a need to access the progression, or hopefully the regression of the disease.

Various methods are used, but each have some weak points. Here is a short list : It could be levels of the drug and of various proteins. It could be the weight, the forced vital capacity volume on the lung function test, the muscle strength measured by handheld dynamometry. Or it could be a test for numeric rating scale for spasticity, or a test for ALS specific quality of life. But one of the two methods described below are used in most cases.

4.1.1.1. ALSFRS-R

This is a questionnaire using observable information by a non-specialist.

The progression and severity of ALS is rated by doctors on the ALS Functional Rating Scale, which has been revised and is referred to as ALSFRS-R.

LSFRS-R scores calculated at diagnosis can be compared to scores throughout time to determine the speed of progression. The rate of change, called the ALSFRS-R slope can be used as a prognostic indicator.

Although the ALSFRS-R score is a recognized prognostic indicator, it is more useful to compare various indicators including vital capacity (FVC%) and the Sickness Impact Profile (SIP) to increase the accuracy of a given prognosis.

4.1.1.2. El Escorial

The El Escorial criteria is often used for diagnosing ALS. It uses physiology elements and includes EMG testing. As it is mainly a diagnosis tool, it enable to sub-categorize the patient in :

- Classical ALS
- Progressive bulbar palsy (PBP)
- Progressive muscular atrophy (PMA)
- Primary lateral sclerosis (PLS)

Over the past two decades, the El Escorial criteria have been used as eligibility criteria in major randomized controlled trials. One of the goals of the revised EEC was to allow earlier diagnosis by introducing a new category, namely « *clinically probable laboratory supported* » ALS. This category allowed EMG findings to be taken into account assuming that EMG is more sensitive than the clinical examination in detecting lower motor neuron signs.

It is criticized because a bias toward slow progressors in the « clinically probable laboratory supported » category[196].

4.1.1.3. Awaji

Awaji criteria was proposed on the background of El Escorial criteria. The Awaji criteria recommended that neurophysiological data should be used in the context of clinical information, not as a separate, stand-alone set of data. In addition, fasciculation potentials associated with signs of reinnervation are considered as evidence of lower motor neuron lesion, in particular in cranial-innervated or strong limb muscles.

---

196 https://www.ncbi.nlm.nih.gov/pubmed/31561715

4.1.2. Lack of biomarkers

In the 20th century, many hypotheses have been advanced to explain the pathogenesis of ALS.

Poliovirus motor neuron selectivity has led to the theory that ALS may be the consequence of atypical poliovirus infection, but traditional culture methods and in situ hybridization of RNA did not detected poliovirus in cerebrospinal fluid and brain samples from ALS.

Because metallotoxins such as lead or aluminum can induce clinical paralysis and motor nerve pathology in some laboratory animals, they have also been implicated in ALS ethiology. But no convincing clinical data or autopsy has corroborated this hypothesis.

The degeneration of spinal and cortico-spinal motor neurons can be induced in autoimmune diseases. This observation and others have led to the hypothesis that ALS could be an autoimmune disease. While the serum of many patients with sporadic ALS has autoantibodies that react with calcium channels, there has been no evidence of a causal relationship between body antibodies and the development of ALS. In addition, patients with ALS have shown no benefit from immunosuppressive therapy.

Several lines of research have indicated that the toxicity of excitatory neurotransmitters such as glutamate may be a factor in the pathology of ALS. Glutamate levels in brain tissue are lowered, while glutamate and aspartate levels in cerebrospinal fluid can be elevated in both sporadic ALS and motor neuron cases. In addition, glutamate transport is reduced in synaptosomal[197] preparations from brains of ALS patient.

---

197 A synaptosome is a synaptic terminal detached from a neuron, with a help of a mechanical device.

4.1. Lack of markers of progression

Scientists also believed that there were two types of familial ALS, one with rapid progression and the other with slow progression. To revive the work on this topic, the Prize4Life Foundation has collected anonymous data on patients with amyotrophic lateral sclerosis who participated in clinical trials of experimental drugs and made them available to researchers in the database. PRO-ACT. This gave rise to some interesting results, but the impossibility of correlating the clusters found with mutations or other markers soon showed the limitations of this approach.

4.2. Animal models

Animal models are important for understanding some points of a pathology. There are about 50 animal models of ALS, but most use mouse models. However, the prefrontal cortex is much less developed in rodents than in primates[198]. Rodents do not have direct projections of cortico-motor neurons[199] that allow precise control of fore-limb movements. The cortico-motoneuronal synapse is a characteristic that distinguishes primates from other mammal species

Many drugs used to treat central nervous system disorders exert their effects via neurotransmitter systems and neuromodulators that differ between primates and rodents, so hybrids animals are designed that incorporate a human gene.

Mouse motor neurons activate muscle motor units at levels close to tetanization, whereas cat and human motor neurons have the ability to generate repetitive excitations capable of modulating efforts finely. So it's hard to think that a rodent can make a good ALS model animal.

It is disconcerting that mice are even considered for ALS research.

The transgenic macaques were first created in 2002 and a model for overexpression of Huntington's disease was described in 2008. Important advances include new viral vectors that can be used in primate research, as well as human gene therapy.

Despite these advances, the creation and analysis of transgenic primate models still represent a major technical challenge. Conducting an ALS study on primates is beyond the

---

198 Kaas, J.H. The evolution of brains from early mammals to humans.
Wiley Interdiscip. Rev. Cogn. Sci. 33–45 (2013).
199 Lemon, R.N. Descending pathways in motor control.
Annu. Rev. Neurosci. 195–218 (2008).

reach of most laboratories because of its cost and stringency. Drug discovery in ALS has suffered from the lack of a realistic animal model. Recently, model pigs of ALS were created. But it's amazing that small animals like Tupaia minor or Tupaia montana are not used in ALS research because they are genetically much closer to the primate than to the rodent, while having dietary habits and a cycle of life comparable to that of the laboratory mouse.

Most of these mouse models involve either genes involved in ALS or TDP-43. But many aspects of ALS are not covered, for example, there is no animal model for excitotoxicity whereas it is a subject that is constantly cited in publications.

4.3. Clinical trials

4.3.1. Designing clinical trials is difficult.

Since ALS is a rare disease, researchers in the field of ALS must work with only a few families, even in countries with a large population. In addition this disease has many different phenotypes, and the lack of recognized biomarkers does not facilitate its study. For example, teams of researchers who discovered the FUS gene involvement in ALS had to sequence nearly 2,000 people, yet found only one case of FUS mutation.

In patients with ALS, time is running fast, half of the motor neurons are already in critical condition at the time of diagnosis, so this emergency is hardly compatible with the duration of a clinical trial. Any successful treatment must manifest itself in visible signs in a few months, or even weeks. This is very difficult to achieve because the health of patients declines very quickly.

In addition, organizing a clinical trial is much more difficult in the case of ALS than in common diseases such as cancer, because to make sense, test participants should not have co-morbidities, take only the drug tested and nothing else, etc. Most patients are often elderly and therefore have significant co-morbidities. Only candidates who meet sometimes extremely strict requirements are selected.

And even if a treatment was found, it might not result in a drug because it had to stay and remain effective in the body for about 24 hours (half-life of 12 hours). Thus, drugs that stay too short (less than a few hours) or more than 24 hours are excluded. This criterion also implies that it is a small molecule to be excreted out of the kidneys. Small molecules have less specificity than long molecules. Some researchers sometimes complain that it would be possible to cure more patients if the pharmaceutical industry was more open to accepting long molecules. But university researchers are not responsible for patient safety, while the pharmaceutical industry is legally responsible for patient safety.

The excessive use of the revised ALS Functional Scale (ALSFRS-R) is a problem for clinical trials. ALSFRS-R is a composite index of parameters that are difficult to accurately assess, leading to many statistical anomalies, such as an improvement when a patient receives a minor treatment for example for excessive salivation[200]. It is difficult to distinguish a small signal in this great sea of noisy parameters. Some even fell into this trap by believing discerning "*reversals*[201]"when they were only statistical anomalies or misdiagnosis.

A subtle point is that there is no way of knowing whether the progression of the control group is normal or not, since the progression of each ALS patient is often different from that of other patients. So, if the control group can not tell the rate of progression, it is impossible to know if a drug is effective or not to slow the progression of ALS. This is why researchers are extremely cautious when selecting patients for clinical trials.

About 5 % of clinical trials have been suspended. There are many possible explanations for these failures, but they are probably due to a lack of improvement or even a clear deterioration in patients. However, the failures of the clinical trials are very instructive on what we think we know about the mechanisms of ALS. Basically, failure teaches us that what we believe we know is incomplete or false. In this respect it is striking to note that while almost all clinical trials have failed, the main principles guiding ALS research have changed little, except that there is a shift towards agnostic treatment proposals (growth factors, correction of adverse effects with ASOs).

---

200 https://jnnp.bmj.com/content/88/2/187
201 https://www.ncbi.nlm.nih.gov/pubmed/29607695

A consequence of this lack of knowledge about the pathology (or pathologies) of ALS is that after having tested about fifty drugs in numerous clinical trials[202], there is still no drug that can slow the progression of the disease satisfactorily for the patients. It must also be said that links are often tenuous between academic research and drugs that are tested in clinical trials by biotechs.

4.3.2. Oddities in clinical trials on ALS

In clinical trials, the location of motoneurons that are affected and therefore should be targeted by the therapy is generally ignored. The therapies are designed to treat all subtypes of ALS, but for example, is it advisable to use a risky intrathecal injection, if the problem is limited to a reduced number of lower motoneurons, as the greater part of them is out of the central nervous system ? Is it advisable to administer an intrathecal lumbar injection to a patient with a bulbar form ?

It is also odd to use intrathecal injections, which in principle bruise the dura-mater whereas it is necessary to preserve it in the case of ALS. And indeed intrathecal injections are also done to patients in the control group, thereby deteriorating deliberately their condition.

---

202 There were 486 ALS clinical trials in June 2019.

5. Panorama of drugs used in clinical trials

This chapter aims at providing a quick glance on drugs in the pipeline of biotechs. Normally drugs are invented in academic premises, the Intellectual Property is bought by biotechs that try to transform what is often a quick and dirty academic experience designed to solve a research question, into a reproducible process to produce a drug that ameliorate the health of animal models.

This involve many aspects that were not envisioned by academics such as the "Pfizer rule of five", that put constraint on drugs in order to make them safe for human beings. The biotechs study the processes of absorption, distribution, metabolization, and excretion of the drug which will condition the administration mode and the dosage of the drug. Indeed it also invents how to produce the drug in a way that is economically sound, and without procurement or logistics risks. Few of the proposed drugs survive at this stage, and it is time for the biotechs to protect their investments by filling patents.

Then the biotechs ask to the regulator for the authorization to make clinical trials. A phase I clinical trial asserts the safety of the drug. It is done on a very small scale, so it does not cost much.

A phase II will assert the efficacy, so it is much more complex as the number of patients must be large enough to statistically be a proxy to the population who will receive the drug. Few drugs will fail to pass successfully a phase II.

Often at this stage the biotech does not have enough resources to proceed to phase III and it tries to gather the interest a much larger company. The phase III will evaluate the drug effectiveness and monitor side effects. At this stage perhaps only one on a thousand academic "breakthrough" will reach this state.

There are three sections in this chapter, the first one is about drugs that have passed a phase I. Those drugs at least are safe at the dosage and with the administration mode that were used in the clinical trial. The second section deals with the two drugs that have successfully completed phase III. These drugs are safe, but few would agree that they are efficient. The last section is about drugs that are currently in phase three. Probably only two or three of them will receive a market authorization, but most of them are interesting.

5.1. List of drugs that have passed Phase I.

The following is a partial list of drugs that have passed Phase I but have still not completed a Phase II or Phase III by mid-2019.

These drugs are interesting as they are safe (they have passed the phase I), and somehow they have attracted the interest of the pharmaceutical industry. Some of those drugs are abandoned, they are still mentioned here because often it is not well understood why they did not worked. In the future they might be used in conjunction with another drug or with a subgroup of patient.

This list only includes drugs that aim to improve most aspects of ALS. So drugs that address only a specific aspect, such as salivation, but without aiming at ameliorating other aspects, are not mentioned here.

5.1.1. Riluzole Oral Soluble

What characterizes this drug : Riluzole is taken orally, but there were concerns about its bio-availability, for example Edaravone is administrated intravenously. The difference in administration mode means that a patient under Edaravone must be cared by a nurse and it is difficult to organize an injection several times a day at home. It was also hypothesized that the problem with Riluzole is not degradation in the digestive tract, but that it is eliminated too quickly from the organism, so an easy way to mitigate this problem would be to ingest Riluzole several times a day. This much easier to organize with an oral formulation than with an injection. Masitinib is currently the only oral drug that has positive effects on ALS.

Relation to the academic research : There is interest in academic research on oral administration of drugs in ALS.

Clinical trials outcome : In 2019, there are about 7 proposals for drug formulations based on Riluzole. Indeed there were some patent litigations between competitors, because it is difficult for competitors to differentiate from each other. MonoSol Rx is a specialty pharmaceutical company that delivers drugs in films, not tablets.

In 2017, the FDA granted MonoSol Rx's request to grant Riluzole OSF the status of a new investigational drug. This means that it can be used to help patients with limited treatment options and for medical needs that are not satisfied.

This designation allowed MonoSol Rx to begin clinical trials on Riluzole OSF. One clinical trial ended after a few months with only 9 patients and the other clinical trial was canceled.

Take home points : This drug should bring minor benefits to all ALS patients.

5.1.2. Talampanel

What characterizes this drug : Talampanel is a drug that has been studied for the treatment of epilepsy, malignant gliomas and amyotrophic lateral sclerosis (ALS).

Relation to the academic research : Talampanel is studied at low intensity for ALS since 2002. Like Riluzole, there are several reasons to believe that it should be effective if our understanding of ALS were correct. Talampanel acts as a noncompetitive antagonist of the AMPA receptor, a type of ionotropic glutamate receptor in the central nervous system.

Clinical trials outcome : Talampanel has completed phase II trials where it may have demonstrated preliminary efficacy, but in May 2010, the results of the trial were found to be negative. Talampanel has been shown to be effective for epilepsy in clinical trials. Talampanel is not in development

244

because of its short terminal half-life (3 hours). This requires administrating several doses per day, however the administration mode is oral so it is not a so important problem.

Take home points : It is unlikely that it may be useful to treat ALS.

5.1.3. Tamoxifen

What characterizes this drug : Tamoxifen is used in the treatment and prevention of breast cancer because it is a selective estrogen receptor modulator (SERM). Its effectiveness depends on the enzyme P450 2D6 creating the active metabolite endoxifene, 4-hydroxytamoxifene.

Cytochrome P450 2D6 (CYP2D6) is an enzyme encoded by the CYP2D6 gene in humans. CYP2D6 is mainly expressed in the liver. It is also strongly expressed in areas of the central nervous system, including the substantia nigra.

Goldenseal, with its two notable alkaloids, berberine and hydrastine, has been shown to modify the enzymatic activities of the P450 marker (involving CYP2C9, CYP2D6 and CYP3A4)

Tamoxifen is also thought to affect the most important factor in the regulation of angiogenesis, vascular endothelial growth factor (VEGF). Therefore, it is considered that the drug prevents tumor-induced angiogenesis. Its neuroprotective action is probably due to its ability to inhibit protein kinase C. This promotes inflammation in the spinal cord of patients with ALS.

Relation to the academic research : Tamoxifen has attracted some interest from ALS scientists. It has shown positive effects in patients with ALS.

Clinical trials outcome : The drug has been well tolerated in clinical trials in both sexes and data from a prolonged follow-up period suggest that patients receiving 20 to 40 mg daily may have longer survival than those receiving only 10 mg daily.

Take home points : This medicine might be important for ALS patients, but it has significant side effects and should not be taken in the long term. Moreover, it interacts with many other drugs in a very complex way.

5.1.4. Dextromethorphan

What characterizes this drug : Dextromethorphan is an opioid most commonly used as an antitussive.

In palliative care of ALS patients, it was observed that these had a positive effect on bulbar function and a clinical trial was conducted.

Dextromethorphan is used in combination with quinidine to reduce demethylation by blocking the P450 CYP2D6 enzyme.

Relation to the academic research : Dextromethorphan has attracted some interest from ALS scientists.

Clinical trials outcome : The clinical study was unique because it was motivated by reports from patients who had improved speech and swallowing by taking a combination of dextromethorphan and quinidine to control emotional lability.

The study was conducted over a short period (70 days) and a self-assessment scale was chosen as the primary outcome measure.

Take home points : The combination therapy is highly indicated for the treatment of pseudobulbar and bulbar symptoms of ALS.

5.1.5. Lithium

What characterizes this drug : Lithium is still considered a first-line treatment for both acute treatment and long-term treatment of bipolar disorder. Before 2011 there was a consensus that lithium would have neuroprotective effects in ALS.

Relation to the academic research : Lithium has attracted a strong interest from ALS scientists because it influence the astrocytes behavior.

Clinical trials outcome : In a clinical trial, lithium-treated transgenic mice indeed showed improved survival compared to normal-type saline-treated mice, and in another clinical trial on lithium in ALS patients, there was a significant effect on survival in the lithium plus Riluzole group compared to the group receiving only Riluzole.

The design of this trial could be criticized, but the difference in survival reported at 15 months (survival of 100 % in the lithium group plus Riluzole compared to 70 % in the group receiving only Riluzole), suggested that a definitive randomized trial placebo controlled was justified. In fact, several clinical trials have taken place which have proved negative. This does not preclude new scientific studies on the impact of lithium on other neurodegenerative diseases.

Take home points : Lithium is probably useless to treat ALS.

5.1.6. Pioglitazone

What characterizes this drug : Pioglitazone is a drug used to treat type 2 diabetes mellitus. It works by improving the sensitivity of the tissues to insulin. It makes sense to use it in ALS because there is a strong presumption that ALS patients are insulin resistant. Pioglitazone acts on the gamma receptor PPAR. PPAR-gamma has been implicated in the pathology of many diseases such as obesity, diabetes, atherosclerosis, cancer and ALS[203].

Relation to the academic research : Like lithium, Pioglitazone has attracted some interest from ALS scientists because it influences the astrocytes behavior.

---

203 https://www.ncbi.nlm.nih.gov/pmc/articles/PMC4923074/

Clinical trials outcome : Pioglitazone is not without health risks. Nevertheless, the clinical trial was discontinued because there was no difference between the placebo group and the drug group.

Take home points : Pioglitazone is probably useless to treat ALS.

5.1.7. Thalidomide

What characterizes this drug : Thalidomide is mainly used as a treatment of certain cancers (multiple myeloma) and of a complication of leprosy. In the past, several ALS model animal studies[204] have shown improvements when these mice were treated with thalidomide.

Relation to the academic research : Neuroinflammation is probably a major contributor to damage to motor neurons. Pre-inflammatory cytokines, such as tumor necrosis factor (TNF), are strongly upregulated in ALS. Thalidomide has attracted little interest from ALS scientists

Clinical trials outcome : A clinical trial was then mounted to examine how ALS patients were responding to thalidomide. Thalidomide may be useful in some cases where standard anti-TB drugs and corticosteroids are not enough to resolve severe inflammation in the brain. Making a clinical with thalidomide is a bit odd, because research has not associated it with ALS. No official information was provided as to why the clinical trial was stopped. It would appear[205] that 23 patients were enrolled, but only 18 were evaluable. There were no improvements in ALSFRS-R or PFT (pulmonary capacity) compared to controls.

Thalidomide has had **several side effects** in patients including sinus bradycardia.

---

204 https://www.ncbi.nlm.nih.gov/pubmed/16510725
205 https://www.ncbi.nlm.nih.gov/pubmed/19922130

Take home points : Thalidomide is probably useless to treat ALS.

5.1.8. Dexpramipexole

What characterizes this drug : Dexpramipexole is the enantiomer of Pramipexole, and has been shown to improve mitochondrial function and to confer significant cellular protection in neurons under stress.

Relation to the academic research : Dexpramipexole has attracted some interest from ALS scientists since 2003, when then found that Pramipexole, a Parkinson drug had some benefit to ALS patients. Then in 2008 it was found that a R+ Pramipexole trial resulted in 17 % reduction in slope of decline of ALSFRS-R, which was qualified as "non significant". In another trial was done with R+ Pramipexole, which was then christened Dexpramipexole.

Clinical trials outcome : Dexpramipexole has been the subject of numerous (+160) clinical trials on many pathologies. 12 clinical trials were conducted on ALS.

Pramipexole acts as a partial/full agonist at the following receptors : D2S, D2L, D3 and D4.

Therefore, with hopes of improving the pathological conditions of ALS, a clinical study was conducted using Dexpramipexole. Dexpramipexole does not have the dopamine receptor agonist activity, so has no adverse drug reactions by the dopamine receptor agonist activity.

A phase I clinical study of Dexpramipexole was conducted as a randomized, double-blind, placebo-controlled study in 54 healthy volunteers. In that study, Dexpramipexole was well tolerated at doses up to 300 mg/data.

In the historical-controlled phase II study that followed, Dexpramipexole was administered to 30 ALS patients at a dose of 30 mg/day for 6 months. It was tolerated and improved the slope of decline on the ALS Functional Rating Scale-Revised (ALSFRS-R) score by 13 %.

In a dose escalation study in 10 ALS patients, the dose of Dexpramipexole was increased to a maximum of 300 mg/day, which was confirmed to be safe and tolerable with no dopaminergic ADRs reported. This study was continued as an extension study, in which Dexpramipexole was administered at doses of 30 mg/day and 60 mg/day for 6 months for comparison. As a result, the decline of the slope of the ALSFRS-R score was smaller at 60 mg/day than at 30 mg/day.

Next, a randomized, double-blind, placebo-controlled, phase II study was conducted, and the safety and tolerability of Dexpramipexole were evaluated in ALS patients. This study was divided into two parts : at Stage 1, 102 subjects were randomized to receive either Dexpramipexole 50 mg/day, 150 mg/day, 300 mg/day, or placebo for 12 weeks.

At Stage 2, 92 subjects who underwent a 4-week washout were randomized to receive either 50 mg/day or 300 mg/day for 24 weeks. Dexpramipexole was generally safe and well tolerated. The slope of the ALSFRS-R score was markedly reduced in the higher dose group at both Stages 1 and 2, and the hazard ratio of mortality was reduced by 68 % in the 300 mg/day group, compared with the 50 mg/day group at Stage 2. Treatment at 300 mg/day was significantly more beneficial in terms of the integrated outcome of the changes in ALSFRS-R and mortality.

Based on these results, a phase III, multicenter, randomized, double-blind, placebo-controlled study of Dexpramipexole (EMPOWER) was conducted in ALS patients in the US, Canada, Australia, and Europe.

However, and very surprisingly, Dexpramipexole did not meet the criteria set in a phase III study. The failure of Phase III was attributed to the difficulty of obtaining reliable results from the ALSFRS-R scale, which led scientists to believe that the results obtained in Phase II were satisfactory, then they were not.

The way to conduct clinical trials, and particularly, the use of futility analysis for high enrollment trials had been criticized[206] and also the validity of the ALSFRS-R questionnaire to measure outcome.

There is currently an ongoing Phase I/IIa clinical trial on Ropinorole, which share some properties with Dexpramipexole. Side effects specific to D3 agonists such as ropinirole and pramipexole can include hallucinations, hypersexuality and compulsive gambling, even in patients without a history of these behaviours.

Take home points : Dexpramipexole is probably effective only on a subset of ALS patients. Given it was originally a Parkinson drug, it may be more suitable for patients with a bulbar form.

5.1.9. Ropinorole

What characterizes this drug : Ropinirole, is a medication used to treat Parkinson's disease and restless legs syndrome. In PD the dose needs to be adjusted to the effect and treatment should not be suddenly stopped. It is taken by mouth.

Relation to the academic research : Ropinirole has attracted some interest from ALS scientists because it belongs to the same class of drugs as Dexpramipexole.

Clinical trials outcome : There is currently an ongoing Phase I/IIa clinical trial on Ropinorole, which share some properties with Dexpramipexole. Some patients on forums report a small improvement, this in itself is very unusual.

Take home points : Ropinorole should receive the attention from ALS patients, for the same reason than for Dexpramipexole. It is not a cure, but so much drugs were

---

206 https://www.ncbi.nlm.nih.gov/pubmed/29486281

found useless, than a drug found having some positive effect for an ALS subgroup is remarkable.

5.1.10. sNN0029

What characterizes this drug : SNN0029 is a recombinant human vascular endothelial growth factor (rhVEGF165) that is administered intracerebroventricularly and acts by inhibiting cell death in motor neurons.

Relation to the academic research : Not much is known. In mutant SOD1 murine models of ALS, sNN0029 is reported by Newron to increase lifespan and slow the progression of the disease. Several studies have indeed shown that VEGF expression is altered in ALS and that VEGF treatment improves disease in murine models of ALS.

Clinical trials outcome : The drug has already been tested in humans as part of a Phase I/II safety study and has shown preliminary evidence of efficacy. The compound is delivered into the brain with an investigational drug delivery catheter from a third-party supplier. The U.S. FDA in April/May 2015, preventing this third-party supplier from commercializing the catheter. The issues raised by the FDA relating to the supplier's quality system led Newron to temporarily interrupt any further patient screening activities, surgical implantation of medical device, or randomization of patients to enable Newron to perform a benefit-risk assessment for sNN0029. This assessment led Newron to discontinue the development of the program.

Take home points : This drug has an obscure origin, and unclear end, so it may not be very important.

5.1.11. IGF-1

What characterizes this drug : Over the past 30 years, glucose intolerance has been reported in a significant percentage of ALS patients. In mammals, there are three Insulin-like peptide receptors in the brain.

The IGF1 receptor and the insulin receptor can form functional hybrids that have similar affinities to IGF1 and insulin, indicating a cooperation. The IGF2 receptor does not bind insulin. These membrane receptors regulate the phosphorylation of various kinases such as PI3 K, GSK2, mTOR SOD that affect protein translation, autophagy, apoptosis, oxidative stress, gene transcription and proliferation among others. Therefore, insulin-like peptides may play a role in various neurodegeneration processes.

Relation to the academic research : The interest of ALS scientists in IGF-1 dates from 1983[207] and is still probably much stronger than for most drugs. Many neurotrophic factors are known to promote neuronal survival and regeneration. As a result, a large number of these factors have been investigated in preclinical models of ALS[208]. These include BDNF, CNTF, GDNF, IGF-1, VEGF, FGF ; HGF, BMP-7, and G-CSF.

Clinical trials outcome : This phase III, randomized, double-blind, placebo-controlled study was undertaken to address whether IGF-1 benefited patients with ALS.

A total of 330 patients from 20 medical centers were randomized to receive 0.05 mg/kg body weight of human recombinant IGF-1 given subcutaneously twice daily or placebo for 2 years.

However there was no difference between treatment groups in the primary or secondary outcome measures after the 2-year treatment period.

Take home points : Given the amount of interest of scientists to IGF-1 in ALS, this is still a drug that must get attention from patients. As for other trials, maybe it benefited to a subset of

---

207 https://www.ncbi.nlm.nih.gov/pubmed/3302111
208 https://www.ncbi.nlm.nih.gov/pubmed/20592948/

patients, or maybe the unusual administration mode (subcutaneous) did not permitted the drug to reach motoneurons.

5.1.12. Tirasemtiv

What characterizes this drug : In 2012, researchers at Cytokinetics suggested[209] that Tirasemtiv, a fast skeletal muscle troponin activator (FSTA), may be beneficial for people with ALS to improve muscle performance. Tirasemtiv is an orally bioavailable molecule that sensitizes the troponin complex in fast-twitch skeletal muscle fibers to calcium. A putative mechanism of action is an improvement in the contraction of muscle in response to diminished neural input thus potentially decreasing muscle fatigue.

Relation to the academic research : This is a rare case where researchers explained extensively[210] how they designed the drug.

Clinical trials outcome : The team reported on the results of the Phase IIb clinical trial, called BENEFIT-ALS, in 2014. Although it did not achieve its primary endpoint of functional decline reduction (ALSFRS-R) in individuals with ALS, the rate of loss of respiratory capacity (SVC) was **slowed by two-third** compared to placebo, which is a potentially very important clinical effect.

Tolerability, in particular the onset of vertigo, was a problem with a high drop-out rate (Shefner and colleagues, 2016). 711 people with ALS participated in the 12-week study.

In the hope of overcoming these difficulties during the Phase III clinical trial, the researchers extended the test period in readable labeling mode, up to two weeks before performing randomization and double blind mode. It was done in order to

---

209 https://www.ncbi.nlm.nih.gov/pubmed/22591195
210 https://www.ncbi.nlm.nih.gov/pmc/articles/PMC5900333/

to eliminate from the trial, patients who could not stand Tirasemtiv and to allow more time for selected patients to acclimate with the drug. In a way it skews the results, it is surprising that this practice is accepted by stakeholders, but it may have been taken into account the lack of medication for ALS.

The dosage was also more flexible, with a maximum target dose of 250, 375 or 500 mg / day, allowing the amount of Tirasemtiv to be adjusted at any time during the study.

The double-blind Phase III clinical trial, VITALITY-ALS, was launched in September 2015. The primary outcome measure was the change in SVC[211] to 24 weeks. Secondary endpoints, measured at 48 weeks, included muscle strength, respiratory capacity (respiratory sub-scores, ALSFRS-R) and function (ALSFRS-R). 743 people with ALS participated in the 54-week study. But the clinical trial failed, and Tirasemtiv did not demonstrate any greater improvements in slow vital capacity, a key measure of lung capacity, over a 24-week period compared with placebo.

Cytokinetics discontinued the development of its muscle enhancer, Tirasemtiv, as a treatment for ALS in November 2017. Jeremy Shefner, principal investigator at the Barrow Neurological Institute in Phoenix, Arizona, reported the results in December 2017.

VITALITY-ALS has not met its primary or secondary criteria, largely because of poor tolerance and side effects, but Cytokinetics is hopeful of success with its new drug. CK-107, the next generation of Cytokinetics, has been clinically tested in people with ALS to determine if the drug can help muscles stay stronger, longer, including the muscles needed for breathing. The primary endpoint was always improvement in SVC.

---

211 SVC = slow vital capacity : The maximum volume of air that can be exhaled slowly after slow maximum inhalation.

But CK-2127107 did neither shown a lower degradation of the slow vital capacity (SVC) after 12 weeks of treatment.

Take home points : Tirasemtiv, like most proposed ALS drugs, has severe side effects. But if it was possible to attenuate those side effects, it might be really useful for slow vital capacity.

5.1.13. Minocycline

What characterizes this drug : The choice of this drug for an ALS clinical trial is a little weird. Minocycline is an antibiotic of the tetracycline family whose penetration by the central nervous system is high orally, which is very rare. The reason for this trial appears to be hypotheses that ALS is a result of severe inflammation.

Relation to the academic research : Nitric oxide synthases are a family of enzymes that catalyze the production of nitric oxide (NO) from L-arginine. NO is an important cell signaling molecule. It helps modulate vascular tone, insulin secretion, airway tone and peristalsis, and is involved in angiogenesis and neural development. It can function as a retrograde neurotransmitter.

iNOS is an inducible NOS, mainly soluble in the cytosol of the cell. As the name suggests, it is inducible and independent of calcium. INOS expression is induced by cytokines and endotoxins. The inducible form is found in macrophages and is part of our immune system. It is able to program cell apoptosis.

NO production via iNOS after macrophage activation plays a major role as a cytotoxic antiparasitic effector molecule. Normally, its concentration is very low. But when the body is attacked by an external agent, an inflammatory mechanism, a production of cytokines, is triggered, which activates the expression of iNOS. Suddenly, the body is confronted with a high concentration of NO. The NO **indiscriminately fights**

everything in its path. It is the ultimate defense of the body. It became a bit weird when the coordinator said that many scientific experiments have shown that minocycline protects nerve cells. He also states that minocycline has been shown to be beneficial in many animal ALS experiments in Europe, Canada and the United States. Actually there is only one study[212] showing that minocycline improves ALS.

Clinical trials outcome : The conclusion of the clinical trial is that minocycline has a detrimental effect on patients with ALS. The principal investigator, Gordon, bitterly concluded that "*the current approach in translational neuroscience is unsatisfactory or the transgenic mouse model is a poor representation of sporadic ALS*". But was there real science behind this clinical trial ?

Another bizarre clinical trial associated minocycline with creatine and celecoxib (a NSAID) with creatine and again claimed that these drugs have shown interest in the central nervous system, which is probably not the case either for creatine and minocycline.

Creatine is a natural compound derived from guanidine, synthesized endogenously in humans in the liver and mainly in the muscles and brain.

Additional doses of creatine may increase the energy efficiency of anaerobic activities and may also stimulate mitochondrial respiration and phosphocreatine synthesis.

These mechanisms may help to explain the apparent neuroprotective properties of creatine observed in a mouse model of ALS in mice, as well as some cases of increased energy in patients with ALS.

Take home points : Minocycline may be useful in ALS, but those clinical trials above, did not help us to know more about this topic.

---

212 https://www.ncbi.nlm.nih.gov/pubmed/12270689

5.1.14. TRO19622

What characterizes this drug : Trophos is a biopharmaceutical startup headquartered in Marseille, France. In 2015, its flagship product candidate, Olesoxime, was conditionally purchased by Roche but in 2018, Roche announced the discontinuation of the product development after inconclusive clinical trials

Relation to the academic research : The first article about Olexime in 2007[213], was well cited by other scientists. Among articles citing it, one discussed about a supposedly better drug : Kenpaullone.

In vitro, Oresoxime also called TRO19622, promoted the survival of motor neurons in the absence of trophic support[214] in a dose-dependent manner. In vivo, TRO19622 rescued motor neurons from axotomy-induced[215] cell death in neonatal rats and promoted nerve regeneration after crush of the sciatic nerve in mice.

In SOD1 (G93A) transgenic mice, TRO19622, improved motor performance, delayed the onset of clinical disease, and prolonged survival.

TRO19622 binds directly to two components of the mitochondrial permeability transition pore : the voltage-dependent anion channel and the 18 kDa translocator protein (or peripheral benzodiazepine receptor), suggesting the potential mechanism of its neuroprotective activity.

Clinical trials outcome : There have been a number of clinical trials with TRO19622, but they have been unsuccessful.

---

213 https://www.ncbi.nlm.nih.gov/pubmed/17496168
214 "Trophic support" implies "nourishing and caring" as do astrocytes or oligodendrocytes for neurons.
215 An axotomy is the cutting or otherwise severing of an axon from the neuron's soma.

In addition to ALS, Olesoxime has already been studied as a potential treatment for spinal muscular atrophy (SMA), a liver disease called non-alcoholic steatohepatitis and peripheral neuropathy. However, research was discontinued for these diseases because Olesoxime failed to achieve the desired therapeutic effects during the trials.

Take home points : Olesoxime has probably little to chance to again rise interest in it.

5.1.15. Sodium Valproate

What characterizes this drug : Valproate (VPA), and its valproic acid, sodium valproate, and valproate semisodium forms, are medications primarily used to treat epilepsy and bipolar disorder and to prevent migraine headaches. It is unclear exactly how valproate works. Proposed mechanisms include affecting GABA levels, blocking voltage-gated sodium channels, and inhibiting histone deacetylases.

Relation to the academic research : Previous studies have investigated the role of the survival motor neuron (SMN) gene in ALS. SMN mutations are the cause of spinal muscular atrophy (SMA), a disease similar to ALS but affecting young people and toddlers. Recent data suggest that SMN genotypes producing less SMN protein increase the susceptibility and severity of ALS. This led to the hypothesis that the clinical expression of ALS was influenced by the total level of SMN protein in affected patients.

Sodium valproate (SVP), an HDAC inhibitor, has been shown to increase SMN protein levels in vitro. From these results and data suggesting the neuroprotective properties of sodium valproate, it was therefore assumed that sodium valproate could prolong the survival of patients with ALS.

In addition, sodium valproate significantly prolonged the survival time in the SOD1 transgenic mouse.

Clinical trials outcome : Since sodium valproate is an FDA-approved compound with well-known pharmacokinetic and toxicity profiles, it was an attractive candidate for a clinical trial in patients with ALS. The clinical response of 18 enrolled patients was compared to the evolution of 31 ALS out-patients, carefully paired by age, gender, evolution rate and time of the disease, who never received treatment with lithium and/or valproate. The ALS functional rating scale, revised version (ALSFRS-R), was applied at baseline, 1 month, and every 4 months until the outcome (death or an adverse event). Biochemical markers, such as Cu/Zn superoxide dismutase and glutathione peroxidase activity, and reduced glutathione were assayed in plasma samples obtained at the baseline visit and after 5 and 9 months of treatment. The results showed that lithium and valproate co-treatment significantly increased survival, and this treatment also exerted neuroprotection in patients because all three markers reached levels that were not significantly different from the matched samples of healthy donors. The trial stopped after 21 months, when the sample was reduced to under two-thirds, due to the late adverse events of the treatment. The results call for large randomized clinical trials with the dual association, but at low doses to avoid adverse events.

Take home points : Like several other proposed drugs for ALS, Sodium valproate has severe side effects.

5.1.16. Ceftriaxone

What characterizes this drug : Ceftriaxone, sold under the trade name Rocephin, is an antibiotic used for the treatment of a number of bacterial infections.

Relation to the academic research : Ceftriaxone upregulates the excitatory amino acid transporter 2 (EAAT2) of astrocytes, which recycles synaptic glutamate to counter the excitotoxicity of ALS (Rao and Weiss, 2004).

Clinical trials outcome : The clinical trial used an adaptive design, designed to seamlessly move from phases I to III as long as the data suggested that this would make sense. The clinical trial had reached Phase III, with 513 subjects enrolled, when organizers who belong to the Northeast ALS Consortium in Charlestown, Massachusetts, decided to stop everything because it did not seem like the drug was effective. There was no improvement in survival, ALSFRS-R score, or lung capacity.

Take home points : Not very interesting.

5.1.17. Memantine

What characterizes this drug : Memantine is an N-methyl-D-aspartate (NMDA) receptor antagonist capable of blocking glutamate-related excitotoxicity (currently used for Alzheimer's disease). It had been used in no less than 230 clinical trials conducted on fifty different diseases, including kleptomania !

Relation to the academic research : In 2005, a group at the Burnham Institute in La Jolla, California reported a 7 % increase in survival in memantine-treated SOD1 mice.

Clinical trials outcome : In 2010, a group from the Institute of Molecular Medicine at the University of Lisbon in Lisbon, Portugal, presented its results of a phase II/III study on memantine. The study showed that memantine was safe and well tolerated in patients with ALS. Unfortunately, the researchers were unable to highlight the effect of memantine on patient survival.

Another Phase II study commissioned by the University of Alberta in Canada examined the effect of memantine on functional outcomes (no results reported).

Finally, a third phase II study tested both the tolerability and safety of memantine in ALS. The study also investigated whether drug therapy could be correlated with changes in a

CSF[216]. biomarker. Unfortunately, as this study was open, no conclusions could be drawn as to the efficacy of the drug.

Take home points : Although many clinical studies have been conducted, we still have no clear answer as to the efficacy of memantine in ALS.

5.1.18. Methylcobalamine

What characterizes this drug : Methylcobalamin (E0302) is a form of vitamin B12 active in the cytosol, it differs from adenosylcobalamin which is active in mitochondria. Methylcobalamin is physiologically equivalent to vitamin B12 . It can be used to prevent or treat conditions resulting from a lack of vitamin B12 intake. Methylcobalamin is also used in the treatment of peripheral neuropathy and diabetic neuropathy.

Relation to the academic research : There is little interest from ALS scientists, it appears that only one Japanese team did research (and four clinical trials) on Methylcobalamin.

Clinical trials outcome : In 2015, Eisai initiated a double-blind, placebo-controlled, Phase II/III clinical trial investigating the value of a high dose of mecobalamin in ALS, using the delay before the ventilation or death event and the modification of the Japanese ALSFRS-R as the main criteria. The results of the study suggest a trend towards a beneficial effect, but the difference between the primary endpoints between treated and untreated patients was not statistically significant.

In 2016, Eisai Co. withdrew its application for new drug status for high-dose methylcobalamin for ALS in Japan. Meetings with the Japanese regulator, the Pharmaceuticals and Medical Devices Agency (PMDA), clarified that the current application

---

216 Le liquide cérébrospinal est un liquide transparent dans lequel baignent le cerveau et la moelle spinale.

was insufficient to be approved and Eisai subsequently withdrew its application. It is not clear whether the company will continue its efforts to develop methylcobalamin in ALS.

A phase III clinical trial has been ongoing since 2017 by Tokushima University in collaboration with Eisai Co. It is expected to end in March 2020.

Take home points : Probably not very interesting, but the current clinical trial may surprise us.

5.1.19. Masitinib

What characterizes this drug : Masitinib is a tyrosine kinase[217] inhibitor, it is used in the treatment of mast cell tumours in animals, specifically dogs. Convergent evidence suggests that tyrosine kinase inhibitors may slow the progression of ALS, perhaps through multiple mechanisms.

Relation to the academic research : Haruhisa Inoue and colleagues reported that many inhibitors of Src and c-Abl tyrosine kinases improved the survival of motor neurons in ALS patients. The compounds act by stimulating autophagy, which accelerates the elimination of toxic proteins. One of the most potent inhibitors, Bosutinib, improved motor neuron survival by 50 % and slightly prolonged the life of ALS model mice, the authors report.

Tyrosine kinase inhibitors may help in other neurodegenerative diseases such as Alzheimer's disease and Parkinson's disease, which also accumulate toxic proteins and cause

---

217 Tyrosine kinases are a subgroup of the larger class of protein kinases that attach phosphate groups to other amino acids (serine and threonine). Phosphorylation of proteins by kinases is an important mechanism in communicating signals within a cell (signal transduction) and regulating cellular activity, such as cell division. It functions as an "on" or "off" switch in many cellular functions. A number of viruses target tyrosine kinase function during infection.

neuroinflammation, and they can be used at much lower doses for neurodegenerative diseases only for cancer.

Masitinib (marketed as Kinavet or Masivet) is a c-kit tyrosine kinase inhibitor and was originally developed for the treatment of tumors in dogs. Masitinib is currently being tested in patients for the treatment of multiple indications, including cancer, inflammatory diseases, and central nervous system disorders such as multiple sclerosis and ALS.

Masitinib works by targeting and inhibiting the « survival, migration, and activity of mast cells," which are involved in the inflammatory response and regulate the permeability of the blood-brain barrier. Neuroinflammation is a hallmark of ALS, and a potential reduction in neuroinflammation via Masitinib could provide a therapeutic benefit to ALS.

Preclinical studies have suggested that Masitinib inhibits CSF-1R and C-kit tyrosine kinases in microglia, macrophages, and mast cells, which are circulating white blood cells that trigger allergic and inflammatory reactions. In animal models, Masitinib prevents microgliosis and astrogliosis in the spinal cord, as well as the infiltration of mast cells and macrophages into neuromuscular junctions (see Trias and colleagues, 2016).

Clinical trials outcome : In 2013, AB Science, a French company, announced that its phase II clinical trial of Masitinib for the treatment of ALS was extended in a phase III trial. The initial phase II of ALS involved the recruitment of 45 patients. The European Phase III would expand recruitment to 210 patients and evaluate the safety and efficacy of Masitinib for the treatment of ALS.

On March 20, 2015, AB Science announced that its drug candidate, Masitinib, has been designated an orphan drug by the FDA. This status is on a practical level, an important step for conducting clinical studies in the USA.

5.1. List of drugs that have passed Phase I.

In the phase III trial, 394 patients from nine countries took 4.5 mg / kg Masitinib, 3 mg/kg or placebo for almost a year. According to a predefined plan, the researchers stratified the participants into either fast progressors (those who lost more than 1.1 points per month on the revised ALS functional assessment scale) or normal progressors.

About 85 % of participants were normal progressors. In this group, patients receiving 4.5 mg/kg Masitinib retained 3.4 ALSFRS-R points more than the placebo group during the study. This resulted in a 27 % lower functional decline over this period, a clinically significant difference, according to Jesus Mora of Carlos III Hospital in Madrid, who presented the results of the clinical trial at ENCALS 2017. Participants treated patients maintained greater lung capacity and reported a better quality of life than the placebo group. They were able to live 20 months before their disease progressed by nine or more points under ALSFRS-R, compared to 16 months for those taking placebo.

Participants who took the lower dose of 3 mg / kg also reported a better quality of life, but their tendency to a slower functional decline was not significant. Treatment of normal progressors with low dose Masitinib at 3.0 mg / kg / day did not significantly reduce functional decline.

The researchers found no significant benefit for both doses in those with rapid progression rates or in the entire cohort.

The results suggest, according to Mora, that Masitinib may be « an important new therapeutic option » for people with ALS who are progressing 1.1 points or less per month. But Jeremy Shefner warns that additional studies on Masitinib are needed before drawing any conclusions. A key question is why no effect is observed in people progressing rapidly. According to Shefner, it is in this sub-group of patients that the effect of a therapy is most likely to be detected (it seems however that this is not an opinion shared by the majority of specialists). « If you're looking at a subgroup and trying to figure out which subgroup is most likely to be sensitive to disease-modifying therapy," Shefner said, « it's usually the other way around. fastest progressors are those in would see an effect more easily. But according to Mora, this subset could simply have a different form of ALS based on a separate mechanism.

According to Shefner, another concern is that people with ALS in the placebo group appeared to be progressing faster than expected, which could adversely affect the interpretation of the results of the clinical trial by artificially introducing the drug as more effective. Among the normal progressors, whose initial progression rate was 0.5 points per month on the ALSFRS-R[218], scoring scale, those randomized on placebo decreased by 1.1 points per month during the treatment phase. treatment, while the declining slope of the Masitinib group has changed very little, Shefner explained.

In 2018, the European Medicines Agency voted against Masitinib's approval as a treatment for ALS, in part for reasons related to concerns about the results of Phase III clinical trials and their subsequent analysis.

AB Science withdrew its appeal to the European Medicines Agency in 2018. The decision announced by AB Science is based in part on the inability to provide additional data during this "reconsideration" proceeding. These results include the results of the Phase III clinical trial examining the safety of Masitinib and additional preclinical analysis to further elucidate its mechanism of action.

---

218 ALSFRS-R includes 12 questions that can have a score of 0 to 4. A score of 0 for a question would indicate no function, while a score of 4 would indicate a complete function (that of a person without disease). This scale is useful for physicians to diagnose patients, measure disease progression, as well as for researchers when selecting patients for a study and for measuring the potential effects of a clinical trial. The ALSFRS-R scale has some limitations, as it is not useful to compare the scores of people with different beginnings.

found that Edaravone reduced the functional decline of 2.49 points ALSFRS-RR over six months compared to placebo in a subgroup of people recently diagnosed with the disease.

It is not clear whether the benefit observed in the clinical trial could benefit people with long-term ALS. It is also not known how to recognize ALS patients who would respond positively to this treatment.

Take home points : Some patients may benefit of Edaravone.

5.2.2. Treeway

Some people were worried about the cost and the logistics of Edaravone treatment, which required repeated infusions. Muller from Treeway hopes to solve this problem. Muller heard about Edaravone for the first time during a trip to Japan. His company, Treeway, is looking for an oral version of the drug, which would be more practical for the chronic treatment of ALS. (People who receive Edaravone after a stroke only need it for two weeks.) In the two phase I clinical trials, Treeway administered several doses of the oral preparation to healthy volunteers and single doses to people with ALS. The company had planned to launch a phase II / 3 trial in 2016, but at mid-2019 there is still no plan announced.

5.2. Drugs that have successfully completed a phase III (2019).

5.3. Drugs currently in phase III (2019).

As those drugs are still in trial, there is less to recount about them.

5.3.1. ACTH

Identifier on ClinicalTrials.gov : NCT03068754

Adrenocorticotropic hormone (ACTH, also adrenocorticotropin, corticotropin) is a tropic polypeptide hormone produced and secreted by the anterior pituitary gland. It stimulates the adrenal cortex to release glucocorticoids. It is also used as a drug and diagnostic agent.

In SOD1 mice, and for a specific dose range, ACTH significantly delayed the onset of disease and paralysis. ACTH significantly reduced soluble SOD1 levels in the spinal cord and CNS tissues of G93A-SOD1-treated mice, as well as in fibroblasts in culture.

End date : October 2021

5.3.2. Arimoclomol

Identifier on ClinicalTrials.gov : NCT03491462

Arimoclomol is an experimental drug developed by CytRx Corporation. It is thought that Arimoclomol works by stimulating a normal cellular protein repair pathway by activating molecular chaperones. Because damaged and localized protein aggregates play a role in many diseases, CytRx believes that Arimoclomol could treat many of these diseases.

ORARIALS-01 is a randomized, double-blind, placebo-controlled trial (NCT03491462) in progress in 30 centers in North America and Europe. It evaluates the efficacy and safety of Arimoclomol capsules in 245 adults with ALS.

The trial has now completed recruitment and Arimoclomol has started to be administered since August 2018. Following initial screening, patients were randomized to a 2 : 1 ratio of Arimoclomol or placebo for 76 weeks. Up to 18 patients under stable treatment with Radicava (Edaravone), by Mitsubishi Tanabe, will also participate in the study in the United States.

Its main objective is to measure the efficacy of Arimoclomol through a combined evaluation of function and survival. The first results are expected in the first half of 2021.

In 2011, global rights to Arimoclomol were purchased by the Danish biotech company Orphazyme ApS. Orphazyme concluded a partnership agreement with Worldwide in late 2017, a global contract research organization.

Patients who have completed ORARIALS-01 will be allowed to continue or start treatment with Arimoclomol as part of the open study (NCT03836716), which is due to be completed by August 2020.

5.3.3. CannTrust CBD Oil

Identifier on ClinicalTrials.gov : NCT03690791

This is a randomized, double-blind, placebo-controlled study conducted on a CannTrust CBD Oil extract in patients with amyotrophic lateral sclerosis or motor neuropathy. Participants will be randomized to a ratio of 1 : 1 to receive CannTrust CBD oil or placebo (both in capsules). The duration of treatment is 6 months with a safety follow-up of one month. Participants will be monitored monthly, either face-to-face or by telephone, and will be assessed to collect data for the study objectives, such as ALSFRS-R, Forced Vital Capacity, Pain and Spasticity Score. and quality of life. Thirty participants will be randomized.

End date : January 2021

5.3.4. Cu(II)ATSM

Identifier on ClinicalTrials.gov : NCT04082832

Cu(II)ATSM Oral Suspension Powder, 36 mg, should be reconstituted with diluent (15 mL of sugar-free flavored pharmaceutical syrup) to provide an oral suspension for immediate consumption. The recommended dose is 72 mg (2 bottles) on an empty stomach each day before breakfast.

Collaborative Medicinal Development, LLC is a portfolio company of Cthulhu Ventures LLC.

In addition to Cu(II)ATSM, CMD is also developing novel small molecule ferroptose inhibitors as leading treatments for the treatment of neurodegenerative diseases, including Alzheimer's disease, Huntington's disease and Parkinson's disease.

End date : December 2020

5.3.5. Deferiprone

Identifier on ClinicalTrials.gov : NCT03293069

The alteration of iron metabolism is reported in animal models of amyotrophic lateral sclerosis (ALS) as well as in sporadic and genetic forms (SOD1 and C9orf72) of ALS. The high concentration of iron in the brain, due to its high energy demand (high oxygen consumption), makes the motor neurons particularly vulnerable to energy deficit and oxidative stress. Post mortem examinations and MRI examinations in patients with ALS revealed evidence of iron accumulation in the central motor tract ; and a high level of serum ferritin, which is a marker of iron levels, is associated with a poorer prognosis.

In ALS mouse models, the use of iron chelators has demonstrated neuroprotection and increased life expectancy, suggesting that removal of excess iron from the brain can prevent neuronal loss and, therefore, promote slow progression of the disease.

Conservative iron chelation refers to a modality whereby much of the iron that binds to the chelator is redistributed in the body rather than exhausted.

By using a conservative iron chelator, Deferiprone, a very good safety profile was observed in a pilot safety study. Deferiprone removed excess iron from the brain regions, reduced the damage caused by oxidation and cell death associated with regional iron deposition without any apparent negative impact on the iron levels required. Today, the efficacy of this new therapeutic modality of neuroprotection is being evaluated in a randomized, double-blind, placebo-controlled, multicenter trial.

The clinical trial ends in April 2022.

5.3.6. Ibudilast

Identifier on ClinicalTrials.gov : NCT04057898

Ibudilast (AV-411 or MN-166) is an anti-inflammatory drug used primarily in Japan. It acts as a phosphodiesterase inhibitor, maximally inhibiting the PDE4 subtype, but also showing significant inhibition of other PDE subtypes.

The clinical trial ends in June 2022.

5.3.7. NurOwn

Identifier on ClinicalTrials.gov : NCT03280056

NurOwn is an experimental cell therapy of BrainStorm Cell Therapeutics that contains mesenchymal bone marrow stromal cells, secreting neurotrophic factors, including BDNF, GDNF and HGF. Bone marrow stem cells are collected from each patient, differentiated into cells that produce neuroprotective growth factors, and then re-injected into the muscle or spinal cord.

Brainstorm therapy differs from that of Neuralstem, Inc., which transfuses neural stem cells from fetal tissue into the spinal cord of people with ALS, while that of Neuralstem hopes to promote the birth of new motor neurons[221], that of Brainstorm encourages the survival of the neurons in place.

This therapy should be given every few months.

The clinical trial ends in July 2020.

5.3.8. ODM-109

Identifier on ClinicalTrials.gov : NCT03505021

ODM-109 aims in part to improve breathing during ALS by improving the performance of the diaphragm muscles. The drug that is administered orally, increases the force of contraction of certain muscles by increasing the calcium sensitivity of troponin C.

This medication is an oral formulation of levosimendan. An intravenous formulation of levosimendan, marketed as Simdax, is clinically approved in some countries for the treatment of acute heart failure.

The positive inotropic[222] and vasodilative effects of Levosimendan are related to its ability to increase sensitivity to calcium and to open ATP-sensitive potassium ion (K +) channels (mitoKATPchannels)

Levosimendan positively affects the synthesis of mitochondrial adenosine triphosphate, conferring cardioprotection and possible neuronal protection during ischemic trauma. In a spinal cord injury model, it has been reported that levosimendan attenuates neurological motor dysfunction. This finding is supported by the fact that diazoxide is an effective

---

221 One may wonder why they would not be sick, in the very unlikely case, where they could develop and replace existing motor neurons.

222 An inotrope is an agent that alters the force or energy of muscular contractions.

neuroprotectant, as demonstrated by a rat ischemia reperfusion study.

The clinical trial ends in October 2020.

5.3.9. Tofersen

Identifier on ClinicalTrials.gov : NCT02623699 and NCT03070119

IONIS-SOD1Rx or BIIB067 is a 2.0 generation antisense drug specifically designed to inhibit the production of mutant superoxide dismutase (SOD1). SOD1 mutations account for about 20 % of familial ALS cases.

This medicine is the result of a collaboration between Biogen and IONIS Pharmaceuticals (formerly ISIS). A Phase III clinical trial is recruiting participants in April 2019. The study is scheduled to be completed by May 2020. The researchers are also considering antisense treatment for another genetic form of ALS caused by C9orf72 gene extensions.

The clinical trial ends in May 2020.

5.3.10. Tudca

Identifier on ClinicalTrials.gov : NCT03800524

Patients enrolled will be randomized into one of two treatment groups : TUDCA or an identical oral placebo. Randomization will be done in a one to one ratio for both arms.

TUDCA will be administered orally at a dose of 1 g twice daily (2 g daily) for 18 months. Patients will also take riluzole at a dose of 50 mg twice daily (100 mg daily).

The randomization of patients will take place after a screening period (introduction) of 12 weeks (3 months) with 3 evaluations spaced 6 weeks apart. Clinical evaluations during the trial phase will be conducted every three months. This will measure the rate of progression before and after the start of treatment (active or placebo).

It is a European project, the end date is June 2021.

5.3. Drugs currently in phase III (2019).

5.4. Which drug for each ALS subtype ?

Now that a doctor has a number of ALS medications at his disposal, how can he choose the best for his patient's situation ? Are there practical approaches to finding this with acceptable uncertainty for each patient ?

Yes, since research has been very focused on the different gene mutations involved in ALS, drug development has often been specific to a target gene. So if the patient's genome is completely sequenced, we will know whether or not there are mutations, and if the patient has been diagnosed but has no mutations, then it is most likely a TDP-43 type of proteinopathy.

- If the patient has a SOD1 mutation with or without a CCS mutation, Cu(II)ATSM will be useful, but even more if there is a CCS mutation. Edaravone also seems to be useful in this case. There is also a gene therapy, Tofersen (BIIB067), in clinical trial phase III.

- If the patient has a FUS mutation, their doctor may seek to increase the expression of one of the PARPs.

- If the patient has the TDP-43 mutation, an ASO might be helpful. It is surprising that there are ASOs for SOD1 and C9orf72 and no ASOs have been developed for TDP-43, which affects more than 90 % of ALS cases. This ASO[223] may be interesting, but it is neither tested nor marketed.

- If the patient has a C9orf72 mutation, some ASOs have also been discussed in the literature (uniQure's miQURE and Biogen's BIIB078). But in this case, the doctor might also be interested in PARP inhibitors.

---

223 https://www.ncbi.nlm.nih.gov/pmc/articles/PMC5902603/

- If there are no mutations or mutations in the list below, this is probably the most common case and for the moment, Arimoclomol is the best option. The ASO[224] may be interesting, but it is neither tested nor obviously marketed.

- If the patient has another mutation, it involves only very few cases and there is not enough room to discuss about it here.

- In all cases, it is advisable to obtain neurotrophic factors in addition to other treatments. For now, Nurown seems a good choice, but different neurotrophic factors have been tested for decades and have sometimes worked well. Masitinib is also an interesting option in this case. If they existed, ointments locally applying neurotrophic factors on the nerves and muscles affected, would probably be a good choice.

---

224 https://www.ncbi.nlm.nih.gov/pmc/articles/PMC5902603/

5.5. Different types of therapies.

5.5.1. First glimpse of gene therapy for SMA.

The following text is about spinal muscular atrophy, but it is really interesting for patients with ALS and Alzheimer's because similar drugs could be made to target TDP-43.

Research on motor neuron diseases has resulted in a drug to treat motor neuron spinal muscular atrophy (SMA). This medicine is called Zolgensma.

This disease is also a motor neuron disease, such as ALS. But while the cause (or causes) of ALS is not known, that of SMA is very well identified and originates from a defect on a gene, so a gene therapy is ideally suited to remedy this situation. This is also the same situation in familial ALS, where a large number of genes are mutated.

The most obvious target case for familial ALS, would be SOD1, which represents a minor percentage of cases, but where restoring proper functioning should halt the progression of the disease because it is point mutations, or a nucleotide is replaced by another nucleotide. For other genes, such as C9orf72 where the repeats are considerably large, it will probably be necessary to both inactivate the mutated gene and substitute it with a gene that functions correctly. For both types of genes, gene therapies have already been developed and are in clinical trials, but these two experimental therapies seem rudimentary because they only make the gene silent, which does not seem very desirable.

A gene therapy is really desirable in general, because it only takes one injection, where therapies like Nurown require a dangerous intrathecal injection every few months and probably for life. In addition, the cost of producing and administering gene therapy is in the order of a few thousand euros[225], even if Novartis sells the injection for the SMA at more than 2 million euros.

The most severe version of motor neuron atrophy (SMA), usually causes paralysis and death two years after birth. SMA results from missense or deletion mutations of the SMN1 gene, which encodes the survival of the motor neuron protein. Once the motor neurons die, the muscles wilt without stimulation causing the atrophy that gave the disease its name.

Humans have a second SMN gene, SMN2, but a single nucleotide difference from SMN1 code leads mainly to an alternative splice form lacking exon 7. This shorter isoform is unstable and degrades rapidly. Nevertheless, the small amount of complete SMN protein produced by SMN2 may be sufficient to allow people with two mutated copies of SMN1 to survive. In fact, the disease has a spectrum of gravity based on the amount of SMN2 expressed.

Some SMN1 mutation carriers with type IV have no symptoms for up to 30 years, but the most severe and common form of SMA, type I, which has almost no expression of SMN2, is the disease that paralyzes infants.

At the 26th International Symposium on ALS / MND in 2015, Brian Kaspar of the National Children's Hospital in Columbus, Ohio, showed the results of a Phase I clinical trial for infants with SMA. The babies who had participated in Brian Kaspar's Phase I clinical trial were alive and squirming in a delicious way. He showed a video of a little girl, at six months of her treatment, who could sit without support, something that infants with SMA are unable to do.

---

225 The cost of producing an AAV9 viral load, which is commonly used in gene therapies, is less than 500 euros (for example at AddGene).

For the clinical trial, Kaspar and colleagues used the innocuous AAV9 adeno-associated virus to transmit a functional SMN1[226] gene to motoneurons. There are different types of AAV viruses, and the AAV9 virus is able to cross the blood-brain barrier and bind to cellular proteins incorporating galactose (Foust and colleagues, 2009, Shen and colleagues, 2011). One dose contains about 200 trillion viruses per kilogram. Although the AAV9 virus preferentially transduces[227] astrocytes in adult mice, in larger animals it also targets motor neurons and oligodendrocytes.

Once it has found its target cells, the virus slides its genetic material into the nucleus, where it persists as an extrachromosomal DNA fragment, so that a treatment should theoretically provide the SMN protein for life.

Kaspar's organization has granted a treatment license to AveXis Inc. (now owned by Novartis) gene therapy company. The rest is history.

---

226 This is a "small" gene, only 28913bp, but special methods of viral load transfer have to be implemented, since it is more than 10 times the capacity of an AAV9

227 Transduction is the process by which DNA is transferred from one bacterium to another by a virus.

5.5.2. Therapies with local production of neurotrophic..

Although motor neurons can be created from induced and transplanted pluripotent cells in the spinal cord, *these motoneurons do not generally integrate well with neuromuscular networks*. Moreover, these neurons would probably be subject to the same degeneration as that affecting the original motor neurons. It is therefore necessary to help these motor neurons by means of neurotrophic factors. Assistance to lower motor neurons, however, has never been studied in the context of ALS, which is another mystery of ALS research.

5.5.2.1. Continuous infusion administration

It has been shown that certain trophic factors promote cell survival and are protective *in-vitro* and *in-vivo* models of neuronal degeneration. These are ciliary neurotrophic factor (CNTF), brain-derived neurotrophic factor (BDNF), glial-derived neurotrophic factor (GDNF), insulin-like growth factor-1 (IGF-1), vascular endothelial growth factor (VEGF) and granulocyte colony stimulating factor (G-CSF).

The CNTF, one of the first NTFs studied in ALS model animals, was injected intra-peritoneally to SMA model mice as early as 1992 or subcutaneous to wobbler mice in 1994. In addition, Mitsumoto and colleagues, demonstrated at the same time a synergistic effect of CNTF and BDNF.

Intra-peritoneal or intra-cerebroventricular injection of VEGF into ALS model mice and rats around 2005 prolonged their lifespan and improved their motor performance. Similar data were observed at the same time in a sporadic model of ALS rats induced by excitotoxic administration of AMPA.

But permanently opening the central nervous system to receive an infusion of neurotrophic factor has never been considered in the case of ALS because it would expose the patient to too many risks.

5.5.2.2. Administration by viral load

GDNF injected intramuscularly in SOD1 G93A in 2002, was associated with delayed onset and delayed progression of the disease[228].

Many studies have focused on IGF-1. Intramuscular injection of AAV virus carrying DNA capable of secreting IGF-1 in infected cells to SOD1 G93A mice in 2003 by the Kaspar team before or at the time of the symptoms of the disease delayed the onset of the disease and increased their lifespan[229].

Intraparenchymal perfusion of the spinal cord, with similar therapy, was also tested in 2008, showing higher expression of IGF-1 but no more efficacy, whereas stereotactic injection into deep cerebellar nuclei in 2008 significantly extended the lifespan of mice[230].

Recently, injection of the adeno-associated auto-complementary viral vector 9 (scAAV9), a more efficient transducing agent for IGF-1, prolonged the survival and motor performance of SOD1 G93A mice during intramuscular or intravenous injection.

The efficacy of intraspinal delivery has been demonstrated for AAV-G-CSF in SOD1 G93A mice with minimal systemic effects in 2011[231].

---

228 https://www.ncbi.nlm.nih.gov/pubmed/12177190
229 https://www.ncbi.nlm.nih.gov/pubmed/12907804
230 https://www.ncbi.nlm.nih.gov/pubmed/18388910
231 https://www.ncbi.nlm.nih.gov/pubmed/21139572

5.5.3. Stem cell therapies

5.5.3.1. Distribution of neurotrophic factors by stem cell-based therapy

Different types of stem cells exist, depending on their source, potential for differentiation and availability, and are suitable for the treatment of neurodegenerative diseases such as ALS.

A study in 2001 tested 3 patients using a G-CSF subcutaneous treatment protocol and CD34 + stem cell isolation, followed by intrathecal administration of the collected stem cells and showed minimal adverse effects[232].

It was demonstrated in the mid-2000 s that the transplantation of human neural stem cells into the lumbar protuberance of SOD1 G93A rats delayed the onset and progression of the disease[233], [234]. Intraspinal administration of human neural progenitor cells retarded disease progression in SOD1 G93A mice in 2017.

Neural stem cells have also been designed to secrete one or more specific neurotrophic factors. Intrathecal transplantation of VEGF overexpressing human neural stem cells in SOD1 G93A mice, as early as 2009, delayed the onset of the disease and increased survival with the integration and differentiation of NSC-VEGF in the spinal cord[235].

Human neural progenitor cells have also been genetically engineered to secrete GDNF. Transplantation of such modified cells in the SOD1 rat was integrated into the spinal cord, resulted in limited motor neuron degeneration but failed to improve motor function[236].

---

232 https://www.ncbi.nlm.nih.gov/pubmed/11798518
233 https://www.ncbi.nlm.nih.gov/pubmed/17038899
234 https://www.ncbi.nlm.nih.gov/pubmed/19326469
235 https://www.ncbi.nlm.nih.gov/pubmed/19626053
236 https://www.ncbi.nlm.nih.gov/pubmed/15871682

In 2018, it has been shown that hPNC-GDNF transplantation into the cortex can prolong survival of SOD1 G93A rats and is safe for primates[237].

5.5.3.2. Mesenchymal stromal cells (MSC)

MSCs derived from the bone marrow can exert neuroprotective effects via paracrine, or control mechanisms, such as the release of anti-inflammatory, anti-apoptotic and neurotrophic factors, and by inducing other types of cells to adopt a protective phenotype. Neuroinflammatory markers have been detected in the neural tissues of patients with ALS. Mesenchymal stromal cells exhibit immunomodulatory properties by secreting anti-inflammatory cytokines such as TGF-β or IL-10. Promising results can therefore be expected with treatment with mesenchymal stromal cells.

There have been about twenty clinical trials, provided by about fifteen groups, who use MSCs in the framework of ALS.

MSCs also offer the following advantages :

- They are easy to obtain.

- They have an in-vitro expansion capacity.

- Lack of immunosuppressive therapy to prevent rejection.

- Reduced risk of malignant transformation[238].

- MSCs are able to differentiate into lines that resemble neurons and glial cells.

Italian researchers led by Mazzini, as early as 2008, intraspinally injected bone marrow mesenchymal stromal cells into SOD1 G93A mice[239].

---

237 https://www.ncbi.nlm.nih.gov/pubmed/29656478
238 https://www.ncbi.nlm.nih.gov/pubmed/20937945
239 https://www.ncbi.nlm.nih.gov/pubmed/18586098

Also in 2008, the intramuscular transplantation of human BM-MSC genetically modified to secrete GDNF in SOD1 G93A rats showed a decrease in motoneuron loss and an increase in overall lifespan[240]. The researchers attribute synergistic effects attributed to the production of vascular endothelial growth factor (VEGF).

In 2010, one study administered intrathecal in 19 patients, MSCs obtained by bone marrow aspiration. Although all patients received MSC by intrathecal lumbar puncture, 9 of the 19 patients also received intravenous MSC[241]. No serious adverse events and a 6-month period of disease stability were reported following the procedure. This team is behind the treatment named Nurown.

In 2012, the Italian team injected [242] mesenchymal bone marrow stromal cells (BM-MSC) intravenously into SOD1 G93A mice, which led to a decrease in motor neuron degeneration, an improvement in survival and motor function, as well as pro-inflammatory factors. This team will have conducted 5 trials in total.

5.5.3.3. Therapies for non-neuronal cells

The surrounding non-neuronal cells in the spinal cord and at the neuromuscular junction appear to play an important role in the pathogenesis of ALS. The potential therapeutic benefit of modifying the microenvironment of motor neurons has therefore been the focus of many studies aimed at modifying non-neuronal cells and providing them with support for neurotrophic factors.

---

240 https://www.ncbi.nlm.nih.gov/pubmed/18797452
241 https://www.ncbi.nlm.nih.gov/pubmed/20937945
242 https://www.ncbi.nlm.nih.gov/pubmed/22481270

5.5. Different types of therapies.

In a 2008 astrocyte study, SOD1-G37R mice with reduced expression of mutant SOD1 in astrocytes exhibited delayed microglial activation that slowed disease progression[243].

Other studies have investigated the transplantation of glial-restricted precursors into the cervical spine of SOD1-G93A mice. The result of this intervention was prolonged survival, reduced motor neuron loss, and decreased motor functional decline[244].

243 https://www.ncbi.nlm.nih.gov/pubmed/18246065/
244 https://www.ncbi.nlm.nih.gov/pubmed/18931666

5.5.4. Therapies using an anti-cancer drug

Studies by McGurk, Gomes, Guo and their colleagues have identified Tankyrase, a poly (ADP-ribose) polymerase, or PARP, as a potent regulator of TDP-43 protein characteristics in Drosophila cell models and mammals of ALS.

5.5.4.1. Cytoplasmic aggregates

They also showed that veliparib, an inhibitor of PARP-1/2 nuclear activity, attenuated the formation of TDP-43-induced cytoplasmic aggregates in mammalian cells. The treatment of rodent spinal cord cultures with Veliparib has been shown to attenuate TDP-43-induced neuronal cell loss.

In recent years, it has become apparent that many ALS proteins, such as TDP-43, may undergo a phase transitions, and this process may contribute to both their biological function and their their propensity for aggregation in the disease.

More specifically, TDP-43 and other ALS proteins converge to membrane-free organelles. Although these granules are only formed during periods of cellular stress and retain highly dynamic liquid-like characteristics, it is thought that persistent granules could potentially cause pathological aggregation of TDP-43 via a liquid-solid switch during maturation of granules. Otherwise, the TDP-43 protein could also pass directly from a diffuse state to an aggregated state.

Moreover, the manipulation of proteins regulating the stress response is beneficial in animal and cellular models of ALS[245], [246]. Despite the elements involving stress pathways in ALS, it is not clear whether they are the cause or the consequence of the disease process.

---

245 https://www.ncbi.nlm.nih.gov/pubmed/28405022/
246 https://www.ncbi.nlm.nih.gov/pubmed/19330001/

5.5.4.2. Over-activation of PARPs

It has been known since 2003 that PARP is somewhat weakly linked to ALS[247]. In 2014, it was suggested that FUS as belonging to PARP family, were components of the cellular response to DNA damage, and that defects in this response (such as mutations) could contribute to ALS.[248].

Recently, this response to DNA damage (DDR) has been shown to be induced by the repeated expansion of C9orf72 in amyotrophic lateral sclerosis.[249]. Cells activate the DNA damage response (DDR) to repair this damage. However, if the damage can not be repaired, apoptosis is triggered.

Poly (ADP-ribose) polymerase (PARP) is a family of proteins involved in a number of cellular processes such as DNA repair, genomic stability, and programmed cell death. PARPs are a family of enzymes that add PAR groups to other proteins. There are 17 known PARPs in mammals and they perform many functions. One function is to locate DNA breaks by recruiting the DNA repair mechanism, which includes ALS-related FUS protein (Naumann and colleagues, 2018).

Could the over-activation of PARPs contribute to ALS ? Maybe the energy demand of DNA repair mechanisms is too high and it kills the cell, just as a cancer patient often dies, not cancer, but pneumonia or thrombosis.

The big advantage of PARP inhibitors is that a few are already approved for clinical use. The FDA has approved three PARP1/2 inhibitors for ovarian cancer.

Most cancer patients using these drugs tolerate them well compared to chemotherapy, at least in the short term (for a review, see Mirza and colleagues, 2018). The use of pre-

---

247 https://www.ncbi.nlm.nih.gov/pubmed/12528821
248 https://www.ncbi.nlm.nih.gov/pubmed/24049082
249 https://www.ncbi.nlm.nih.gov/pubmed/28481984

approved drugs may accelerate the development of treatment for ALS.

Of course, to treat ALS, medications must cross the blood-brain barrier. Veliparib and niraparib are known to do this.

Many questions remain unanswered :

- This involvement of PARPs in the pathology of ALS does not explain the very localized onset or the spread observed in ALS.

- We do not know why PARP activity is high in ALS. It could force the aggregation of TDP-43 into the cytoplasm, but it could also be a defense against another stress that will be reinforced if PARP is inhibited.

- It will be important to determine if this strategy works in the mammalian models of the disease, because flies are very different from mammals.

- It is unclear whether PARP inhibitors, in addition to preventing the formation of new aggregates, destroy existing aggregates of TDP-43 in neurons. This is important because, since neurons in people with ALS already have TDP-43 pathology, PARP inhibitors would be useless if existing aggregates are not destroyed.

- In addition, it is unclear if this strategy could be beneficial. For example, some scientists have suggested that it would be beneficial to stimulate, not inhibit, PARS activity in FUS ALS. The idea would be to give these enzymes more time to repair breaks in DNA in ALS neurons. In fact, treatment with vagiparib, a PARP 1/2 inhibitor, can lead to poor localization and aggregation of FUS in the cytosol of cells in culture, contributing to cytotoxicity (Naumann and colleagues, 2018).

- In addition, PARP-1 inhibitor 5-iodo-6-amino-1,2-benzopyrone did not provide any benefit in a mouse model of SOD1 ALS (Andreassen and colleagues, 2001).

- Neurologists are concerned about the long-term use of these drugs in the treatment of chronic neurodegenerative diseases such as ALS. Interfering with the long-term process of DNA repair would be dangerous for cells that reproduce rapidly.

- It may be more appropriate to use tankyrase inhibitors (PARP5) instead of PARP1 / 2 because these enzymes probably do not participate in the DNA repair process, making them potentially safer. Several highly selective PARP5 inhibitors are under development for cancer (Haikarainen and colleagues, 2014), but none have been clinically tested.

5.5.5. **Antisense oligonucleotide therapies.**

Antisense oligonucleotides are single strands of DNA or RNA that are complementary to a chosen sequence. They are short : the therapeutic ASOs have a length of between 18 and 30 base pairs. In the case of antisense RNAs, they prevent the translation into protein of certain strands of messenger RNAs by binding to them.

When the genetic sequence of a particular gene is known to cause a particular disease, it is possible to synthesize a strand of nucleic acid (DNA, RNA or a chemical analogue) that will bind to the messenger RNA (mRNA) produced by this gene and prevent its translation into protein, which amounts to disabling this gene for this protein (but not for other proteins from different "splicing"). This is possible because mRNA is a simple strand.

This synthesized nucleic acid is termed "antisense" oligonucleotide (ASO) because its base sequence is complementary to the messenger RNA of the gene (mRNA), which is called "sense" sequence (so that a sense segment of mRNA « 5'-AAGGUC » -3 '"would be blocked by the antisense mRNA segment » 3'-UUCCAG-5' ").

Spinraza (Nusinersen) is a drug used in the treatment of spinal muscular atrophy. In December 2016, it became the first approved drug used in the treatment of this disorder.

Like any ASO, it needs to be administered periodically, so it is less attractive than competing Zolgensma gene therapy. It also has several side effects. Most current ASO treatments do not cross the blood-brain barrier. Therefore, CNS targets should be administered by intraventricular injection into mice or by lumbar puncture in humans.

Nusinersen costs $ 750,000 the first year and $ 375,000 a year in the United States, starting from 2019.

It is interesting to wonder about the cost, because producing antisense oligonucleotides is very easy, it can probably be done in any hospital or university laboratory. Indeed, once someone knows the correct sequence, it is trivial to buy one among the many companies[250] that synthesize this product as a service, those companies will sell it as long it will not being used on humans.

However finding which ASO will be useful is incredibly complex. Researchers need to design many (thousands) ASOs, each designed to combine with different extracts of the RNA sequence, to find those that have most effectively knocked down the expression of the target protein.

Absorption in the CNS is an active process and is not uniform for all types of cells or neurons. Nucleic acids are susceptible to nuclease degradation and have low protein binding and thus ineffective tissue uptake, preventing their use as drugs.

Many types of modifications to nucleotides and their linkages can enhance various properties, thus increasing the relevance of ASO as drugs. Most of these modifications modify the pharmacokinetics (improvement of nuclease resistance leading to a longer half-life), pharmacodynamics (higher affinity for the target RNA) or endocytic absorption, controlled by specific sets of surface proteins cellular.

And then this drug should be tested on animal models and in case of success in humans. All this requires years, staffing and money and often this process fails, so the cost of research must also factor in the cost of unsuccessful attempts.

5.5.5.1. List of antisense oligonucleotides for ALS :

- ATXN2 (the gene that encodes Ataxin-2 protein) is a disease susceptibility gene for ALS and the interruption

---

250https://www.bio-rad.com/en-us/applications-technologies/oligonucleotides-design-applications of the interaction between TDP-43 and Ataxin-2 is a promising target for the treatment of ALS and other diseases. In 2010, the work of Aaron Gitler and Nancy Bonini at the University of Pennsylvania showed that repeated expansions of mid-size CAG are significantly associated with the risk of developing amyotrophic lateral sclerosis. ATXN2 is therefore an interesting target for a therapy using antisense oligonucleotides.

- A reformulated version of IONIS-SOD1Rx (BIIB067) is undergoing Phase I clinical trials by Ionis Pharmaceuticals and Biogen. In 2019, Biogen develops its drug BIIB078 which targets the specific messenger RNA emerging from the C9orf72 gene in order to degrade it, eliminating RNA and preventing the production of the abnormal protein that it encodes. BIIB078 largely preserves normal C9orf72 protein.

- Ionis Pharmaceuticals and Biogen have initiated a Phase I clinical trial of a therapeutic ASO targeting C9orf72 for ALS.

For those who are interested, there are bioinformatic tools for designing ASOs[251], [252].

---

251 https://github.com/MirkoLedda/polyoligo
252 https://github.com/davidhoover/DNAWorks

5.5.6. Other Therapies

5.5.6.1. Metals : Cu(II)ATSM

A comparison has been made between different metals and ALS, particularly the metals involved in oxidation reactions such as iron, but also copper and zinc, since the SOD1 protein contains some. It is estimated that about half of all proteins contain a metal, either to stabilize the protein at one fold or to lower the energy cost of a chemical reaction.

Therapeutic Cu(II)ATSM was found to increase the life expectancy of mice expressing human transgenes SOD1 G93A and SOD1G37R. In addition, Cu(II)ATSM is currently undergoing a Phase I / II clinical trial in Australia for the treatment of ALS.

Several studies show that when human CCS is coexpressed in low expression SOD1 G93A mice, an apparent deficiency of copper appears in the spinal cord. These animals die eight times faster than those carrying only the SOD1 mutation. These results suggest that overexpression of CCS alters the copper import into mitochondria by creating a copper deficit by giving priority to copper over SOD1.

Non-metallized ATSM has a high affinity for Cu2+. However, there was no evidence of improvement or exacerbation of ALS in SOD1 mouse models (Vieira and colleagues, 2017). But as Cu(II)ATSM, it has consistently and independently demonstrated distinct salvage and neuroprotective properties in various mutant SOD1 mouse models. This success led to the use of Cu(II)ATSM in clinical trials of ALS patients[253].

The results were favorable and prompted to continue phase II trials of Cu(II)ATSM in Australia.

253« *Phase 1 Dose Escalation and PK Study of Cu(II)ATSM in ALS/ MND* », 2016

In addition to ALS, Cu(II)ATSM has been shown to be effective in reversing parkinsonism defects in various disease models, both in-vitro and in-vivo (Hung and colleagues, 2012). What is extremely interesting is that it is thought that these models are not related to the activity of the SOD1 protein.

In the context of Parkinson's disease, peroxynitrite induces nitration and aggregation of α-synuclein. Nitrated α-synuclein is neurotoxic and injection of this molecule into rat rat substantia nigra (SNPC) produces many pathological features of Parkinson's disease.

In mid-2019[254], the scientists used a mouse model induced by an environmental neurotoxin, which produces features resembling the Guamean variants of ALS and parkinsonism (ALS-PDC).

Unlike the widely used transgenic ALS mouse models, their model shows a much slower evolution of neuronal changes, but it is progressive and provides well-defined sequential deficits that occur initially in the mouse as motor neuron degeneration, as in the Classic ALS, sometimes followed by deterioration of the cortex and hippocampus, leading to cognitive decline.

The BSSG produces features resembling the Guamean variants of ALS and Parkinsonism. DMSO is known to be neurotoxic

The animals were randomly divided into five groups, with five animals per group (n = 5) :

- Control,
- DMSO control,
- BSSG treatment,
- Cu(II)ATSM treatment,
- BSSG / Cu(II)ATSM treatment.

---

254 https://www.ncbi.nlm.nih.gov/pubmed/31181282

Experiments have shown that in this model, the toxicity of DMSO did not lower the level of functional motoneurons below the threshold that would affect the motor functions of animals, and these animals were able to maintain their performance during behavioral evaluations.

Treatment with Cu(II)ATSM lowered the elevation of microglia in the BSSG group. However, the difference between the BSSG group and the BSSG group treated with Cu(II)ATSM was not significant.

Interestingly, although motor neurons were reduced in the DMSO group, the level of microglia remained comparable to that of the control group. It is possible that the degradation of motor function requires microglial activation as well as neuronal loss. Alternatively, the ability of Cu(II)ATSM to prevent cell degeneration may be specific to certain cell types.

This article shows that Cu(II)ATSM can be used far beyond SOD1-like ALS, it is even surprising that it could include parkinsonism-like manifestations, which involve an attack on very different neurons in terms of anatomy, motor neurons. It is a study not only on mice not on humans, but moreover on an unusual ad-hoc mouse model, and curiously the number of mice is very low. Given the financial stakes for scientists and investors in the Cu(II)ATSM business, one would have thought that a study would have been mounted on a much more classic mouse model and on many mice.

5.6. Biology's tools and ALS research

Oligodendrocytes were first described in 1921 by the neuroanatomist Pío del Río Hortega and Schwann cells were named after the anatomist and physiologist Theodor Schwann in 1871. Both were identified with the development of pioneering histological staining that are still used today.

5.6.1. A change of scale

From 1960 on, biology gradually changes scale. Until then, physiology is an excellent link between biology and medicine. Physiology deals with organs, tissues and hormones, all in a framework that is often very mathematical. The main tool is the optical microscope.

But there are problems that are difficult to treat by physiology, for example why some hormones are secreted by certain tissues and especially why the intensity, timing and type of secretion can change. Scientists realized that it was difficult to make progress without understanding the functioning of the cells, fortunately a few years ago in the 1950 s, biology has provided a simple explanation for the production of protein by cells via the cell. DNA and RNA.

In addition microscopes become difficult to use in the increasingly smaller biological targets, because a photon (a "grain" of light), has the same size as a bacterium. A virus, a protein or a hormone is impossible to visualize with an optical microscope. The fluorescence microscope is then invented and a fluorescent antibody is used which binds to the molecule of interest. Although the molecule of interest is not observable, the glow created by fluorescence is quite observable. This allows to continue to progress, but around 1990 it becomes untenable. Four other problems related to microscopes are :

- It is necessary to prepare the samples, concretely to cut slides which tears the cells and creates parasitic artifacts.

- It is necessary to "fix" the slides thus obtained with biologically active products, or even of relatively vague composition, which limits the repeatability of observations, or even their credibility.

- that the temporal dimension is totally absent, we can not observe interactions.

- that one can observe only tiny specimens, how to observe a motor neuron axon in all its extent under a microscope ?

However, the antibodies are not selective enough, they bind to molecules that are not the ones we believe in, and there is clearly a need for another paradigm in the tooling. A striking example is the study of the misfolding of SOD1 (wild-type) in ALS, which is mainly based on the immunohistochemical staining of formalin-fixed spinal cord tissue and embedded in paraffin with the aid of conformation-specific antibodies[255].

However, new techniques appear, the first studies devoted to the understanding of the border between the CNS and SNPs in the late 1960 s, owe much to the invention of transmission electron microscopy (TEM), a technique capable of a resolution of the order of a nanometer, which was developed after the second world war.

Electrophoresis techniques are also widely diversified around this time. Unlike microscopes that require long learning and often specialized staff, electrophoresis techniques are simple and inexpensive, students can master them in a few days. In addition, there is no longer any need to chemically alter the tissues to make observations. This is the time when scientists are looking for genetic modifications which would cause ALS.

---

255 https://www.ncbi.nlm.nih.gov/pmc/articles/PMC6094144/

A perverse effect of these techniques is that the mental models of the problems to be studied are considerably influenced by the tools. Scientists now study the expression of a molecule through high throughput biology technologies, there are talk about electric fields or quantum effects but human physiology, tissues, organs and even the organization and diversity of cells are forgotten. Whereas in the past, ALS researchers worked mainly in hospitals, they will now come from universities.

It is also a time of massive recruitment and new generations are seizing these molecular technologies and intellectual tools such as "pathways" describing the modifications and interactions between molecules. But these tools are essentially non-formal, we are far from the differential equations of Dr. Guyton[256]. The Systems biology that wants to systematize biology by borrowing a lot from engineering, will not succeed in being adopted.

But in the mid-2000 s there will be a return of imaging with the introduction of high-performance and low-cost cameras, because the localization of molecules is very important for understanding interactions. It is also the arrival of super-resolution techniques that can visualize objects smaller than photons, as well as light-beam microscopes that can observe tissue without shredding. The return of the imagery, also allows to observe events and interactions throughout their course and thus to avoid making hazardous assumptions. This is the case for example with the discovery in 2005 that extracellular mutated SOD1 can induce gliosis that causes ALS, or in 2014, when the displacement of TDP-43, is filmed from the nucleus to the end of the axon.

This kind of discovery is impossible with high-throughput tools.

---

256 https://en.wikipedia.org/wiki/Arthur_Guyton

5.6. Biology's tools and ALS research

5.6.2. Critique of ALS research practices.

For an outside observer of ALS research, there are some questionable practices :

- Model animals are created by genetic engineering. How can sporadic disease be studied in genetically engineered animals ? We can only find problems related to genetics !

- Scientists often use humanized model animals, that is, a human gene has been introduced into an animal. The motivation is that often animal models do not allow a good translation of the results in humans, but how could putting a human gene in a mice, make the animal model closer to the human disease ?

- ALS affects motor neurons, but only higher primates share an identical physiology of the central nervous system. Yet scientists are studying "their" ALS on model animals that are not primates.

- Flies, which are very often used as model animals, do not have a spine : They have an exoskeleton. The notion of inferior and superior motoneurons has absolutely no sense in the fly.

- Researchers have studied ALS in unicellular organisms such as yeasts (for example, to study the localization of TDP-43), ignoring the fact that ALS clearly does not attack all cells, there is a specificity concerning neuronal cells in the broad sense.

- Why are there no studies on the absence of similar pathology on sensory neurons ? In general they follow courses similar to neuromotors and at the cellular level these two types of neurons are quite similar, so why ALS is not affecting them ?

- Most of the axon of the lower motor neurons is outside the blood-spinal barrier. But all the ALS scientists act as if lower motoneuron were inside this barrier, it influences the choice of drugs which becomes therefore very restricted.

- Researchers are studying motor neurons in flies, zebrafish. They are a few millimeters long and are make assumptions about the movement of molecules in human motor neurons 100 times longer. Moreover, we know that the typical cell of mammals is quite different from that of other living beings.

- Scientists did publish mainly on SOD1 mutations from 1993 to 2006, and with a decline only after 2013, while mutations of SOD1 represent only 2 % of cases. Why were the scientists so badly inspired in the choice of their research ?

- Another example of weird behavior is the considerable number of contradictory studies that abound in the field of ALS research. Almost all discoveries have been reversed without anyone knowing in the end who is right. Which does not seem to bother anyone. This seems so unprofessional.

- Yet another example is that over the last 40 years, only a dozen laboratories seem to have made important discoveries, most of them in the United States, but only a few drugs have emerged and only for the family form of the ALS. With more than 10,000 scientists involved in the field of ALS, new scientific leaders would surely have appeared ? Is there a filter that eliminates outsiders ? Is university research the right tool for medicine ? The role of powerful associations like ALSA may need to be examined more closely.

5.6. Biology's tools and ALS research

5.6.3. An alchemy of modern times ?

In terms of **philosophy of science**, ALS research is "unusual". A science is necessarily empiric and falsifiable and its theories must have a strong internal coherency and great predictive power. ALS research demonstrated it does not fit in this frame : Many explanations are provided, many experiences made, many of them contradictory with each other, with nobody caring to provide some global explanation. Many drugs that have been tested in clinical trials do not come from academic research on SLA, like Thalidomide or Minocycline or on contrary are tested on hundreds of unrelated diseases like Dexpramipexole. Academic research have "discovered" hundreds of compounds that were supposed to be effective in treating ALS while pharmaceutical research was unable to translate them into treatments.

The fundamental characteristics of a science are the existence of a conceptual framework (for example : notions of logic, causality, geometry, operators allowing a form of calculation) and theoretical models based on this conceptual framework, capable of to formulate hypotheses that we will then test. For example in cancer research there are more than 7000 mathematical models[257]. An article like *"The Hallmarks of Cancer"* present a consistent, global framework of the disease that is built on a few principles.

In ALS research there is no conceptual framework, no formal models. The description in ALS articles is qualitative, descriptive, linear and imprecise « such molecule influences such phenomenon ». It completely ignores the existence of interlocking physiological systems (metabolic, hormonal, nervous, immune) that maintain a homeostasis called "life".

For decades ALS research ignored complexity, and it relied on molecular biology toolset, where all the cells and all the tissues are equivalent, indeed its tools (blotting, Electrophoresis, PCR),

257 https://www.ebi.ac.uk/biomodels/search?query=cancer

detect molecular effects only on the macroscopic scale. With these tools it is impossible to detect localizations of molecules on a microscopic scale, so problems like protein aggregates can not be identified.

We have seen how difficult it has been to realize that the central nervous system is a place where a population of cells interact (and sometimes compete) within the tissues they inhabit, and that the functioning of the CNS was not just about expressing a few genes.

Moreover, the only attempts at modeling are via model animals, and there is no formal framework for linking a model animal to a human disease. It's just declarative, a science team publishes an article that can be summarized as « *Our team has designed a model animal for ALS* » and it stops there. No one takes the trouble to provide comparative scales (in the absence of a mathematical model) of the intensity of symptoms and progression of the disease between the model animal and the human, nor how similar interventions will have effects in correspondence (or not) in model animals and humans.

Part II, An overview of a future therapy

6. An overview of a future therapy

The purpose of this chapter is to discuss a possible future therapy that has the potential to stop the progression of ALS. The next chapter will aim to discuss ways to heal.

Indeed until today the best experimental therapies only succeed in slowing the progression of the disease. The main progress over the last 20 years is in reducing side effects compared to early therapies. But in 20 years there have been no major reductions in ALS progression between Riluzole and Masitinib, and an Edaravone seems to be even less effective than Riluzole. Perhaps this is an effect of drug marketing policies for rare diseases, where efficiency is not a primary goal[258], while safety and health are considered very important.

It is therefore necessary to deliberately seek therapies to first completely stop the progression of the disease for most of patients, and in a second time recover speech and restore a minimum of autonomy in everyday life.

By stopping the disease, we mean a therapy that does not require dangerous periodic intervention such as an intrathecal injection. We also expect a therapy that is based on a rational design, and that we know is viable in the long term. It is therefore a different approach from that of clinical trials where pragmatic, non-explanatory criteria determine success or failure and drugs could be whatever fancy the principal investigator without any need to provide a convincing argumentation.

---

258 Public opinion will not understand that an authorization for an ineffective drug is refused, if it means a lack of medicine to cure a pathology.

6.1. A proposal to reduce aggregates of TDP-43

This section is a proposal open to the pharmaceutical industry to create a drug targeting TDP-43 proteinopathies such as amyotrophic lateral sclerosis (ALS).

It is also a way to fight an exorbitant price for this future therapy, by establishing a prior art, which could be useful to counter future attempts to patent this proposal.

A TDP-43 gene therapy is important because most ALS patients suffer from dysfunctions of TDP-43, which appear as aggregates of TDP-43 in the cytoplasm.

This document describes how such a drug could be designed, realistically with common laboratory technologies such as antibodies or transfection. The recently approved Zolgensma (AVXS-101) for spinal muscular atrophy (SMA) probably shows the way forward for designing this new drug.

Proteinopathy TDP-43 is not exclusive to ALS. This ensures that investments in gene therapy for ALS, a rare disease, can still find a significant market after being re-targeted.

6.1.1. Secondary goals

Mitigating inflammation is a secondary goal compared to reducing aggregates of TDP-43, but attractive.

Another secondary aim is to promote the destruction of the aggregates and the means of this destruction by the normal cellular pathways, for example the proteasome.

A third secondary goal would be to administer neurotrophic factors, especially around the target axon.

6.1.2. What is the state of the art of gene therapy for TDP-43 ?

This proposal is at state of the art in 2019. It is motivated by several successes in ALS mouse models published over the last five years[259]. Similar reports have been made in a Drosophila model of ALS[260]. Related work has been done for SOD1 mouse

259 Pozzi S, Thammisetty SS, Codron P, Rahimian R, Plourde KV, Soucy G, Bareil C, Phaneuf D, Kriz J, Gravel C, Julien JP. Viral-mediated delivery of antibody targeting TAR DNA-binding protein 43 mitigates associated neuropathology. J Clin Invest. 2019 Jan 22. pii : 123931. doi : 10.1172/JCI123931.

260 Gao, N., Huang, Y.-P., Chu, T.-T., Li, Q.-Q., Zhou, B., Chen, Y.-X.,… Li, Y.-M. (2019). TDP-43 specific reduction induced by Di-hydrophobic tags conjugated peptides. Bioorganic Chemistry, 84, 254–259. doi:10.1016/j.bioorg.2018.11.042

6.1. A proposal to reduce aggregates of TDP-43

models[261] [262] [263]and even macaques[264]. In total, some 100 articles have been published since 2007 on these topics.

261 Tommaso Iannitti, Joseph M. Scarrott, Shibi Likhite, Ian R.P. Coldicott, Katherine E. Lewis, Paul R. Heath, Adrian Higginbottom, Monika A. Myszczynska, Marta Milo, Guillaume M. Hautbergue, Kathrin Meyer, Brian K. Kaspar, Laura Ferraiuolo, Pamela J. Shaw, and Mimoun Azzouz Translating SOD1 Gene Silencing toward the Clinic : A Highly Efficacious, Off-Target-free, and Biomarker-Supported Strategy for fALS Mol Ther Nucleic Acids. 2018 Sep 7 ; 12 : 75–88. Published online 2018 May 3. doi : 10.1016/j.omtn.2018.04.015

262 Maria Grazia Biferi, Mathilde Cohen-Tannoudji, Ambra Cappelletto, Benoit Giroux, Marianne Roda, Stéphanie Astord, Thibaut Marais, Corinne Bos, Thomas Voit, Arnaud Ferry, and Martine Barkats A New AAV10-U7-Mediated Gene Therapy Prolongs Survival and Restores Function in an ALS Mouse Model Mol Ther. 2017 Sep 6 ; 25(9) : 2038–2052. Published online 2017 Jun 26. doi : 10.1016/j.ymthe.2017.05.017

263 Patel P, Kriz J, Gravel M, Soucy G, Bareil C, Gravel C, et al. Adeno-associated virus-mediated delivery of a recombinant single-chain antibody against misfolded superoxide dismutase for treatment of amyotrophic lateral sclerosis. Mol Ther. 2014 ; 22(3) :498-510.

264 Kevin D Foust, Desirée L Salazar, Shibi Likhite, Laura Ferraiuolo, Dara Ditsworth, Hristelina Ilieva, Kathrin Meyer, Leah Schmelzer, Lyndsey Braun, Don W Cleveland, and Brian K Kaspar Therapeutic AAV9-mediated Suppression of Mutant SOD1 Slows Disease Progression and Extends Survival in Models of Inherited ALS Mol Ther. 2013 Dec ; 21(12) : 2148–2159. Published online 2013 Oct 15. Prepublished online 2013 Sep 6. doi : 10.1038/mt.2013.211

6.1.2.1. Summary of steps in the design process :

- One or more therapeutic goals and molecular targets are defined to decrease the amount of aggregated TPD-43 in the cytoplasm of the cell.

- Epitopes are defined for these targets.

- Nanobodies are made from these epitopes.

- Plasmids are then produced which encode the combination of heavy and light chains from the selected hybridoma cell.

- These plasmids are inserted into AAV viral vectors.

- Once inserted behind the blood-brain barrier, these viral vectors infect the cells that then produce the nanobodies.

- Nanobodies bind to TDP-43 in aggregates and report it to be degraded by chaperone-mediated autophagy.

- The addition of chaperone-mediated autophagy (CMA) signal induces transcription of HSP70, further enhances the overall clearance of TDP-43 in aggregates by the proteasome.

6.2. What are the theoretical foundations and steps on which this therapy would be based[265] ?

The 43 kDa TAR DNA binding protein (TDP-43) is a DNA/RNA binding protein mainly located in the nucleus under normal physiological conditions.

However, hyperphosphorylated, fragmented and ubiquitinated forms of TDP-43 can be identified as essential components of cytosolic inclusions in sporadic ALS and frontotemporal lobar degeneration (FTLD).

It is therefore reasonable to think that removing the cytoplasmic aggregates of human TDP-43 protein even after the onset of the disease[266] can reverse the pathology of the TDP-43 protein.

The rational for the therapy design is therefore to use intrabodies[267] to target those aggregates in the cytosol. Those intrabodies will bear a destruction signal which will be understood by the cell's proteasome.

---

265 This section is based on the following document :
   Elimination of TDP-43 inclusions linked to amyotrophic lateral sclerosis by a misfolding-specific intrabody with dual proteolytic signals
Yoshitaka Tamaki, Akemi Shodai, Toshifumi Morimura, Ryota Hikiami, Sumio Minamiyama, Takashi Ayaki, Ikuo Tooyama, Yoshiaki Furukawa, Ryosuke Takahashi & Makoto Urushitani
   https://www.ncbi.nlm.nih.gov/pmc/articles/PMC5902603/
266 Walker, A. K. and colleagues
Functional recovery in new mouse models of ALS/FTLD after clearance of pathological cytoplasmic TDP-43.
   Acta. Neuropathol. 130, 643–660 (2015).
   https://www.ncbi.nlm.nih.gov/pmc/articles/PMC5127391/
267 An intrabody (from intracellular and antibody) is an antibody that works within the cell to bind to an intracellular protein.

6.2. What are the theoretical foundations and steps on which this therapy would be based ?

6.2.1. How are these aggregates formed ?

Under conditions without cellular stress, the TDP-43 protein interacts with the mRNAs on which the ribosomes are located separately, forming polysomes.

A polysome or polyribosome is a set of ribosomes linked together by a messenger RNA. This set looks like a pearl necklace.

They are the place of protein biosynthesis whether they are in free form in the hyaloplasm or linked to the endoplasmic reticulum to form a rough endoplasmic reticulum.

Various stresses induce ribosome clustering in a "blocked" state, resulting in the formation of stress granules (stress granules) usually containing the TIA-1, G3BP, ataxin-2 and eIF4G1 / 2 proteins.

In the blocked state, ribosome transcription is inhibited in a homeostatic response.

However, the prolonged stress, and the resulting misfolding of the TDP-43 protein, create stress granules and pathogenic aggregates of TDP-43. These granules also contain fragments of TDP-43. The TDP-43 protein contains a nuclear localization signal (NLS) as well as a nuclear export signal (NES) 10, which allows the cellular transport mechanisms to displace this TDP-43 protein between the nucleus and the cytosol.

In addition, membrane-free organelles in the cytosol formed by the liquid-liquid phase separation of RNP and RNA are involved in TDP-43 proteininopathy.

Misfolding and poor cytosolic localization also result in a loss of normal TDP-43 protein function, and the disruption of protein homeostasis and resulting RNA is considered to be another likely pathogenic mechanism in more toxicity of inclusions.

6.2. What are the theoretical foundations and steps on which this therapy would be based ?

Inclusions of TDP-43 can be identified in the majority of ALS patients, suggesting that these aggregates are a fundamental pathology of sporadic ALS.

Aberrant inclusions of TDP-43 are also observed in familial cases of ALS associated with various mutations such as C9orf72, MATR3, hnRNP1, UBQLN2, SQSTM1, VCP and OPTN, as well as in cases of TDP-43 gene (TARDBP) mutations itself, indicating that the misfolded and poorly localized TDP-43 protein is a common pathogenic molecule in familial as well as sporadic ALS.

6.2.1.1. What is a single-chain antibody and why use it ?

Because naturally occurring antibodies are optimised to be secreted from the cell, cytosolic **intrabodies** require special alterations, such as the use of **single-chain antibodies** (scFvs), for being stable and resistant to the reducing cytosolic environment.

Their small size makes it possible to use them in the context of gene therapies, because the viral vectors only allow small payloads.

Single-chain variable fragments (scFv) were introduced two decades ago through the generation of a variety of recombinant antibodies binding to various pathological protein epitopes involved in the field of neurodegenerative diseases. Clinical demonstration of their effectiveness in alleviating pathological symptoms is well established.

Due to their small size, good tissue penetration and low immunogenicity, scFv antibodies have been produced for various neurodegenerative diseases.

6.2. What are the theoretical foundations and steps on which this therapy would be based ?

Some single-chain antibodies have been studied for ALS [268] [269] [270], but only scFv targeting misfolded SOD1 has been shown to be effective in-vivo for improving pathological changes and slowing disease progression in a murine model with a SOD1 mutation linked to ALS [271] [272] [273].

The production of an anti-TDP-43 scFv antibody and its therapeutic effect when administered in ALS / FTD patients with TDP-43 pathology have been reported in several studies in 2019, in the United States, Canada, in France and Japan.

6.2.1.2. How to target the deleterious aggregates of TDP-43 ?

How to reach these aggregates of TDP-43 located in the cytoplasm of motor neurons ?

268 Ghadge GD, Pavlovic JD, Koduvayur SP, Kay BK, and Roos RP. Single chain variable fragment antibodies block aggregation and toxicity induced by familial ALS-linked mutant forms of SOD1. Neurobiol Dis. 2013 ; 56:74-8.

269 Patel P, Kriz J, Gravel M, Soucy G, Bareil C, Gravel C, et al. Adeno-associated virus-mediated delivery of a recombinant single-chain antibody against misfolded superoxide dismutase for treatment of amyotrophic lateral sclerosis. Mol Ther. 2014 ; 22(3) :498-510.

270 Tamaki Y, Shodai A, Morimura T, Hikiami R, Minamiyama S, Ayaki T, et al. Elimination of TDP-43 inclusions linked to amyotrophic lateral sclerosis by a misfolding-specific intrabody with dual proteolytic signals. Sci Rep. 2018 ; 8(1) :6030.

271 Patel P, Kriz J, Gravel M, Soucy G, Bareil C, Gravel C, et al. Adeno-associated virus-mediated delivery of a recombinant single-chain antibody against misfolded superoxide dismutase for treatment of amyotrophic lateral sclerosis. Mol Ther. 2014 ; 22(3) :498-510.

272 Ghadge GD, Kay BK, Drigotas C, and Roos RP. Single chain variable fragment antibodies directed against SOD1 ameliorate disease in mutant SOD1 transgenic mice. Neurobiol Dis. 2018 ; 121:131-7.

273 Dong QX, Zhu J, Liu SY, Yu XL, and Liu RT. An oligomer-specific antibody improved motor function and attenuated neuropathology in the SOD1-G93A transgenic mouse model of ALS. Int Immunopharmacol. 2018 ; 65:413-21.

6.2. What are the theoretical foundations and steps on which this therapy would be based ?

Due to the lack of a reliable mechanism for introducing antibodies into a living cell from the extracellular environment, this requires expression of the antibody in the target cell, which can be accomplished by gene therapy.

In molecular biology, an "antibody" is an antibody that acts in the cell to bind to an intracellular protein.

Since natural antibodies are optimized to be secreted by the cell, intracellular bodies require special modifications, including the use of single-chain antibodies (scFvs, also called nanobodies or nanobodies), or other techniques.

Tamaki and colleagues developed in 2018[274], an intra-body expressing only the VL and VH domains of the region determining the complementarity of their previously designed antibody (Shodai and colleagues, 2012) that specifically related to cytoplasmic aggregated TDP-43.

---

274 https://www.ncbi.nlm.nih.gov/pmc/articles/PMC5902603/

6.2. What are the theoretical foundations and steps on which this therapy would be based ?

Domain VH

EVQL QQS GAE LVKP GAS VKL SCTA SGF NIK DYYM

HWV KQR TEQG LEW IGR IDPE DGE TKY APKF QGK

ATI TADT SSN TAY LQLS SLT SED TAVY YCT IIY

YYGS RYV DYW GQGT TLT VS

Domain VL

EIVL TQS PTT MAAS PGE KIT ITCS ASS SIS SSYL

HWY QQK PGFS PKL LIY RTSN LAS GVP ARFS GSG

SGT SYSL TIG TME AEDV ATY YCQ QGSS IPL TFG

SGTK LEI

They first sought to develop intrabodies derived from monoclonal antibody 3B12A[275], targeting only the pathogenic structure of TDP-43. To apply this antibody within the cells as a potential scavenger of intracellular aggregates of TDP-43, they generated a single-chain variable fragment (scFv) for use as an **intrabody**.

The cDNAs encoding variable fragments of the heavy chain (VH) and the light chain (VL) were obtained from the mRNA of the hybridoma 3B12A and the domain profiles were studied.

6.2.1.3. Destruction of aggregates

If we want the target protein to be destroyed by the internal mechanisms of the cell, the nanobody must make the target protein to display a signal of destruction. This can be

---

275 The monoclonal antibody 3B12A selectively reacts with mislocated, aggregated and cytosolic TDP – 43 in cultured cells and in the postmortem spinal cord of patients with sporadic ALS.

6.2. What are the theoretical foundations and steps on which this therapy would be based ?

implemented by two proteolytic signals, a PEST endogenous signal and a chaperone-mediated autophagy (CMA) signal.

Proteolytic CMA is a selective pathway associated with the heat shock family member HSC70, which functions as a molecular chaperone for the removal of misfolded proteins.

The analysis of the DNA sequence of the intrabodies that will be chosen must show that their VH domain contains a sequence (for example RIDPEDGETK) with a PEST score as high as 9 at the region determining the complementarity, potentially conferring the ability to induce proteasome-mediated proteolysis[276].

In the article on which this chapter is based, analysis of the DNA sequence of the generated intrabodies showed that the VH domain contains a RIDPEDGETK sequence with a PEST score of up to 9.02 at the complementarity determining region 2 (see sequence of domains VL and VH above), potentially conferring the ability to induce proteasome-induced proteolysis.

A PEST sequence is a peptide sequence rich in proline (P), glutamic acid (E), serine (S) and threonine (T). This sequence is associated with proteins having a short intracellular half-life. Therefore, it is assumed that the PEST sequence acts as a signal peptide for protein degradation. This degradation of the protein can be mediated via proteasome or calpain.

Since self-degradation is a desirable property for a therapeutic intrabody, the scientists associated with Tamaki have therefore investigated the effects of the VH domain PEST sequence and protein disassembly signals on scFv degradation.

To this end, they constructed several VH_VL intra-bodies containing two protein disassembly signals, CL1[277] for

---

276 https://www.ncbi.nlm.nih.gov/pmc/articles/PMC5902603/
277 https://www.ncbi.nlm.nih.gov/pmc/articles/PMC2728579/

6.2. What are the theoretical foundations and steps on which this therapy would be based ?

proteasome localization and CMA for chaperone-mediated autophagy[278] [279], assuming that the interaction between scFv and antigen alone can not suffice for clearance of proteins.

The intrabody then consists of 4 segments :

Domain VL, linker, Domain VH, label Myc, sequence KFERQ

The details of the construction of the intrabody are provided in Annex S1 of their article[280].

This intrabody suggests that exploitation of both the proteasome and autophagy could be a valuable therapeutic method.

---

278 Lysosomes absorb and degrade intracellular proteins in cultured cells in response to serum deprivation, and in the tissues of organisms in response to starvation. A mechanism by which proteins enter the lysosomes for further degradation requires that the substrate proteins contain peptide sequences biochemically related to Lys-Phe-Glu-Arg-Gln (KFERQ).

279 https://www.ncbi.nlm.nih.gov/pmc/articles/PMC3408550/
280 https://www.ncbi.nlm.nih.gov/pmc/articles/PMC5902603/

6.2.2. Taking into account the AAV gene therapy vector in ALS.

6.2.2.1. AAV is safe.

Despite limited packing capacity (about 4.5 kb for a single strand and about 2.4 kb for self-complementary AAV), the AAV vector is the most promising for gene delivery in neurological diseases. It maintains exogenous gene expression for long periods of time (Murlidharan and colleagues, 2014).

6.2.2.2. AAV is used successfully in a similar disease.

A gene therapy of SMA, called Zolgensma (AVXS-101), which delivers the SMN1 gene using scAAV9, has shown significant clinical potential. AVXS-101 is administered intravenously or intrathecally. Upon administration, the AAV9 self-complementary viral vector delivers the SMN1 transgene to the cell nuclei where the transgene begins to encode the SMN protein, thereby attacking the root cause of the disease.

With a capacity about twice that of AAV, lentivirus has also been used as a proof-of-concept vector in the preclinical models of SMA (Azzouz and colleagues, 2004) and ALS, since lentivirus can be inserted randomly into the host genome, its clinical application poses significant safety concerns (Imbert and colleagues, 2017). The benefits of AAV have led to the choice of scAAV9 for the delivery of SMN1 in Zolgensma gene therapy, indeed serotype 9 has a relatively strong tropism towards lower motor neurons in the spinal cord in various species (Foust and colleagues, 2009). Bevan and colleagues 2011, Federici and colleagues 2012).

6.2.3. Administration considerations

6.2.3.1. Timing considerations

Successful treatment of any disorder is more likely to occur when treatment is administered early in the pathogenesis rather than later, and particularly at the final stage of the disease. While intuitive, this underscores the importance of earlier diagnosis, especially for ALS, where most ALS are thought to be very advanced in diagnosis.

AAV9-based approaches for some neurodegenerative diseases such as ALS are less effective in old age, which is a challenge since ALS usually occurs in elderly people (Foust and colleagues, 2010).

It has been considered safest to use virus-derived vectors that normally infect humans, but at the cost of the immune system recognizing them as pathogens and attempting to eliminate them. These immune responses have the effect of eliminating transduced cells and limiting the efficiency of gene therapy.

It is therefore essential when translating AAV9-mediated gene therapy for clinical applications, to first determine whether the patient has pre-existing immunity to AAV, and then to mitigate the development of potentially damaging immune responses to therapy, especially when gene therapy is to be done intravenously.

Toxicities associated with AAV accumulation are likely to occur. The immune response may start late in treatment when the increase in viral load reaches a certain threshold.

AAV9 has a neuronal tropism and can induce long-term stable expression with a single administration, which is important given the immunogenicity problems associated with viruses (Lorain and colleagues, 2008). This contrasts with multiple invasive intrathecal injections of nusinersen, which may have undesirable side effects (Haché and colleagues, 2016).

6.2.3.2. Injection site

Contrary to practice, it is important to take stock of the most affected nerves for each patient. From this information we will select the vertebra which should benefit from the treatment as soon as possible. If multiple vertebrae are affected, multiple injection sites will be required.

It might be interesting to inject the therapy in muscles as well. The mechanism is then that of a retrotransport of the viral load, from the muscle to the lower motoneuron, as described in a 2003 article by Kaspar and colleagues[281].

6.2.3.3. Treatment dosage

Thus, there is a fair balance between administering sufficient gene therapy to ensure proper targeting in an effective amount without causing systemic toxicity accumulation and undesirable side effects.

It is difficult to monitor the benefits of an intervention if, like in ALS, the natural history of the disease is variable and the phenotypic traits are not quantitative and prolonged over time. There is a strong need for reliable biomarkers of ALS to discern sufficient target commitment and correct dosage.

It should also be remembered that once AAV is delivered, it is relatively difficult to control the expression of the transgene.

---

281 https://www.ncbi.nlm.nih.gov/pubmed/12907804

6.3. Conclusion

Hopefully, new experiments to reduce the amount of misfolded and poorly located TDP-43, with the technologies summarized in this paper, will soon be performed on a pig model of ALS. The following steps could be :

- Start trials on humans.

- Extend this work to other proteins involved in ALS, such as FUS.

- Extend this work to Alzheimer where a third of cases, have a pathology type TDP-43.

Any medical or pharmaceutical entity wishing to discuss a follow-up to the therapy presented in this chapter, should not hesitate to contact the author : jeanpierre.lerouzic@wanadoo.fr

Part III.

7. Restoring the motor function.

This chapter does not present any work that could lead to therapies in only a few years, but it wants to show that there is a continuous progression of research on this point and that we can hope that the research will not encounter any roadblock in the next decades.

A key factor in moving forward in this area will be to get closer to the spinal cord specialists who have made considerable progress in recent years. Obviously this will involve a new type of researchers, closer to medicine and clinical interventions, which may include surgical operations.

7.1. Restoring cells that are dying.

ALS patients often ask : Are half of their motor neurons already dead when the diagnosis is made, as they can often read, or are they simply atrophied as they their muscles ? In fact the scientific literature is not very clear, in general it speaks of « *neurons that are dying* », but there are also a non negligible number of articles that talk about recovery of motor capacity on animal models[282]. There are also atrophied and inactive motoneuron observations in case of rupture of the axon, for example in case of spinal cord section, but perhaps not dead.

The barrier between life and death is porous, even at the cell level. Perhaps the most dramatic evidence of this concept came in April 2019, when a team of researchers from the Yale School of Medicine caught the attention of the world by briefly

---

282 https://www.ncbi.nlm.nih.gov/pmc/articles/PMC5127391/

restoring cellular activity in dead brains. It was there to revive cells of the central nervous system.

Any hope is perhaps not lost to restore the existing motor neurons, which would obviously be the most appropriate solution. Another element that is only rarely taken into account is that the axon of the lower motoneurons is outside the central nervous system, and the regeneration exists in the peripheral nervous system, even if it is slow and limited in distance, it could be helped with neurotrophic factors.

Of course, if one day we managed to restore motor neurons or to create new ones, the muscles would have to be innervated again and that they would acquire mass in their turn. In any case, it would surely be a case of several years of painful rehabilitation.

7.1.1. Neurons can recover even after the onset of neurodegeneration.

In 2015, for the first time in ALS research, it was shown that motor neurons could recover after the onset of the disease. The primary goal of the researchers was not this one, it was to create a credible model animal of ALS characterized by inclusions of TDP-43[283].

Proteinopathy TDP-43 proved difficult to model in mice. The protein, which provides the link between the nucleus and the cytosol to handle RNA, is essential for cell viability. Thus, as with any gene, eliminating TARBDP alters many internal mechanisms of the cell, so mice where this gene was rendered inactive (knock-out), did not survive.

As the pathological aggregates of TDP-43 are located in the cytoplasm, the scientists decided to delete only the nuclear localization sequence of the human gene protein before putting it in a mouse. In this way, the TARBDP gene is still able to produce the TDP-43 protein, but it does not remain in the nucleus. As long as the mice is fed with some doxycycline, the modified gene is inactive.

The researchers referred to these mice as « NLS regulable mice » or rNLS. When the mice reached the age of about five weeks, the researchers changed their diet to a diet without doxycycline and observed the evolution of the disease. The mice developed TDP-43 inclusions in the spinal cord and brain. In addition, the animals' brains narrowed and their motor neurons retracted from the muscles and died. Compared with other TDP-43 models, the pathology in rNLS mice was more similar to that in humans.

The animals also presented progressive neuronal motor disease. They developed leg tremors and lost the ability to

---

283 http://www.ncbi.nlm.nih.gov/pubmed/26197969

grasp a wire or balance a rotating rod. They lost weight and died about 10 weeks of that new diet without doxycycline.

When Walker and colleagues again started to give doxycycline to some of the mice that did not have doxycycline for six weeks, after one week of this diet, the animals began to seize a wire more closely and were less oscillated on the rotating stem. They gained weight and lived a normal life. Aggregates of TDP-43 began to disappear in two weeks with this diet incorporating doxycycline and disappeared completely after three months. The cortical and motor neurons stopped degenerating.

The first motor neurons to die in these mice correspond to those who are the most vulnerable in humans : fast motor neurons but quickly fatigable. Slower and more resistant neurons caused additional axons to sprout and muscle fibers were taken over after inactivation of the TDP-43 transgene.

In six weeks of inactivating transgene, the percentage of neuromuscular junctions innervated by motor neurons had doubled. Spiller analyzed this re-innervation further. First, she determined which motor neurons were most vulnerable to the toxicity of the TDP-43 protein and which persisted.

Previously, scientists had reported that rapidly fatigable motor neurons, which innervate fast-twitch muscles and facilitate rapid movements such as jumping and running, are the first to degenerate in humans and in ALS model mice.

On the other hand, fast fatigue-resistant motoneurons, which activate fast movements but get tired more slowly, and those who manage activities such as standing or strolling, take longer to degenerate.

Spiller observed that in rNLS mice it was the fast fatigable motoneurons that had disappeared. This raises an intriguing question : How did the mice recover traction once the TDP-43 expression normalized, when their fatigued neurons were gone ?

To identify the mysterious motoneurons that were connected to the re-innervated muscles, the researchers injected into the muscles a fluorescent tracer. This confirmed that the slowest neurons, which resisted fatigue, had developed new connections.

These same slow-moving and fatigue-resistant motor neurons have also begun to express MMP-9, a metalloproteinase that is usually found only in rapidly fatigable neurons. The metalloproteases have the role of reshaping the tissues. They are generally poorly expressed in healthy tissues, but their expression increases during physiological or pathological tissue remodeling processes, under the effect of factors capable of modulating the expression of their genes (IL-1, TNFα, prostaglandin, cellular lesion...). They participate in various phenomena such as angiogenesis, tissue repair, embryogenesis or skin scarring.

MMP-9 has been shown to express itself specifically in motor neurons most vulnerable to ALS. MMP-9 is strongly expressed by the vulnerable motor neurons of the spine, but not the oculomotor motor neurons, nor those of the Onuf nucleus that are only rarely affected by ALS. MMP-9 also increases the stress of the endoplasmic reticulum.

Edaravone, a free radical scavenger that inhibits the expression of MMP-9, has recently been approved for the treatment of ALS.

However a 2019 study, by Krista J. Spiller[284] and his team, who were already authors in the study above, found that strategies that reduce the level of MMP-9 beyond motor unit resulted in premature deaths in a subset of rNLS8 mice. Therefore, selective targeting of MMP-9 in motor neurons may be

---

284 https://www.ncbi.nlm.nih.gov/pubmed/30458231

beneficial for ALS, but adverse effects outside the motor circuit may limit the most commonly used clinical targeting strategies.

The researchers suggest, and this seems to have not received the hearing that it deserves, that several different etiologies may result in toxicity in the same vulnerable predisposed motor neuron subtype (fast-fatigable motoneurons), and that MMP-9 is in the pathway that mediates this toxicity. They believe that MMP-9 targeting may still be a useful therapeutic strategy in ALS, but that only the administration of drugs targeting MMP-9 of the spine would be necessary.

7.2. Transforming healthy cells into motor neurons

7.2.1. Trans-differentiation of cells excluding motor neurons

At the beginning of the 20th century, the prevailing view was that mature cells were permanently blocked in the differentiated state, cell differentiation being a unidirectional process.

But in 1962, John B. Gurdon demonstrated that the nucleus of a differentiated intestinal epithelial cell of frog can generate a fully functional tadpole by transplanting on an enucleated egg. Gurdon concluded that differentiated somatic cell nuclei could potentially return to pluripotency, with the potential to restart development.

Since Takahashi and Yamanaka's demonstration in 2006 that only a few transcription factors are needed to transform differentiated somatic cells into a pluripotent state, efforts have shifted to direct reprogramming of a differentiated cell to another type of differentiated cell. Direct neuronal reprogramming was performed by Vierbuchen and colleagues, in 2010, by transfecting fibroblasts with three transcription factors Ascl1, Brn2 and Mytll.

Oligodendrocyte precursor cells (OPCs) originate from neural progenitor cells located in embryonic ganglionic eminences that also generate inhibitory neurons. They are ubiquitous in the central nervous system, continue to proliferate throughout life and generate oligodendrocytes in the gray and white matter. The OPCs have a certain lineage plasticity and attempts have been made to reprogram them into neurons with varying degrees of success.

7.2. Transforming healthy cells into motor neurons

Attempts have been made to reprogram neurons directly from OPCs. Glutamatergic and GABAergic neurons would have been generated from reactive glial cells in the wounded neocortex after retroviral transduction with the bHLH Neurod1 proneural transcription factor by Bertrand as early as 2002 and more recently by Guo in 2014. However, cell identity remained uncertain.

During these various attempts, the neurons that were derived from astrocytes were not able to establish functional synapses, which considerably limits the interest of this technology.

Heinrich and colleagues, showed in 2010, that the fate selection of neurotransmitters among astrocyte-derived neurons can be controlled by the selective expression of distinct neurogenic transcription factors.

A mapping of genetic fate was then used by Heinrich and colleagues in 2014 to show that Sox10-expressing oligodendrocyte precursor cells (OPCs) in the injured and non-intact neocortex could be converted to neurons by retroviral administration of Sox2 and Ascl1, another member of the bHLH family.

While these two studies by Heinrich's team only succeeded in reprogramming OPCs in the context of an injured cortex, another study by Torper and colleagues in 2015, showed that neurons could be generated from OPCs in adult striatum. It was done by administrating an AAV associated to three transcription factors Ascl1, Lmx1a and Nurr1, which are known to promote reprogramming of fibroblasts in dopaminergic neurons.

Pereira and colleagues, showed in 2017 that converted neurons were stably integrated among the other cells and many of them had the electrical properties of mature GABAergic neurons. In the same year, Weinberg's team was successful in transducing oligodendrocytes to neurons in adult rats using oligodendrocyte-tropic AAV harboring a microRNA against the polypyrimidine tract binding protein.

However, the mechanisms by which direct neuronal conversion from glial cells occurred, remained unclear.

7.2.2. Trans-differentiation in the brain from astrocytes to neurons

The human brain contains billions of neurons and even more glial cells. Neurons can not divide, so they do not regenerate themselves after an injury. On the contrary, glial cells can proliferate in case of injury or disease.

The first discovery of neurogenesis in adult rodents in the 1960 s was only recognized much later. Today, it is widely recognized that neurogenesis in adults in the mammalian brain is possible, but it is limited to a few distinct niches such as the hippocampus and the subventricular zone (Ming and Song, 2011). But neurogenesis in the hippocampus of the adult human brain is the subject of much discussion.

It was known that in case of trauma, brain neurons could be replaced by astrocytes that change their phenotype. Indeed it has been shown that glial cells migrate to injured sites to differentiate into neurons.

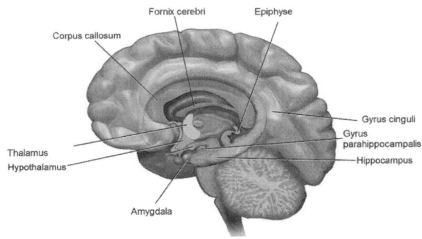

Source Wikipedia

We will see in the following pages that artificial neurogenesis in vivo, tries to reproduce this phenomenon and uses glial cells to generate neurons. This technology eliminates the in-vitro steps of stem cell culture and transplantation procedures and involves promoting the phenotype change of a cell located near the location where a neuron is desired.

Thus, nerve regeneration in-vivo could be applied to Alzheimer's or Parkinson's disease to provide a large number of new functional neurons, repairing the brain in situ. Regenerating upper motor neurons seems yet far away. If changing the phenotype (shape and behavior) of a cell is now possible, however, the phenotypes of a motor neuron and a glial cell are profoundly different, a motor neuron has an axon that is a thousand times longer than an extension of an astrocyte.

Moreover, creating a motor neuron is only half of the problem, it is also necessary that this neuron be interfaced with a muscle fiber. The neuromuscular junction is something specific to motor neurons. Even if this interface resembles of that between an astrocyte and a motor neuron, the biology is not the same and the connection will not be automatic.

7.2.3. Creating new neurons using gene therapy

In June 2019 in Keystone, Colorado Don Cleveland suggested that instead of inhibiting this or that ALS protein, ASOs could give rise to brand new neurons in a diseased and aging brain.

Xiang-Dong Fu, a colleague from Cleveland, simplified the conversion processes that were discovered in previous years and presented in the previous pages. He found that inhibiting the expression of a unique protein, the binding of the pyrimidine tract (PTB), led fibroblasts to become true neurons that give rise to axons and are able to trigger action potentials.

To achieve this conversion, the researchers inhibited the production of PTB with ASO in astrocyte cultures. This oligonucleotide then induced the differentiation of astrocytes from mice or humans into cells expressing typical and differentiated neuronal markers into different types of neurons. A small proportion of the converted neurons expressed tyrosine hydroxylase (Th), a marker of dopaminergic neurons.

The next logical step was then to try to reproduce this conversion in the very brain of a living being. The researchers then injected into a wild-type mice an adeno-associated virus expressing a hairpin RNA (shRNA) in order to inhibit the expression of PTB, as well as a red fluorescent protein allowing to mark infected cells.

Cleveland reported that one month after injection, 80 % of red blood cells expressed neuronal and non-astrocytic markers. A quarter of the converted cells also expressed Th, suggesting that they could make dopamine. In animals that received a control virus expressing nonspecific shRNA with the red fluorescent protein, the labeled cells remained astrocytes.

Next, the scientists tested the strategy in a murine model of Parkinson's disease, in which they destroyed dopaminergic neurons on one side of the dark substance by injecting the 6-OHDA neurotoxin. After this destruction, the researchers injected the virus controlling PTB directly into the dark substance. One month later, they found, that in mice not receiving treatment no new neurons had formed around the toxin lesion, but on the contrary in mice that had received gene therapy, converted neurons abounded.

Injection lesion of 6-OHDA decreased dopamine levels in the neighboring striatum by 80 %, which receives dopamine from nigral neurons. Treatment with the PTB-reducing virus had restored dopamine levels to 66 % of normal. The benefits of the PTB-reducing virus lasted up to a year and a half after the injection.

Overall, the results suggest that the conversion of astrocytes to neurons not only restored dopaminergic function in 6-OHDA-poisoned mice, but also provided a long-lasting rescue of motor deficits caused by ablation.

The excitement was palpable in the room as researchers bombarded Cleveland with questions. Charles Meshul of the Oregon University of Health Sciences in Portland asked if converted neurons formed functional circuits with the striatum. Cleveland said that although patch-clamp experiments suggest that neurons are functional and that dopamine levels suggest that they pump the neurotransmitter, it is unclear whether they form similar connections to native neurons.

Martin Kampmann from the University of California at San Francisco wondered what caused astrocytes to become dopaminergic neurons in place of another type of neuron. Cleveland hypothesized that different subtypes of astrocytes might be prone to turn into neuronal subsets in the event of PTB inhibition, but local signals in nigra, where the virus was injected, directed probably also converts to the dopaminergic type.

Others questioned the potential disadvantages of astrocyte exchange for neurons. Cleveland acknowledged that it had not yet studied the consequences of reducing the astrocyte pool and noted that any company developing ASOs against PTB should conduct dose studies to evaluate side effects.

Others asked how the strategy would work in the context of Parkinson's disease while in the study that was recounted by Cleveland, it was an acute neurotoxic lesion. Cleveland replied somewhat evasively that it remained to be determined.

A little later, he said that in patients with Parkinson's disease, converted neurons would have to withstand an intense neurodegenerative environment. Therefore, he assumes that the astrocyte conversion will give better results in combination with other treatments that would target the processes leading to neurodegeneration.

And in a particularly important issue for us, it was asked whether this strategy could mitigate the neuronal loss in other diseases ? Cleveland said "**yes**", although a targeted approach to replacing dopaminergic neurons lost in the dark substance has the greatest chance of success.

Aaron Gitler of Stanford University was impressed by the discoveries of Fu and Cleveland. He agreed that neuronal replacement could theoretically work for Parkinson's disease, but that it would be difficult to bring functional motor neurons back into ALS. Motor neurons must germinate axons that form connections over great distances.

7.2.4. **In vivo conversion compared to stem cell treatments.**

In vitro stem cell-based neurogenesis currently dominates the field of regenerative medicine, largely because stem cells are easier to grow in an in-vitro environment than to evolve within an organism where many vital mechanisms try to maintain homeostasis.

The last decades have led to a better understanding of the molecular mechanisms of stem cell self-renewal and differentiation. However, there is still no widely applicable stem cell treatment to treat severe neurological disorders.

The reasons for this discrepancy between basic research and clinical applications could be related in particular to the effectiveness of neuronal differentiation, the purity of differentiated neuronal subtypes, the potential for tumorigenesis associated with stem cells, the potential genetic mutations accumulated during multiple generations in culture, potential immuno-rejection after transplantation and ethical concerns related to aborted embryonic stem cells and fetal tissue.

On the other hand, all the disadvantages associated with cell culture are automatically solved by an in-vivo cell conversion approach.

In addition, the designed in-vivo cell conversion technology also has a number of advantages over endogenous neurogenesis in the adult. The use of endogenous glial cells near lost neurons for regeneration is perhaps the most economical way to reconstruct lost neurons and restore lost functions. Since glial cells are widespread in the CNS, in-vivo glia-to-neuron conversion technology can regenerate a large number of new neurons throughout the CNS.

7.2.4.1. Challenges to overcome for making functional motor neurons

Like any revolutionary new technology, the *in-vivo* conversion approach from glial cells to neurons also faces many challenges before being translated into clinical therapies. A big challenge is to convert local glial cells into neurons with a similar identity to that of regional neurons. This may require identifying an optimal combination of transcription factors that mimic the early neuronal specification process. The recent advent of algorithms to predict the transcription factors involved in cell-to-cell conversion could help accelerate this process (Rackham and colleagues, 2016, Ronquist and colleagues, 2017).

Another challenge is to convert glial cells into fully functional neurons and to ensure the long-term survival of the adult brain. Numerous published studies have shown successful conversion of astrocytes to neurons in vivo, but only a few studies demonstrate highly functional neuronal properties through electrophysiological recordings.

The third challenge is to demonstrate the integration of newly converted neurons not only in local neural circuits but also in global neural circuits and with muscle fibers.

7.2.4.2. Limitations of cell conversion in vivo.

In addition to these challenges, there are certainly some limitations to *in-vivo* cell conversion. An obvious limitation is that when degeneration is too severe, such as massive loss of advanced tissue, *in-vivo* cell conversion may not be sufficient to generate enough cells. It may be necessary to graft external cells or artificial tissues to repair tissue loss.

With prolonged denervation there is a loss of myofibrils and possibly death of the muscle cell. Once these changes have occurred, it is impossible to restore a functional neuromuscular unit. Thus, the goal of any reconstruction strategy aimed at restoring motor function is to restore a functional neuromuscular unit before these irreversible changes occur.

Another limitation is that if neurodegeneration is caused by a genetic mutation, the converted neurons would always carry the mutation and could still degenerate later. Although in the case of neurodegenerative disorders, neonatal neurons can survive for a long time before degenerating again, the ideal strategy may be to combine cell conversion with genetic editing technology to correct the mutation so that converted neurons can survive even longer.

7.2.4.3. In vivo cell conversion by oral therapy

The overexpression of transcription factors via viral vectors has the advantage that it can be delivered accurately to the brain or spinal cord, where neurons are failing. However, such an intervention requires high technical skills on the part of neurosurgeons and well-equipped hospitals.

In rural areas where medical facilities are scarce, gene therapy will be difficult to implement. To overcome this limitation of gene therapy, researchers have tested the possibility of oral drug therapy. In 2015 Zhang and colleagues succeeded in transforming human astrocytes into functional glutamatergic neurons by using a combination of small molecules under *in-vitro* conditions. In 2017, Gao researchers also reported that adult human astrocytes isolated from glioma patients can be chemically transformed into glutamatergic neurons in cell cultures.

In 2019 Yin and colleagues, have successfully converted human astrocytes into neurons using 3 to 4 small molecules, which is obviously closer to drug development.

These studies have paved the way for future pharmacotherapy, but in-vivo studies on direct chemical reprogramming and effective drug delivery across the blood-brain barrier have yet to be performed before potential clinical translation.

7.2.4.4. Generation of a motor nerve for a transplant.

A limitation to *in-vivo* conversion is that motor neurons are very different from other cells ; they have an axon that is several decimeters long.

An alternative to in-vivo conversion could be the complete transplantation of a functional motor nerve that has been developed in-vitro from stem cells. Of course such an operation would necessarily be limited to a few nerves, but for example, recovering the use of the hands would be a spectacular progress.

The first successful transplants of motoneurons in small mammals date back to 1993[285]. Researchers tested the possibility of local transplantation of embryonic motoneurons to restore innervation of denaturated somatic muscle as a first step in the recovery of muscle function.

Ventral spinal cord cells (lower motoneurons) from rat embryos were transplanted into the distal stump of the axotomized tibial nerves (axon cut) of adult rats.

The animals were sacrificed 3 to 18 weeks after transplantation. After 3 weeks, large, multipolar cells, resembling alpha motor neurons, were observed in the graft site surrounded by myelinated and unmyelinated axons and dendrites. The axons emanating from these grafted motor neurons formed neuromuscular junctions. Grafted motoneurons survived up to 18 weeks.

This study demonstrates that embryonic spinal motoneurons, transplanted into the distal adult peripheral nerve block, are able to survive and re-innervate the denervated target muscle.

---

285 https://www.ncbi.nlm.nih.gov/pubmed/29107592

7.2. Transforming healthy cells into motor neurons

In 2017, to build an organoid mimicking the developing nervous tissue, Japanese researchers[286] first differentiated human-induced pluripotent stem cells (hiPSCs) into spinal motor neurons. More than 60 % of the cells differentiated and formed a cluster of neurons.

The newly formed cluster was then transferred to a custom culture device for the formation of axonal fascicles. The culture micro-device contained a chamber for receiving the cluster of neurons, a microchannel for the formation of axonal fascicles and a target chamber for containing axonal endings.

Neurons spontaneously extended axons out of the chamber's cluster of neurons. These axons spontaneously formed a single, straight and unidirectional fascicle into the microchannel after being cultured in the spheroid for approximately 20 days.

The efficiency of axonal fascicle formation was greater than 90 % at day 30 for three hiPSC lines derived from different individuals, demonstrating that this process of forming nerve organoids was robust and reliable.

However, in this case axons are very short, so to form motor neurons likely to be grafted on humans, it would probably require much more maturation time. As the axons of the fascicle progress, the problems of nutrition, protein transport and myelin creation become more and more urgent.

---

286 https://www.ncbi.nlm.nih.gov/pubmed/29107592

Conclusion

Before 2006 with discovery of the TDP-43 involvement in sporadic ALS, not much happened in the ALS research field. But then it accelerated, 2011 saw the discovery of C9orf72, which is implicated in half of the familial cases.

But in other areas the mystery deepens, for example some SOD1 mutations found in ALS, have a somber prognostic and other SOD1 forms have a life expectancy of decades. And despite an incredible amount of invested resources, we still do not really know what deleterious mechanism is associated with SOD1.

It is nice also that scientists are now more interested in complex answers than the simplistic « all is genetic » of the turn of the century. Some good examples are the study of the burden of DNA repair on cellular metabolism, or how a pattern of misfolded or mislocated proteins is implicated in many neurodegenerative diseases.

It would be nice to reconcile the different and incompatible ways to categorize ALS, some typologies look at the anatomy (bulbar/spinal/...), other looks at the genome (SOD1/C9orf72/...), some differentiate SOD1 forms from proteinopathies, etc. The ALS research might benefit from a new classification of diseases, because the ALS bulbar form may look closer to Alzheimer, Parkinson or multiple sclerosis, than to the spinal form. On contrary the spinal ALS form resembles to some kind of extreme axonopathy and it could benefit from progresses in this field.

We need the equivalent for ALS of the famous « hallmarks of cancer » by Weinberg.

On the pharmaceutical side, we can expect in the short term good news of drugs, like Arimoclomol, that disaggregate protein clumps in the cytosol, and also of treatments that will bring neurotrophic factors close to motoneurons like Nurown.

In a more distant future, therapies will replace failing motoneurons with new ones. After all who would have expected the arrival of induced pluripotent stem cells in 2006, who would have predicted how easy to induce ? There is a silver lining on the horizon.

Table of Contents

Made in the USA
Monee, IL
11 February 2020